FAMILY INVESTMENTS
IN CHILDREN'S POTENTIAL
Resources and Parenting Behaviors
That Promote Success

MONOGRAPHS IN PARENTING

Marc H. Bornstein, Series Editor

For more information on LEA titles, please contact
Lawrence Erlbaum Associates, Publishers, at www.erlbaum.com.

FAMILY INVESTMENTS IN CHILDREN'S POTENTIAL

Resources and Parenting Behaviors That Promote Success

Edited by

Ariel Kalil
Thomas DeLeire
University of Chicago

2004

LAWRENCE ERLBAUM ASSOCIATES, PUBLISHERS
Mahwah, New Jersey   London

Lawrence Erlbaum Associates, Inc., Publishers
10 Industrial Avenue
Mahwah, New Jersey 07430

Cover design by Kathryn Houghtaling Lacey

Library of Congress Cataloging-in-Publication Data

Family investments in children's potential : resources and parenting
   behaviors that promote success / edited by Ariel Kalil, Thomas
   DeLeire.
      p. cm.
   Includes bibliographical references and index.
   ISBN 0-8058-4871-1
      1. Family—Psychological aspects. 2. Family—Economic aspects.
   3. Parenting. 4. Parent and child. 5. Child development. 6. Child
   welfare.   I. Kalil, Ariel.   II. DeLeire, Thomas.

HQ728.F3155 2004
649'.1—dc22   2003060133
                                                        CIP

Books published by Lawrence Erlbaum Associates are printed on acid-
free paper, and their bindings are chosen for strength and durability.

Printed in the United States of America
10 9 8 7 6 5 4 3 2 1

For Karl, Henry, and Elinor
—A. K.

For Jenny
—T. D.

Contents

Series Foreword
Monographs in Parenting

Parenting is fundamental to the survival and success of the human race. Everyone who has ever lived has had parents, and most adults in the world become parents. Opinions about parenting abound, but surprisingly little solid scientific information or considered reflection exists about parenting. *Monographs in Parenting* intends to redress this imbalance: The chief aim of this series of volumes is to provide a forum for extended and integrated treatments of fundamental and challenging contemporary topics in parenting. Each volume treats a different perspective on parenting and is self-contained, yet the series as a whole endeavors to enhance and interrelate studies in parenting by bringing shared perspectives to bear on a variety of concerns prominent in parenting theory, research, and application. As a consequence of its structure and scope, *Monographs in Parenting* will appeal, individually or as a group, to scientists, professionals, and parents alike. Reflecting the nature and intent of this series, contributing authors are drawn from a broad spectrum of the humanities and sciences—anthropology to zoology—with representational emphasis placed on active contributing authorities to the contemporary literature in parenting.

Parenting is a job whose primary object of attention and action is the child—children do not and cannot grow up as solitary individuals—but parenting is also a status in the life course with consequences for parents themselves. In this forum, parenting is defined by all of children's principal caregivers and their many modes of caregiving. *Monographs in Parenting* will encompass central themes in parenting ...

WHO PARENTS?

Biological and adoptive mothers, fathers, single parents, divorced and remarried parents can be children's principal caregivers, but when siblings, grandparents, and nonfamilial caregivers mind children their parenting is pertinent as well.

WHOM DO PARENTS PARENT?

Parents parent infants, toddlers, children in middle childhood, and adolescents, but special populations of children include multiple births, preterm, ill, developmentally delayed or talented, and aggressive or withdrawn children.

THE SCOPE OF PARENTING

Parenting includes genetic endowment and direct effects of experience that manifest in parents' beliefs and behaviors; parenting's indirect influences take place through parents' relationships with each other and their connections to community networks; and the positive and negative effects of parenting are both topics of concern.

FACTORS THAT AFFECT PARENTING

Evolution and history; biology and ethology; family configuration; formal and informal support systems, community ties, and work; social, educational, legal, medical, and governmental institutions; economic class, designed and natural ecology, and culture—as well as children themselves—each helps to define parenting.

THE NATURE, STRUCTURE, AND MEANING OF PARENTING

Parenting's pleasures, privileges, and profits as well as frustrations, fears, and failures are all explored.

Contemporary parenting studies are diversified, pluralistic, and specialized. This fragmented state needs counterforce in an arena that allows the extended in-depth exploration of cardinal topics in parenting. *Monographs in Parenting* vigorously pursues that goal.

—Marc H. Bornstein
Series Editor

Preface

What makes some children flourish in life and others flounder? Is it the resources that parents have, or how parents behave and use those resources that matters? The chapters in this volume focus on parents' abilities and choices regarding investments in their children. Investments have the return in improved child and young adult outcomes that parents both care about and are willing to make sacrifices for. Yet, parents differ in terms of the resources they have available to invest, the choices they make, and the behaviors they engage in. Questions posed in this volume address the extent to which child investments derive from resources relative to behaviors, how resources and behaviors are related and allocated, and whether they can compensate for one another. Is it what parents have or what they do that matters for children? On the other hand, are these parental behaviors merely responses to children's genetic predispositions? The chapters in this collection answer these questions through the lens of economic, biological, and developmental psychological theory.

In doing so, this volume strives to conceptualize an interdisciplinary framework of investments in children. This framework is loosely built around the idea that two broad dimensions of parental investments exist. These include resources (economic as well as psychological) on the one hand and behaviors (e.g., parents' provision of instrumental support, emphasis on education, and purchasing decisions) on the other. The authors of these chapters also recognize the role of genetics in their assessment of the relative role of parental influence, and they recognize that parenting represents a complex interplay between the child, the family, and the broader social environment. For instance, chapters in this volume take note of the ways in which characteristics such as immigrant status and family structure affect parents' allocation of resources and how these characteristics constrain or support parental behavior. And equally importantly, the chapters recognize the influence of child characteristics, such as child gender or disability status, on parental behavior.

Moreover, new and provocative evidence from several of the chapters suggests that characteristics of the current generation of parents that might be viewed as a "resource" are actually the result of behaviors of the prior generation. Authors' creative use of multigenerational panel data sets allows insights into this question. Finally, several of the chapters recognize the possibilities and limitations of public policy interventions. Governmental investments in children often seek to offset inequities in, or compensate for the lack of, parental investment. However, parents are and likely will remain the primary source of investments in children including the provision of cognitive stimulation, supervision and discipline, skill, health, education and other components of human capital as well as the provision of family social support, culture, and social competence. Thus, developing a better understanding of which parental investments matter, when they matter, and how resources can be successfully invested in children's potential is key to shaping efficient interventions and social policies that reflect all sources of child investments. Understanding which parental investments matter will also help policymakers design government interventions—and decide whether to intervene at all—so as to avoid their crowding out investments by parents.

The contributors to this book are developmental psychologists, economists, sociologists, and others who work on different components of a theoretical framework of family investments in children. In bringing these chapters together in one volume, we hope to foster cross-disciplinary communication, generate new ideas, and strengthen existing ones for a multifaceted research agenda on the role of parents and families (as opposed to government policies and institutions) in promoting children's success.

WHAT DO PARENTS DO?

Within the family environment, parents create a microcontext that affects children's development (Bronfenbrenner, 1986). According to developmental psychologists, the triumvirate of "good" parenting behaviors consists of parental nurturance, consistent discipline, and appropriate provision of autonomy (Chase-Lansdale & Pittman, 2001). Specific dimensions of effective parenting include parents' warmth and responsiveness; limit setting and supervision; provision of cognitive stimulation; modelling of attitudes, values, and behaviors; management of the world outside the home; and creation of family routines and traditions (Chase-Lansdale & Pittman, 2001). These aspects of parents' behavior help infants and young children to develop secure attachments to their caregivers, which lays the foundation for children's successful emotional development and self-regulation and promotes social competence, positive behavior, and academic success in middle childhood and adolescence (Conger, Ge, Elder, Lorenz, & Simons, 1994; Connell, Spencer, & Aber, 1994). For example, warm and supportive parenting, positive parent–child relationships, and developmentally appropriate levels of parental monitoring and involvement in children's lives predict high self-esteem, positive psychosocial development, low levels of behavior problems, and academic competence (Steinberg, 2000). Parents' ability to organize and monitor their children's social and extrafamilial environments has important implications for children's exposure to dangerous and risky situations (Furstenberg, Cook, Eccles, Elder, & Sameroff, 1999). These findings have been demonstrated repeatedly in the developmental literature.

Most economic approaches to family investments in children date to the path-breaking work of Gary Becker, much of which is collected in Becker (1991). The economic approach to family investments, as in the developmental approach, assumes that parents care about the lifetime well-being of their children. It recognizes that some children have distinct advantages over others resulting from their (genetic and other) endowments received at birth. However, parents not only pass on some of their endowments to children, they also influence the well-being of their children by making investments in their human capital (their skills, education, health, and other attainable characteristics that will enable the children to become productive and happy adults). These investments are most often characterized in terms of effort, time, and money. Economic models of parenting behavior are concerned with the choices that parents make in organizing and allocating the resources that can be invested in children's human capital. The economic approach, unlike the developmental approach, is less concerned with explaining the mediating pathways through which these investments yield their effects (Duncan & Magnuson, 2002) but instead focuses on the trade-offs parents face in their choices of whether and how much to invest.

Parental investment decisions to allocate effort, time, and money to children's well-being can be analyzed using the tools of economics. The theory suggests that the determinants of parental investments in children can be broken down into the following components: parents' income, prices (which might be determined by the abilities of the child—i.e., the "returns" from investments and the costs of borrowing), and parental preferences. Many of the chapters in this volume explicitly or implicitly take up these themes in their examination of the factors that influence parents' inputs into their children's well-being.

Much modern research on families and children is influenced by either the economic or the developmental approach to parental investments in children—and is often influenced by both approaches. This volume collects 10 chapters that reflect this diversity of backgrounds.

In the first chapter, developmental psychologists Bradley and Corwyn present a useful taxonomy to describe the types of parental investments that research has shown matter to child development. They label them the "five S's": safety/sustenance, stimulation, socioemotional support, structure, and surveillance.

Safety and sustenance can begin before birth, with prenatal care, and continue throughout the child's life. *Stimulation* also is a lifelong pursuit but is especially important in the early stages of development, when neural development is underway. *Socioemotional support* spans both economic and emotional supports that imbue a sense of belonging and worth and socialize children to the norms and expectations of society. *Structure* involves setting appropriate limits for the youth, as well as regulating parental expectations to align with the child's developmental stage. *Surveillance* is keeping track of a child's whereabouts and ultimate safety.

Of course, although these factors matter, they are not all that matters. Genetics, for example, can mediate the responses of children to various inputs from parents, as can peers and other outside influences. Children and parents interact with and are influenced by the larger world. Even parents' own upbringing influences the way they parent their children.

In chapter 2, Neiderheiser and Reiss draw our attention to the important role of genetic influences on children's development. The most direct personal characteristic of a parent is, of course, his or her genetic make-up. Until recently, efforts to understand the contributions of biology to parenting and child development were constrained by the invasiveness of biological assays and by fears that biological research would engender deterministic conceptions of individual behavior (Campbell, Shaw, & Gilliom, 2000). In the past, it was not possible to distinguish environmental effects from genetic effects on parenting and child outcomes. Recent advances in behavioral genetics, however, have opened the door to such exploration, and Neiderhiser and Reiss examine these recent advances and their meaning for child development research.

Genetics can play an important role in parenting. Parents may pass on genes related to a "difficult temperament" to their children. In parents, these genetic traits may be expressed in irritable and negative parenting, which is also subsequently correlated with the child's difficult temperament. Or it may be the case that parents are responding to the genetically influenced characteristics of a "difficult" child. Understanding the process through which genetic traits influence parenting—whether from parent to child, or child to parent—can ultimately lead to more accurate interventions to improve parenting.

Genes are not the only characteristics that are passed on from parents to children. A wide body of research discusses the intergenerational transmission of parenting behavior. Although genetics might account for some of these similarities, a "family capital" or set of motivational goals might also be at work. In chapter 3, Michael takes up this hypothesis. Michael, an economist, draws on unique British panel data providing information from three generations of family members. He finds a correlation between maternal breastfeeding and children's verbal abilities, even controlling for family economic resources. He also finds a correlation between the grandmother's breastfeeding of the target child's mother and the child's verbal ability, and this effect is mediated by the mother's own breastfeeding behavior. Families can influence their child's development even when economic resources are lacking, he concludes, and this is especially true if the parent grew up in a home that also saw the importance of investing in children with time and commitment. Family dynasties, as he puts it, are not only built on economic wealth. Dynasties can be created by passing down the importance of investing in human capital. As Michael concludes, behaviors that are within the reach of nearly all parents, not just those with financial means, can substantially influence their child's healthy development.

In chapter 4, Dunifon, Duncan, and Brooks-Gunn also argue for the importance of a family shared culture, as distinct from families' economic resources, in their analysis of data from the Panel Study of Income Dynamics. These data, like the ones that Michael uses, provide information on three generations of family members, thus allowing the authors to identify the relative contribution of parental behaviors versus economic resources. Like Michael's study, this research suggests some positive intergenerational effects—in particular, growing up with parents who are organized and efficient (as measured by the cleanliness of their home) increases subsequent educational attainment and earnings of children. These results could be either because organization and efficiency is an inherited trait, or because parental organization leads to better parenting behaviors.

In sum, these studies suggest that parental investments are critically important for children, within and across generations. However, any strong conclusion on the role of parental behaviors should be tempered by the studies of the importance of genetics to both child outcomes and parental behaviors.

THE EXPANDING ENVIRONMENT OF INFLUENCES ON CHILD DEVELOPMENT

Although the consensus is that parents play a considerable role in the development of their children, parents often face factors beyond their control that ultimately influence their children. A basic tenet of child development is that it is viewed as an ongoing interplay among the child's inherent predispositions, the family's characteristics, and the wider environment. A variety of influences at these various levels interact with each other to shape development and adaptation over time and across contexts. Importantly, patterns of influence within families are seen as reciprocal and bidirectional; children's characteristics elicit and influence parents' behavior as much as parents' behavior shapes that of their children. Put in the terminology of economic theory, children with different characteristics or who live in different environments may have different returns to parental investments. These characteristics and environments, therefore, may affect the incentives parents have to make these investments. Several of the chapters in this volume address these themes with their focus on the role of children's disabilities, immigration status, the gender of the child, and family structure on parental investments.

In chapter 5, Guralnick, a developmental psychologist, describes the influence of children's disabilities on parental behavior. Parents of children with disabilities often face extreme stress in both their interpersonal and family lives. Greater demands are placed on their time and money, and parents are often forced to adjust their behavior to accommodate their child's needs. The author proposes three categories of family interaction that can be applied generally to both typical development and conditions related to risk and disability: the quality of parent–child transactions; family-orchestrated child experiences; and health and safety provided by the family. Taken together, these three family interaction patterns are essential to optimal social and cognitive competence of young children with disabilities. Finally, Guralnick stresses the importance to these families of outside supports and early interventions. Given these great demands, intervention programs, he argues, should better tailor their offerings to the family situation, or risk alienating the parent and losing the benefits of intervention. Assistance programs must adapt to the parent, not the other way around, allowing for a high degree of individual tailoring.

Parenting takes place in a cultural context. For example, the United States is a land of immigrants, and immigrant parents face a number of often bewildering changes to which they and their children must adapt. Developmental psychologists Fuligni and Yoshikawa discuss the strategies of parental investment employed by immigrant parents in chapter 6. The authors note that immigrant parents are often faced with a non-native language and culture, a potentially new socioeconomic and educational status, and a confusing set of rules regarding their eligibility for social assistance, institutions, or other programs. As a result, immigrant parents often adjust their parenting style or choices. Fuligni and Yoshikawa's chapter helps us better understand the adaptive strategies immigrant parents develop in response to both majority and minority cultural influences on their development.

For instance, one area in which immigrant families adjust parenting is education. According to Fuligni and Yoshikawa, immigrants often left their home countries for the perceived economic benefits, and they see education as key to those prospects for their children. As a result, they often place great weight on the importance of education and hold high aspirations for their children. Often, the authors find, these aspirations encourage the pursuit of "practical" degrees. Children of immigrants, for example, are more likely to pursue technical and business degrees, which have a clear link to future jobs, over degrees in the social sciences and humanities. This encouragement may pay off in that foreign-born children are more likely to financially support their families as young adults than American-born children. Education, on the other hand, can be compromised if the family faces financial distress and needs the child to provide economic support, a situation that is much more common in immigrant families. This chapter provides insights into the complex interplay between parental preferences and the constraints imposed by the social environments in which they live.

The characteristics of the child, as well as those of the parents, can influence parental investment behavior. One characteristic of the child that may lead to different behavior by parents is gender, particularly if parents have a preference for sons. In chapter 7, economists Lundberg and Rose examine whether parents invest differently in sons versus daughters in their analysis of how the child's gender influences the family's spending patterns.

The ways in which families spend their money can benefit children. For example, greater expenditures on essentials such as education and medical care may benefit children more than spending on other goods. Lundberg and Rose find that housing expenditures are substantially higher in families with only a son, compared with families with only a daughter. Although families with only a son do not spend more on other durables, such as cars and furniture, these families do spend more on other "investment-type" goods, such as recreation and sports equipment, health insurance and medical costs, and books and toys, particularly in low-income families. Furthermore, parents in families with only a boy also spend more on jewelry and personal care services for the mother as well as other discretionary consumption goods. The extent to which families with sons behave differently from households with daughters may suggest that the expenditures of families with boys exhibit a greater investment component and that parents of sons have a greater optimism in the long-run prospects for the family.

Investments in children are also influenced by family structure. In chapter 8, Ziol-Guest, Kalil, and DeLeire examine whether spending patterns differ between single-parent and married-parent families with children in ways that might affect child well-being.

The authors find that single parents allocate their resources differently than do married parents. In particular, compared with married parents, divorced parents spend a lesser share of their budget on food consumed at home, whereas never-married parents spend a greater share on food consumed away from home. Both divorced and never-married parents spend a greater share of their budgets on alcohol and tobacco products than do married parents. The authors argue that these differences in how parents allocate resources likely reflect differences in non-economic parental resources—for example, time and information—between single and married parents.

WHAT CAN PUBLIC POLICIES DO?

In recent years, there has been a surge of interest in family-based prevention and intervention, fuelled in part by an increased awareness of the crucial role played by the family in shaping the development of children. Parent-based intervention strategies focus on enhancing parental skills or resources in the hope that these enhancements will translate into improved child outcomes. Such programs may be aimed at improving parental income, parental education, or parental behaviors. The specific nature of the intervention varies from program to program and may encompass home visits, group support, and informational sessions. Some interventions include a child component in addition to a parent component. Home visiting programs, for example—which typically serve pregnant women and families with young children—have many different goals, including the promotion of good parenting skills, prevention of child abuse and neglect, and improving children's school readiness and healthy development. To a lesser extent, these programs aim to improve maternal well-being by promoting maternal education and employment and deferral of subsequent pregnancies. In chapter 9, Magnuson and Duncan examine these programs and ask whether it is more effective to improve the parent's educational and economic circumstances or to focus the approach on the children.

With a few noteworthy exceptions, they find that most parenting programs aimed at changing parental behavior appear ineffective at improving children's outcomes. In contrast, a different type of intervention seeks to improve family well-being and child development by moving parents into work and boosting their incomes. A set of recent experimental interventions has identified generally positive outcomes of mandated work programs for families receiving cash assistance, particularly when the programs not only require participants to work but also "make work pay."

Magnuson and Duncan also describe the relative merits of child-focused programs. Intensive programs that target preschoolers have had the most success. In contrast, less intensive programs have had more mixed success, and programs targeted at adolescents (e.g., those that focus on preventing school drop-out or pregnancy) show very little evidence of being effective. Interventions early in life can help children attain the developmental skills they need to take advantage of opportunities later in life. It is likely that this is part of the explanation for early interventions being more effective than later interventions—because they have the capacity to set children on a different trajectory that has enduring effects over the life course.

Government policies have often targeted income as a key route to improving child welfare. In chapter 10, Waldfogel presents an overview of the effects of government policy on child well-being. She compares government programs and initiatives across different countries, with a specific focus on the U.S. and U.K. approaches.

Waldfogel finds that the United States spends less on social welfare benefits than many other countries and that these benefits are spent differently at different income levels. However, as she stresses, comparing policies that promote child investments is more complicated than simply adding up the money spent on social welfare programs. It is also about the range of policy instruments that governments use to make those investments. Such instruments can range from cash benefits, to voucher programs and related benefits, employment and earnings improvement programs, and educational or health programs. The recent U.S. welfare reforms, for example, have focused primarily on policies to increase parents' employment and earnings. Reforms in the United Kingdom, in contrast, have set more ambitious goals with a broader range of policy initiatives, including improving benefits to children and communities, promoting work among parents and making work pay, and increasing and improving benefits to children when parents cannot work. As Waldfogel notes, it is still too early to determine which approach works best in promoting the health and well-being of a country's children.

The chapters in this volume are concerned with how parents help to ensure their children's fullest potential. As this collection shows, this question remains at the heart of social scientists' endeavors and continues to present new challenges and opportunities for policy-makers. A multidisciplinary approach, combining, for example, economic and psychological perspectives on parents' investments in children's futures, offers new insights and holds much promise for future research.

ACKNOWLEDGMENTS

Family Investments in Children's Potential: Resources and Parenting Behaviors That Promote Success derives from original presentations delivered at a workshop of the same name held in Chicago, Illinois in September 2002. The workshop was sponsored in part by the Northwestern University/University of Chicago Joint Center for Poverty Research. We are grateful to the William T. Grant Foundation and the Foundation for Child Development for their support of the workshop and the production of this volume. Finally, we thank Barbara Ray for excellent editorial assistance, and we thank also the production staff at LEA.

REFERENCES

Becker, G. (1991). *A Treatise on the Family (enlarged ed.)* Cambridge, MA: Harvard University Press.

Bronfenbrenner, U. (1986). Ecology of the family as a context for human development. *Developmental Psychology, 22,* 723–42.

Campbell, S. B., Shaw, D. S., & Gilliom, M. (2000). Early externalizing behavior problems: Toddlers and preschoolers at risk for later maladjustment. *Development and Psychopathology, 12,* 467–88.

Chase-Lansdale, P. L., & Pittman, L. (2001). Welfare reform and parenting: Reasonable expectations. *The Future of Children, 12,* 167–85.

Conger, R. D., Ge, X., Elder, G. H. Jr., Lorenz, F. O., & Simons, R. L. (1994). Economic stress, coercive family processes, and developmental problems of adolescents. *Child Development, 65,* 541–61.

Connell, J. P., Spencer, M. B., & Aber, J. L. (1994). Educational risk and resilience in African American youth: Context, self, action, and outcomes in school. *Child Development, 65,* 493–506.

Duncan, G. J. & Magnuson, K. (2002). Economics and parenting. *Parenting: Science and Practice, 2,* 437–450.

Furstenberg, F. F., Cook, T. D., Eccles, J., Elder, G. H. Jr., & Sameroff, A. (1999). *Managing to make it: Urban families and adolescent success.* Chicago: University of Chicago Press.

Steinberg, L. (2000, March). *We know some things: Parent adolescent relations in retrospect and prospect.* Presidential address, biennial meeting of the Society for Research on Adolescence, Chicago, IL.

1

"Family Process" Investments That Matter for Child Well-Being

Robert H. Bradley
Robert F. Corwyn
University of Arkansas at Little Rock

INTRODUCTION

Parental investments in children have been defined in a variety of ways to suit a variety of purposes. For example, Trivers (1972), operating from the framework of evolutionary biology, defined parental investment as any act by a parent of an individual offspring that increases that offspring's chance of survival and reproduction at the cost of that parent's ability to invest in other offspring. Becker (1991), using principles from economics, considered parental investments as those aimed at maximizing the lifetime earnings of the child. Hertwig, Davis, and Sulloway (2002) extended this approach, giving it a somewhat more psychological quality. Specifically, they argued that parents use multiple investment strategies that essentially involve a kind of negotiated compromise among competing goals for their children, social norms, and the nature and extent of resources present at any given time. Each perspective on parental investments has merit, certainly within its own frame, but a more holistic frame permits the full range of motivations that influence human behavior.

In this chapter, family process investments in child well-being are defined as those parental actions aimed at preserving or enhancing child development. Another way to think about these family process investments is as actions aimed at preserving or building a child's "personal assets" (Scales &

1

Leffert, 1999). This definition implies an intention on the part of the parent, a conscious decision to do something that will make a child's life better. Most of the scholarly literature focuses on parental actions aimed directly at the child, such as providing food and shelter, ensuring a child's health, responding to a child's cries of distress, and so forth. These "direct investments" in child well-being are the focus in this chapter, but they are not the only types of investments parents make in behalf of their children.

Parents make numerous "indirect investments" as well. That is, they take actions whose purpose is to make the child's life better but that may not be directed at the child per se. Indirect investments include such things as deciding where to live, determining what school or daycare a child will attend, joining the PTA, deciding to spend extra hours at work so that the family will have more money, taking part in a social or political organization, and so forth. For much of the 20th century and into the 21st, evidence has accumulated on the value of direct parental investments in children. By contrast, there is almost no information on the value of indirect investments. Although this chapter only briefly discusses these indirect investments in child well-being, it is critical that the research community begin investigating these investments to fully understand parents'role in human capital formation, particularly with regard to fathers and members of certain cultural groups.

As conscious actors in their children's lives, parents do not inevitably act in their children's best interest. An overall review of the literature suggests that three conditions are necessary for parents to make positive investments in their children: a sense of future, a sense of purpose, and a sense of connection.

WHICH INVESTMENTS MATTER?

The answer to this question is, at once, both simple and complicated. The fact is, what adults do in their role as parents has changed over the centuries, a function of technological, social, and economic adjustments. The goal of parenting, however, has remained essentially the same—to enable children to become competent, caring adults who are able to function well within society (Maccoby, 1992). In any place or in any era, attaining the goal is no mean feat. This seemingly innocuous generic prescription requires a variety of specific parenting actions carried out over a lengthy period of time, fitted to a particular child's needs, and executed within the boundaries of the resources and constraints present. These actions may take time, energy, or expenditure on the part of parents and, therefore, can rightly be thought of as investments.

Bradley and Caldwell (1995) recently constructed a system for organizing the tasks of parenting around the concept from systems theory that parents help to regulate the course of children's development (Sameroff, 1995). Central to the framework is the notion that optimal parenting (a facilitative home environment) is best conceived of as a set of regulatory acts and conditions aimed at successful adaptation and at successful exploitation of opportunity structures for children (Saegert & Winkel, 1990). Such a conception is in keeping with ecological developmental theories that place value on person–environment fit as the basic way of insuring maximum adaptability and optimal well-being. Moreover, the notion that parents are regulators of child–environment fit connects with the idea from systems theory that human beings are advanced, self-constructing organisms that actively engage their environments (Ford & Lerner, 1992). This framework is also consonant with the idea that children are conscious agents who are active in adapting to and constructing their environments (Lewis, 1997; Shonkoff & Phillips, 2000).

Starting from this basic notion, Bradley and Caldwell (1995) identified five basic regulatory tasks (or functions) performed by parents: safety/sustenance, stimulation, socioemotional support, structure, and surveillance—the "five S's," if you will. These five S's constitute the classes of investments that parents must make to both protect children from harm and promote their well-being. The first three types of investments (or regulatory functions, to use systems theory nomenclature) derive from what is known about human needs and arousal systems. Specifically, Maslow (1954) contended that human beings need environments that promote survival, provide information (including enlistment of attention), and affirm worth. Relatedly, Ford and Lerner (1992) identified three major domains of functioning, each with its own arousal processes: biological/physical (activity arousal); cognitive/attention arousal; and social/emotional arousal. For complex living systems such as human beings, the task of maintaining internal unity is quite complicated due to the large number of component subsystems involved and the elaborateness of their organization (Ford & Lerner, 1992; Shonkoff & Phillips, 2000). To deal with children's individuality and complexity, parents must perform other functions that assure that the "direct inputs" designed to sustain, stimulate, and emotionally support the child are maximally fitted to the child's current needs, proclivities, and competencies—hence, structure and surveillance.

Safety and Sustenance

From the standpoint of investing in children, of primary importance to parents is assuring the physical well-being of their children. Parents provide adequate nutrients, shelter, and conditions to maintain health and insure both survival and physical and psychological development (Pollitt, 1988). Parents also often seek to protect children from pathogenic conditions such as pollutants, passive cigarette smoke, physical hazards, and exposure to heavy metals. That said, parents obviously differ in the degree to which they protect their children from physical hazards overall and from any specific physical hazard (Evans, Kliewer, & Martin, 1991; Jacobson, Jacobson, Padgett, Brummitt, & Billings, 1992; Tong & McMichael, 1992).

In America, threats to well-being such as malnutrition are relatively rare. However, many American children suffer from poor nutrition and poor eating habits, resulting in compromises to their health (e.g., many children suffer vitamin and mineral deficiencies and obesity) and increasing the likelihood of poor immune response and abnormal brain growth (Lozoff, Jiminez, & Wolf, 1991; Ogden, 1998). Dealing effectively with these nutritional problems requires different types of investments, such as being vigilant in what children eat, establishing good eating routines, and helping children monitor their own eating patterns.

Parents, especially mothers, invest in their children's health beginning prior to birth by getting good prenatal care, avoiding smoking, drinking, and drugs during pregnancy, maintaining proper diet during pregnancy, and getting sufficient exercise. There is substantial evidence that these investments increase the likelihood of normal, healthy deliveries and long-term well-being.

The United States ranks 22nd among industrialized nations in infant mortality rates (Guyer, Hoyert, Martin, Ventura, MacDorman, & Strobino, 1999). An important aspect of parental involvement directly affecting the safety of children, therefore, is prenatal care. Mothers who begin prenatal care early are more likely to have a healthier pregnancy and a better pregnancy outcome (Fiscella, 1995). Owing largely to the expansion of Medicaid coverage to poor and near-poor pregnant women, the past decade has seen a significant increase in prenatal care (Dubay, Joyce, Kaestner, & Kenney, 2001). In 2000, 83.2% of U.S. mothers began prenatal care in the first trimester of pregnancy—up from 75.8% in 1990 (Centers for Disease Control, 2002). These figures were lower for American Indians (69.3%), Hispanics (74.4%), African Americans (74.3%), and teen mothers (69.1%). Only 3.9% of all mothers received care beginning in the third trimester or no care at all, falling from 6.1% in 1990.

Two other preventable causes of adverse birth outcomes are maternal smoking and alcohol use. Both show declines during the past decade. Based on birth certificate data, which are likely underreported, cigarette smoking during pregnancy has declined from 19.5% in 1989 to 12.2% in 2000 (Centers for Disease Control, 2002). Not surprisingly, the rates differed dramatically for mothers with less than a high school education and those who were college-educated (25% versus 2%, respectively). The most recent survey that collected data on alcohol use during pregnancy reported a decline in drinking rates during pregnancy from 22.5% in 1988 to 15.3% in 1995 (Ebrahim, Luman, Floyd, Murphy, Bennett, & Boyle, 1998). Among women reporting frequent use (i.e., at least five drinks per occasion or seven drinks per week), the rate dropped from 3.9% in 1988 to 3.5% in 1995. Risk factors associated with alcohol use during pregnancy were college educated, unmarried, employed, and high household incomes.

After birth, parents, again particularly mothers, continue to invest in ways that benefit children's health (e.g., by continuing to avoid smoking, by breastfeeding, and by making sure children have routine well-child visits and immunizations). These investments redound to children's good health, such as by increased immune response and decreased rates of asthma (Committee on Health & Behavior, 2001). Unfortunately, there is a noticeable decrease in the number of well-child visits, and many children do not receive routine care as they move into adolescence (Committee on Health & Behavior, 2001).

The need to protect children from threats to their safety is obvious. The leading cause of morbidity and mortality in children beyond age 1 is accidents, many of which are preventable (Garbarino, 1988; U.S. Dept. of Health & Human Services, 1991). For example, there is evidence that the use of car restraints results in fewer injuries (Christerphersen, 1989). However, there is evidence—mostly anecdotal or from case studies—that parents vary widely in how much time and energy they invest in protecting children from physical hazards, including toxic substances and sharp objects. Analysis of the National Longitudinal Survey of Youth (NLSY), data aggregated over five biennial assessments (1986–1994), shows that the safety of a child's home varies by poverty status (Bradley, Corwyn, McAdoo, & Garcia Coll, 2001). Only 10% of children younger than age 3 and living in poverty had a safe home play area (no potentially hazardous health or structural hazards), compared with 90% of children generally. Homes grow more hazardous as children age. For children ages 6–9, 75.9% of nonpoor White children and 68.9% of poor White children resided in a home with no potentially dangerous structural or health hazards within reach. These figures were approximately 5% lower for African American children (71% nonpoor and 63.8% poor, respectively). For some children, the threats to physical well-being extend beyond the immediate boundaries of home (i.e., children living in war zones, dangerous neighborhoods, and even farms). In such situations, parents often take great care to protect their children from the dangers, sometimes at considerable cost to their own health and safety (Klingman, 2002).

Stimulation

To insure competence and continued effort toward life-enhancing goals, the environment must provide sensory data that engage attention and provide information (i.e., stimulation). There is an abundance of both psychological theory and empirical data to buttress the significance of stimulation for cognitive, psychomotor, social, and sensory development (Bradley, Caldwell, & Rock, 1988; Bradley, Whiteside, Mundfrom, Casey, Kelleher, & Pope, 1994; Horowitz, 1987; Lickliter, 2000; Shonkoff & Phillips, 2002). According to Kagan (1984), the main catalyst for environmentally mediated change is information. Environmental stimuli are received as information through the senses, where they are reacted to immediately. All incoming stimuli have the potential to inform the organism regarding needed action. The salience of the information depends on both the attributes of the stimuli and the internal states of the organism at the time the stimuli are received. This information reacts with qualitative changes in competence and an emerging sense of self in children to generate and excite motives that guide behavior.

The deleterious consequences of understimulation were first brought to light in studies of institutionalized children (Dennis, 1973; Skeels & Dye, 1939). Later evidence revealed the negative consequences of overstimulation and disorganized stimulation (Deutsch and Associates, 1968; Wohlwill & Heft, 1977). Current evidence suggests that a moderate amount of stimulation presented in a variety of forms is beneficial to development (Bradley & Caldwell, 1976, 1979; Elardo, Bradley, & Caldwell, 1975; Kagan, 1984). Illustrative evidence of the value of stimulation comes from studies of parent talk. The research of Hart and Risley (1995) and Hoff (2003) provide compelling documentation of the value in providing children more labels for objects, responding contingently to children's speech, making efforts to elicit conversation from children, sustaining conversations with children, and just talking to them more often.

Researchers in the last three decades have begun to document differences in the level of communication between parents and children. Hart and Risley (1995), in what has become a classic study in the field, found that mothers directed an average of 325 utterances per hour to their children between the ages of 11 and 18 months. However, there was more than a tenfold difference between mothers in the rate per hour, with low socioeconomic status (SES) mothers typically providing fewer utterances than middle SES mothers (SES includes maternal education, parental occupational status, and family wealth). This difference went beyond the number of utterances to the overall quality of communication. Hoff (2003) found that middle-class mothers had higher rates of speech, used more topic-continuing replies and fewer directives, posed more conversation-

eliciting questions and more word tokens. In both studies, children who received more and richer language showed higher levels of language competence. When they analyzed NLSY data, Bradley, Corwyn, McAdoo, and
Garcia Coll (2001) found not only SES differences in how often mothers
spoke to young children, but differences in how often mothers spoke to older
children as well. These SES differences in the level of stimulation extended
to almost every form of stimulation examined.

Stimulation is important because it shapes the course of development, including neural development. Neuronal organization is determined in part
by asymmetries of stimulation. In general, the more stimulation a particular
behavioral system receives, the more the neuronal structures serving it will
gain ascendancy (Rosensweig, Krech, Bennett, & Diamond, 1962). In their
penetrating analysis of how children learn, the Committee on Developments in the Science of Learning shows that people learn by actively en-
countering objects, actions, events, and concepts in their environments
(Bransford, Brown, & Cocking, 2000). To move from novice learner to ex-
pert in any particular area of knowledge or skill requires substantial experience (usually guided experience) in that area (meaning much stimulation).
According to the Committee:

> Along with children's natural curiosity and their persistence as self-motivated learn-
> ers, what they learn during their first 4 or 5 years is not learned in isolation. Infants' ac-
> tivities are complemented by adult–child relationships that encourage the gradual
> involvement of children in the skilled and valued activities of the society in which
> they live. Research has shown that learning is strongly influenced by these social inter-
> actions (pp, 102–103).

A good example of the value of such investments in children is the academic gains made by children whose parents read to them from infancy onward (Bradley, 1994). Reading has long been considered a bellwether of the
quality of stimulation. Sixty-seven percent of White, nonpoor mothers reported reading to their children (birth to age 3) at least three times per week
(Bradley, Corwyn, Mcadoo, & Garcia-Coll, 2001). This compares with only
45% of poor, White mothers. Percentages were lower for African American
(44% nonpoor, 32% poor) and Hispanic (42% nonpoor, 25% poor). For all
three groups, the percentages increased for children aged 3–6. For example,
49% of nonpoor, Hispanic mothers reported reading to their children at
least three times a week, and 30% of poor Hispanic mothers did.

The number of books in a household is another important indicator of
stimulation. More than 60% of infants from nonpoor, White homes have at
least 10 developmentally appropriate books available for reading (see Table
1.1). This compares to only about 40% of poor, White children. The figures
for African American and Hispanic children are far lower (e.g., only 16% of

TABLE 1.1
Percent Responses to HOME Items by Ethnic Group, Poverty Status and Age of Child

	European-American		African-American		Hispanic-American	
	Non-poor	Poor	Non-poor	Poor	Non-poor	Poor
Birth through 2 years						
Child has 10 or more books	63.1	41.8	33.0	19.7	36.5	16.0
Reads to child 3/week or more	66.7	44.9	43.8	31.7	41.9	25.1
Child has 7 or more cuddly toys	81.9	76.6	67.1	52.5	70.3	61.7
3 through 5 years						
Child has 10 or more books	93.4	74.6	67.8	39.9	68.1	37.9
Reads to child 3/week or more	71.4	55.4	45.0	33.3	48.7	29.8
Helps child learn numbers	95.9	93.5	92.9	86.7	93.1	86.7
Helps child learn alphabet	94.4	87.5	91.9	86.3	85.5	74.8
Helps child learn shapes/sizes	87.9	78.7	77.0	63.0	73.2	57.9
Taken to museum monthly or more	8.3	6.0	13.5	10.8	8.8	8.5
6 through 9 years						
Child has 10 or more books	94.7	80.3	75.3	47.8	75.8	43.7

Reads to child 3/week or more	45.2	35.7	30.3	28.0	34.5	20.9
Child has musical instrument	46.8	28.4	36.0	23.1	37.2	25.7
Child gets special lessons	61.0	36.5	44.7	34.6	43.2	23.9
Taken to museum monthly or more	8.2	8.6	15.1	11.6	9.8	9.0
With father outdoors 1/week or more	85.8	61.3	66.9	47.7	81.0	69.8
Discuss t.v. programs with child	89.6	79.1	79.0	61.7	81.5	69.6
10 through 14 years						
Child has 10 or more books	73.5	50.9	41.6	26.1	47.0	20.2
With father outdoors 1/week or more	76.3	57.0	51.0	41.0	71.2	56.7
Discuss t.v. Programs with child	89.0	78.9	72.3	58.5	77.0	62.8
Child has musical instrument	55.3	41.8	39.1	24.8	38.1	23.1
Child gets special lessons	68.7	54.4	60.3	48.6	54.5	31.6
Taken to museum monthly or more	5.2	7.0	10.4	10.7	5.9	9.0

poor Hispanics). The figures for preschool children (ages 3 to 6) are higher across the board, ranging from a low of 38% among poor Hispanics to 93% for nonpoor Whites. The number of developmentally appropriate books available remains fairly constant until adolescence, at which point numbers decline significantly, nearly to levels reported during infancy.

Young children from all ethnic and social class groups tend to have a significant number of toys available. More than 50% of children in all groups had at least seven cuddly or role-playing toys during infancy, with fewer than 5% in any group having none. The majority of preschool children have access to some type of electronic device to play music or story tapes and records. Between one fourth and one half of children from all groups had some type of musical instrument to play when they were between the ages of 6 and 14.

Beyond reading to the child, most parents also report teaching their children specific skills and concepts. As Table 1.1 shows, the vast majority of parents from all groups (75% to 97%) report teaching such basic concepts as colors, shapes, alphabet, and numbers to preschool children. Data from the 1996 National Household Education Survey showed that almost 40% of all families help children with homework at least three times per week. About one third help children once or twice a week, and only about one fourth rarely or never help their children (National Center for Education Statistics, 2002). Although these social interactions are most critical in early childhood, their value continues throughout life. Stimulation is important not only for cognitive and psychomotor growth, but for normal development of many biological subsystems (e.g., vision; Cohen, DeLoache, & Strauss, 1979).

Parent efforts to stimulate children take many forms, from talking to children to reading to them, to teaching specific skills, to involving children in household activities and family projects. As children age, parents may become more reactive and less proactive in the forms of stimulation they provide (e.g., advising and consulting on how to solve problems with school mates or dating partners, Laird, Pettit, Mize, Brown, & Lindsey, 1994). Although research does not exist on every particular type of stimulation, there is ample evidence that the greater the variety of stimulation to which a child is exposed by the family, the greater the likelihood of academic and even social success (Bradley, 1994; Bradley & Corwyn, 2003; Bradley, Corwyn, Caldwell, Whiteside-Mansell, Wasserman, & Mink, 2000; Bradley, Corwyn, Burchinal, McAdoo, & Garcia Coll, 2001). As children enter school, out-of-home experiences constitute a greater part of parental stimulation. That said, fewer than half of all children either receive special lessons or belong to organizations or clubs designed to promote their competence (with notable SES differences in these figures; see Table 1.1). In comparison, more than 60% of mothers reported taking their children to cultural experiences such as museums and art galleries during the past year, albeit only about 10% report doing so once a month or more. Although there are SES differences within each ethnic group studied, there are fewer ethnic group differences in this area of stimulation than in directly providing lessons and club memberships.

Although one certainly might view reading to a child, teaching a child to ride a bike, or taking a child to a museum as leisure activities from which a parent derives pleasure irrespective of benefit to the child, both the time costs and the fact that parents tend to devote energy during the activity to assuring that the child gains something from the experience indicate that parents view such activities as investments in the child's well-being. Moreover, the wide variability in the amount of time parents spend in such activities suggests that they are not just done for the parents themselves but represent variations in how much parents wish to invest in their children.

Socioemotional Support

Optimal socioemotional development depends on having an environment that responds to human social and emotional needs (Bretherton & Waters, 1985). This is an extraordinary challenge in that it means helping children cope with basic anxieties, fears, and feelings of emotional insecurity. It also means inculcating a sense of belonging and worth, facilitating a sense of happiness and fulfillment, and promoting a sense of responsibility and concern for others.

One of the most important investments parents make is assisting their children with emotion regulation (Thompson, 1994). Emotions function to prepare human beings to take action in their own best interest (Grinker et al., 1956). The emotion arousal system is rather easily triggered in conditions that pose threat or conditions that offer opportunities for exploration. Emotions also provide a primitive regulatory process that operates before a person constructs evaluative thoughts and constructs values, preferences, and personal goals (Ford, in press). To ensure optimal fit with environmental affordances and demands, children need parents who invest their time and energy enlisting and modulating the motivational properties of emotions (Eisenberg, Cumberland, & Spinrad, 1998). Sometimes this means that parents must take action in advance of expressed needs (e.g., assuring a child that the babysitter will be there to take care of the child while they are away, or assuring the child that things will be okay at that first day of school). Other times it means taking action after the needs are expressed (e.g., comforting a child awakened by a nightmare). Parents may help the child with emotion regulation by comforting, distracting, or redirecting attention to safer and more enjoyable pursuits. Studies indicate that responsive, social interactions on the part of mothers assist infants in regulating arousal (Fogel, Diamond, Langhorst, & Demos, 1982) and may contribute to a general capacity to regulate arousal (Gable & Isabella, 1992).

According to Erikson, responsive care builds a sense of trust—in others and the environment more generally. Predictable, responsive care also contributes to a secure attachment (Ainsworth, 1973; Bowlby, 1969). Children who are securely attached to their parents are in an advantaged position to develop a balanced sense of self (Cassidy, 1988), positive social relationships (Park & Waters, 1989), and an increased capacity to modulate stress reactions (Caldji, Tannenbaum, Sharma, Francis, Plotsky, & Meany, 1998). Importantly, a secure attachment moves a child toward an orientation of mutuality where there is greater receptivity for other parental investments, such as socialization on getting along with others and investing in learning activities (Kochanska, 1997). An investment in responsive care on the part of parents appears not only to yield positive benefits for emotional well-being but to increase the yield on subsequent parental investments in the child's development.

As children get older, socioemotional support from parents may take the form of assisting them to realistically appraise situations so that stress is minimized, effective coping strategies can be employed, and goals leading to a sense of fulfillment can be pursued (Lazarus, 1993). It may even require "emotion coaching" (Johnson & Lieberman, 1999). A major issue in this regard is to show children how situations can be manageable. According to Rotter (1966), the willingness of a person to perform a particular act is a function of the extent to which the behavior is seen as leading to a desired outcome. Evidence on both infrahuman and human subjects indicates that the environment must be controllable at least to some minimal degree if positive motivation is to be maintained.

Socioemotional support entails more than just responding to expressed needs and helping children regulate their emotions. Children thrive when they feel wanted. Feeling wanted motivates children to pursue life-enhancing goals. Rohner (1986) compiled evidence from several large cross-cultural studies showing that warm, supportive relationships help promote good adjustment, a sense of well-being, good health, and a wealth of other positive developmental outcomes. There is also evidence that children benefit from positive affirmation of worth (Ausubel, 1968; Roberts, 1983). That is, to be supportive, parents must be reinforcing (in a proactive sense) as well as responsive (in a reactive sense). How worth is affirmed varies substantially from culture to culture. In some societies, worth is closely tied to individual accomplishments or status; in others, it is more strongly tied to collective commitments and involvement.

The extent to which parents show affection to their child has been examined in the Panel Study of Income Dynamics (PSID) and National Longitudinal Survey of Youth (NLSY) data sets. Both of these large data sets involve nationally representative cohorts of families in the United States. Ninety-one percent of mothers and 77.2% of fathers in the PSID indicated that they hugged or showed physical affection to their child in the past month (Yeung, 1999). A smaller percentage of mothers and fathers said "I love you" to the child (86.5% and 66.9%, respectively) and even fewer said words of appreciation to the child (35.1% and 38.8%, respectively).

Using NLSY data, Bradley, Corwyn, McAdoo, and Garcia Coll (2001) found ethnic group and poverty status differences in the responsiveness of parents. Eighty-seven percent of nonpoor White, and 73.4% of poor White parents showed physical affection to their infant or toddler during the 1-hour, in-home interview. Hispanic parents showed similar levels of affection, and African American parents showed lower levels of physical affection. Eighty percent of nonpoor, African American families, and 64.3% of poor African American families showed physical affection to the child. Parents were less likely to show physical affection as the child aged. Only 63.2% of nonpoor White, 48.7% of poor White, 46.2% of nonpoor African American, and 31.7% of poor African American parents were observed kissing or hugging their 3–5-year-old child.

A third type of investment is providing encouragement and guidance for adequate functioning outside the family environment (Pettit, Dodge, & Brown, 1988). Part of this takes the form of reinforcing behaviors that lead to competence and engagement in activities that promote success outside the home. Part takes the form of discipline strategies and expressions of expectations for involvement and success (Steinberg, 1986). Finally, part may take the form of modeling of adaptive behaviors (Putallaz, 1987). A good example of the latter is maintaining calm during periods of threat or stress. Such behavior has been shown to reduce the negative impact of events (e.g., storms) and conditions (e.g., war) that often produce traumatic reactions in children (Klingman, 2002). At its base, support is an investment that provides motivation to comfortably and productively engage the broader environment.

Structure

Exceptional parents know that for children to thrive, parents must do more than provide sufficient sustenance, stimulation, and socioemotional support. Although children need these investments, receiving equal amounts of these inputs does not necessarily result in equal amounts of "good" growth and development. Parents must also invest their time and energy managing and arranging the inputs such that they are maximally suited to the child's requirements and environment. Arranging the inputs can be as crucial to development as the amount. For example, preterm infants, infants exposed to drugs prenatally, and some children with autism can be overwhelmed by levels of stimulation that are quite comfortable for normal children (Als, 1986; Friedman & Sigman, 1992).

Children have limitations in their ability to effectively deal with their environments. For instance, the number of objects that a person can manage effectively at any one point in time increases with age (Kuhn, 1992). Children also have less developed cognitive strategies for selecting, remembering, and dealing with information and are, therefore, more dependent on instructional or other environmental aids to assist them in problem-solving (Bjorkland, 1990). The Committee on Developments in the Science of Learning concluded that, "Parents and others who care for children arrange their activities and facilitate learning by regulating the difficulty of the tasks and by modeling mature performance during joint participation in activities" (Bransford et al., 2000, p. 103). Likewise, studies of language development show that parental scaffolding of children's early language experiences (i.e., providing a predictable referential and social context for communication) contributes significantly to language acquisition (Bruner, 1983). The research on dialogic reading tells the same story. Specifically, children's language scores and early competence in reading were superior when adults helped the children tell the story in a book rather than just reading the story to them (Whitehurst, Arnold, Epstein, & Angell, 1994).

Parents invest their time in structuring productive learning activities in a myriad of ways, from placing an object to be manipulated in the hands of an infant, to setting up routine times for homework, to providing increasingly challenging lessons on driving to the adolescent. Learning is also easier in the absence of distracting stimuli (Wohlwill & Heft, 1977). Thus, parents often must ensure that the environment is free of noise and competing inputs when children are trying to learn. In general, the evidence shows that children's cognitive development is influenced by how parents organize the physical and temporal features of the environment (Bradley & Caldwell, 1976).

The domains of cognitive and language development contain the richest array of studies showing the benefits of parental structuring of inputs to children. However, children also have limitations in other domains that require parents to structure children's encounters with the environment in ways that benefit the child. Take, for example, the mundane task of feeding a child. It is not enough that the parent provides sufficient nourishment. Research shows that poor timing and pacing of feeding may contribute to failure-to-thrive (Drotar, 1985).

Parents also assist their children in developing friendships. Ladd and Goltner (1988) found that children whose parents initiated peer contacts had more playmates and more consistent play companions in their preschool peer networks.

Parents tend to invest considerable energy structuring the physical sur-roundings of children. Environmental psychologists have long been inter-ested in how physical structures influence behavior and facilitate adaptive functioning (e.g., how physical arrangements within a home help to insure privacy, Altman, 1977). In effect, the design of the physical space enables and encourages people to do certain things and constrains them from doing others (Rapoport, 1985). Among the most revealing studies of the influence of physical structure are those by Moore (1988) on the spatial organization of daycare centers. He found that, in contrast to children in both fully open-plan and fully closed-plan spatial organization, children in modified open plan environments were more visually and actively engaged in devel-opmentally oriented tasks. Group size was smaller, age mixing was greater, and there was almost twice as much social interaction. In open-plan centers, there was more random nontask behavior. In closed-plan centers, there was more withdrawn behavior and more teacher-directed behavior.

Orderly environments enable children to learn the meaning and func-tion of things more readily. Having distinctive, well-situated landmarks makes it easier for children to orient themselves and to get around in their surroundings (Evans et al., 1991). Parents address the problems of physical space not only by what they do with the space itself but by how they deal with children's access to and use of space. Parents react to phys-ical hazards, for example, by restricting children's freedom to explore (Kaplan & Dove, 1987).

Meaning also comes from having order in one's social environment. This often takes the form of routines and family rituals. Family rituals not only provide a sense of order but serve as a means of socialization (Fiese, Hooker, Kotary, & Schwagler, 1993). One routine that is assessed in national surveys is how often families eat meals together. Analysis of NLSY data show that eating family meals together varies by poverty status ethnicity and the child's age (Bradley, Corwyn, McAdoo, & Garcia Coll, 2001). Among chil-dren younger than age 3, the percentage who ate at least one meal a day with both parents was 74.1% for nonpoor White children; 65.3% for poor White children; 59.9% for nonpoor African American children; and 36.7% for poor African American children. The percentages for Hispanic children were very similar to those of White children. The percentages for children over age 12 were: nonpoor Whites, 64.2%; poor Whites, 51%; nonpoor Af-rican Americans, 37.4%; and poor African Americans, 25.7%.

Children also are limited in their ability to deal with stress and complex-ity, to obtain needed materials for use or consumption, to exercise control over their own bodies, and to manage social situations (Ford & Lerner, 1992). Accordingly, parents must structure the child's encounters with the environment to benefit the child. There is still relatively little information available on how to "best" organize actions, objects, and events to achieve a particular developmental effect in many areas of child functioning. However, there are areas of research such as conscience formation (Kochanska, 1993) and social behavior (Patterson, DeBaryshe, & Ramsey, 1989) for which a reasonable database is emerging. There is also evidence attesting to the general value of establishing family routines, as they provide a kind of overarching structure to the child's daily life, thus making life more predictable and manageable (Melamed, 2002). Bronfenbrenner and Crouter (1983, p. 379) concluded that mothers can encourage and shape the child's psychological growth by structuring the settings the child experiences so as to "evoke certain kinds of activities and discourage others."

Surveillance

To be effective in managing children's lives, parents must keep track of the whereabouts and activities of the child. Most commonly, this investment has been viewed as protecting children from harm (Darling & Steinberg, 1993; Patterson et al., 1989; Peterson, Ewigman, & Kivlahan, 1993; U.S. Dept. of Health & Human Services, 1991). A significant proportion of accidental or unintentional injury occurs often because of parental failure to adequately monitor and supervise children (Garbarino, 1988; Peterson & Gable, 1998). The level of child monitoring and the parent's overall supervisory style (i.e., the parent's degree of active attention to removing or attending to potentially dangerous objects and conditions) directly contribute to the likelihood of injury; and both are connected to parental perceptions about the level of risk present and the controllability of the hazards (Greaves, Glik, Kronenfeld, & Jackson, 1994). Furthermore, the amount and type of supervision needed to prevent injuries change as children grow older (Peterson et al.,1993).

Parents keep track of their children's activities not only to prevent physical harm, but to prevent psychological harm as well. For example, since the advent of the Internet, children have been exposed to on-line victimization by sexual predators (Finkelhor, Mitchell, & Wolak, 2000). The need to monitor children's television viewing and video games has been the subject of much concern and research, with evidence suggesting that exercising control over these media is important for long-term child well-being. That said, the evidence suggests that most parents have relatively few rules regarding television viewing (Dorr, Rabin, & Irlen, 2002).

There is also considerable evidence that surveillance is important to adaptive behavior. For example, Steinberg (1986) found that latchkey children who report home after school, whose parents know their whereabouts, and who have been reared authoritatively are less susceptible to peer pressure than those who "hang out" with peers after school and whose parents provide little supervision. Crouter, MacDonald, McHale, and Perry-Jenkins

(1990) examined relations between parental monitoring and children's school performance and conduct. They found that less monitored boys received lower grades than did other children, and less monitored boys from dual-earner families had poorer conduct.

Studies have shown that parental monitoring is related to substance abuse, juvenile delinquency, and school achievement for children in middle childhood and adolescence (Brown, Mounts, Lamborn, & Steinberg, 1993; Dornbusch, Ritter, Leiderman, Roberts, & Fraleigh, 1987; Loeber & Dishion, 1983). Patterson, DeBaryshe, and Ramsey (1989) concluded from their review of antisocial behavior that poor monitoring and supervision of the child's activities often contribute to the development of antisocial behavior. Unmonitored children, they suggested, are more likely to respond to peer pressure to engage in risky behavior. In their report, the Committee on Community-Level Programs for Youth of the National Research Council and Institute of Medicine concluded that, "Across settings, there is more positive development and fewer problem behaviors with consistent monitoring by parents" (Eccles & Gootman, 2002, p. 92).

Very little is known about how much parents keep tabs on young children. Based on NLSY data on whether the parent kept the focal child in view during a 1-hour home visit, nonpoor families were more likely to keep track of infants and toddlers than poor families (Bradley, Corwyn, McAdoo, & Garcia Coll, 2001). Approximately 90% of nonpoor White and 81% of poor Whites kept the child in view during the interview. Fewer nonpoor and poor African American (85.3% and 78.2%, respectively) and nonpoor and poor Hispanics (84.7% and 82.9%, respectively) kept the child in view. The bulk of research on parental monitoring has focused on adolescence. The National Survey of American Attitudes on Substance Abuse asks teens about 12 surveillance actions they attribute to their parents: monitoring television; monitoring the Internet; restricting music they buy; knowing their whereabouts after school; expecting to be told the truth about where the teen is going; very aware of academic performance; imposing a curfew; making clear they do not approve of marijuana use; eating dinner with teen six or seven times a week; turning off television during dinner; assigning teen regular chores; and being present when teen returns from school. Only 27% of teens indicated that their parents consistently took 10 or more of these actions (National Center on Addiction and Substance Abuse, 2001). Nearly one fifth (18%) of teens reported that their parents took five or fewer of these actions.

Surveillance, however, goes beyond just protecting children from harm and forestalling bad behavior. It also involves tracking what the environment potentially affords the child by way of productive and enjoyable encounters. At present, there are virtually no data on this aspect of parental monitoring.

Darling and Steinberg (1993) offered the proposition that overall parenting style gives meaning to each parenting behavior. They made reference to the conceptualization of parenting style introduced by Baumrind (1980; i.e., authoritative, authoritarian, laissez faire), but the significance of their proposition extends beyond just Baumrind's conceptualization. Their larger point is, the overall manner in which adults execute the job of parenting provides an interpretive frame for each particular thing they do. In effect, when a mother with a generally laid-back style of parenting scolds her child, it is likely to have a somewhat different impact than when a mother with a demanding style does the same thing. Although Darling and Steinberg offered only limited empirical support for their proposition (and there have been few efforts on the part of other researchers to extend their thinking to other areas of parenting style), there is adequate general support in both theory and research to agree with their conclusion. For example, there is evidence that parental expectations and attitudes about achievement set the stage for children's responses to parental requests for doing homework and the like (Alexander & Entwisle, 1988). Style, in effect, can become a means of dampening the impact of particular parenting investments (i.e., a hidden tax) or a means of accelerating the impact (i.e., sheltered wealth). In effect, parenting style changes the "value" of parental actions and, thereby, changes the impact on children. There is a need for substantially more specific research on the relation between overall styles of parenting and the impact of particular investments, but there is little doubt that the relation exists.

THE INVESTMENT PORTFOLIO

Does careful attention to these five parenting investments promote positive adaptation in children? The most straightforward answer is that the research is incomplete. There are hundreds of studies on dozens of populations that show an association between each of the five classes of investments and various aspects of well-being. There is more convincing evidence for particular actions than others, but the evidence is generally compelling (see *From Neurons to Neighborhoods* [Shonkoff & Phillips, 2000], for an excellent synopsis). Much remains undetermined, however, about the nature of these relations (or even their consistency across children). Neiderhiser and Reiss, in chapter 2 of this volume, examine genetic factors, for example, but that is just the tip of the iceberg. Human beings are advanced organisms, actively engaged in complex social and physical ecologies. Not surprisingly, there is no simple formula that will yield certain dividends for all children (Shonkoff & Phillips, 2000). The precise yield on any investment is hard to predict with accuracy.

One reason it is hard to estimate just how much yield will accrue to particular parenting investments is that investments of a particular kind do not occur in isolation from the larger portfolio of family process investments, nor do they function in isolation from those other investments. The same parent who provides a rich array of stimulating experiences for a child also tends to structure those experiences such that they have the intended effect of promoting competence and enjoyment. Likewise, the parent who provides a child with expressions of affection and affirmation is likely to carefully monitor the child's whereabouts. There is ample evidence that parents who score high in one area of investment also tend to score high in other areas of investment (Bradley, 1994). Accordingly, it is difficult to tease apart the value of particular types of investments.

Unfortunately, the literature on parenting and child development is not very helpful in that the vast majority of studies focus on only one type of investment at a time, too often attributing any "effect" observed to that type and ignoring its covariation with other types of investments. An interesting exception is in studies of malnutrition. For several decades, researchers who want to understand the impact of poor nutrition on cognitive competencies have understood the importance of controlling for the level of stimulation available to the child.

We recently conducted a series of analyses on data from the National Longitudinal Survey of Youth (NLSY) that attest to the value of controlling for multiple types of family process investments simultaneously. We examined the relation of learning stimulation and maternal responsiveness to a diversity of outcomes in three different ethnic groups over three developmental periods. In each analysis, we included both types of family process investments. We often found that each type of investment contributed to the prediction of child developmental outcomes when controlling for the other investments, but that the predictions were lower than the simple bivariate correlation between each specific process and each particular outcome.

Another reason it is difficult to estimate the yield for particular family process investments is that these investments occur not only "in time" but also "through time." There is evidence that the impact of particular investments depends not only on when they occur (i.e., the timing) but on how long they continue (i.e., the duration or constancy). A good example of research on the former issue is a study by Duncan, Brooks-Gunn, and Klebanov (1994) that showed that poverty early in childhood has a greater negative impact on intelligence than poverty later in childhood. Likewise, there is evidence that persistent poverty has deeper and more long-lasting effects than transient poverty (Bradley & Corwyn, 2002). Bradley et al. (1988) found that some types of investments seem to have greater impact on particular child outcomes if those investments occur early in life, other types of investments seem to have greater impact if they occur closer in time to when the outcome is measured, and some seem to have more impact as the investment accumulates through time. Recently, based on seven waves of data from the NLSY, maternal responsiveness during early adolescence was found to be related to PPVT scores even when controlling for maternal responsiveness during middle childhood. By contrast, learning stimulation measured when children were in early adolescence was correlated with PIAT Reading scores, but the effect became nonsignificant when controlling for the learning stimulation during prior developmental periods (Bradley & Corwyn, 2003).

Finally, as is the case in so many areas of research on human behavior, inadequacies in measures of key investments and outcomes reduce the likelihood of accounting for substantial amounts of the variance in their relations. It is rare that measures of parenting completely capture the full extent of whatever investment is being made, and some characteristics of children have remained particularly difficult to assess with high validity.

The message from these studies seems to be that life is not just a collection of isolated events or experiences, but a composite of many experiences in and through time. The impact of any one type of family process investment depends on its consistency across time and the array of other investments present. Accordingly, to better understand the yield on any particular investment requires examining that investment in light of other investments using more finely tuned measures, with attention paid to particular investments through time.

THE BROADER CONTEXT OF INVESTMENT

Although we know very little about how often parents engage in most actions designed to assist their children's well-being, one thing is clear: How often parents do any particular thing varies greatly, and the variability is linked to the context of parenting and to characteristics of the child. Over the years, any number of models have emerged that depicted the relation among family processes, child development, and the context in which both occur. The first of these models is Bronfenbrenner's (1995) bioecological systems process–person–context–time model. The essence of his model is captured in two propositions.

Proposition 1. Human development takes place through processes of progressively more complex reciprocal interaction between an active, evolving organism and the persons, objects, and symbols in its immediate environment. To be effective, the interaction must occur on a fairly regular basis over extended periods of time. Such enduring forms of interaction are referred to as *proximal processes.*

Proposition 2. The form, power, content, and direction of the proximal processes affecting development vary systematically as a joint function of the characteristics of the developing person, of the environment, both immediate and more remote, in which the processes are taking place, and the nature of the developmental outcomes under consideration.

Using this broad frame, Belsky (1984) articulated a more targeted model aimed at explaining how family processes help to shape children's development: the parenting process model. He argued that what parents do is influenced by three broad classes of factors: parental personality and psychological well-being, contextual subsystems, and child characteristics. Researchers have applied variants of this basic parenting process model in numerous populations, during every developmental period, and for every developmental domain, in an effort to delineate how particular family process investments play out in children's lives. Findings are neither complete nor fully consistent, but the basic tenets of the model have received convincing support.

Parental Personality and Psychological Well-Being

There have been literally hundreds of studies that examined relations between parental characteristics and parenting behavior. Not surprisingly, a substantial number focused on negative attributes of parents, such as mental illness, substance abuse, and mental retardation. There have, however, been ample studies on positive attributes as well, such as optimism and strong attachments to one's own parents (i.e., the intergenerational transmission of attachment). What follows are a few illustrations from the literature—some positive, some negative.

Mental illness, especially depression, has been the subject of numerous investigations on parenting (for an excellent review, see Zahn-Waxler, Duggal, & Gruber, 2002). Parental psychopathology is a well-established risk factor for both neglectful and harsh parenting. Mental illness corrupts and undermines investments in children in three ways: (a) it decreases positive investments in children's well-being; (b) it establishes a context in which those investments have lesser yield for children because it reduces the child's emotional security and in the process reduces the uptake of positive investments; and (c) it creates a context in which the child is likely to receive fewer positive investments from other adults (either from the remaining parent or from the family support system).

The scenario for alcoholism and other forms of substance abuse is largely the same (Mayes & Truman, 2002). What becomes readily apparent in these parent–child dyads is that the life histories of parent and child are yoked. The dysfunctional aspects of life for the parent are often visited on the child. The damage to children often begins in utero. Life after birth is often filled with chaos, neglect, and abuse. The research speaks not just of negative parental characteristics but of positive ones as well, positive in the sense of increasing the level of investment in children's well-being. Perhaps the most obvious positive characteristic is parental competence, social as well as intellectual. Brighter parents tend to create more nurturing and stimulating environments for their children than do less bright parents (Whiteside, Pope & Bradley, 1996). Their scores on almost every aspect of parenting tend to be higher. For these parents, children tend to benefit from both the genes they inherit and the environments created by their highly competent parents.

There is a growing literature on the intergenerational transmission of attachment. Parents who themselves perceive that they have a strong attachment to their own parents tend to show more sensitivity to their children. In turn, their children tend to be more securely attached to the parents. A recent study showed that this path of intergenerational attachment trends accounts for about 30% of the variance in attachment security (van Izendoorn, 2002).

There are a number of other parental characteristics that are associated with parenting behaviors that appear to foster children's social and emotional well-being, including optimism, agreeableness, conscientiousness, and a sense of calm (Belsky & Barends, 2002; Brody, Stoneman, Flor, McCrary, Hastings, & Conyers, 1994; Klingman, 2002). Parents with these traits make investments in their children that are particularly valuable in helping children cope with adversity (La Greca & Prinstein, 2002).

Contextual Subsystems

The physical and social settings in which families live constitute part of what Harkness and Super (2002) called the *developmental niche*. The developmental niche of families regulates the micro-environment for children. The impact of the developmental niche can be seen in such mundane parental actions as whether babies sleep with their parents or not. The physical environment of cribs and chairs, together with the social environment, sets the structure for the infant's emerging skills (i.e., they set the opportunities and incentives for infant action). In effect, the setting determines what the infant can see, hear, and do. There is considerable variation in what and how parents within any social group or any physical setting invest in their children, but the beliefs, values, and traditions of each group and the affordances of each physical setting are instrumental in determining those investments (Bradley, 2002).

For example, higher rates of divorce and cohabitation leave a higher proportion of children living with a single parent, a stepparent, or an unrelated adult (Smock, 2000). That only 64% of children under age 18 live with both biological parents (Federal Interagency Forum on Child and Family Statistics, 2000, Table POP5.A) means that a sizable portion of children's needs are met by grandparents, cohabiting partners, and single parents. Moreover, some children have only one caregiver whereas others have several caregivers (e.g., two biological parents and two stepparents). As a result, it is important that data on parental involvement take into account the caregiver ratio.

As noted earlier, family income is an important context to consider given that it is clearly linked with every parental input. Likewise, other components of SES beyond income (namely, maternal education, parental occupational status, and family wealth) have consistent impacts on key investments in child well-being (Bradley & Corwyn, 2003). Bradley et al. (2001a), focusing primarily on learning stimulation and maternal responsiveness in the NLSY, found that at almost every age and in all three ethnic groups examined, mothers with higher SES afforded children more stimulation and more socioemotional support. Not surprisingly, these investments produced yields in both child competence and child adaptive behavior.

Although culture and social class (and, to a lesser extent, community) are almost always mentioned when discussing contextual influences on parenting practice, Bronfenbrenner's (1995) model is far more inclusive. Parents are also influenced by governmental regulations and policies (Temporary Assistance for Needy Families regulations have had mixed impacts on the time spent with children), laws (e.g., seat belt laws), public health campaigns (Sudden Infant Death Syndrome deaths have declined), and educational programs. What parents do is often influenced by social institutions. Bronfenbrenner referred to this set of influences as *mesosystem relations*. The activities, practices, and expectations present at school, work, and church often help shape how parents act toward their children.

Finally, it is important to note that in every society, the particular ways parents invest in their children change through time (French, 2002). The 20th century witnessed major changes in everything from sleep patterns to feeding routines to amount of time invested in reading and help with homework to discipline. For example, data from the 2001 National Household Education Survey reveal that today's parents read more to their children than parents of former generations (National Center for Education Statistics, 2002).

Child Characteristics

It is a dictum of every systems theory concerned with human development that children with different characteristics "attract" different types of investments—not only from their parents but from peers and other adults as well (Belsky, 1984; Ford & Lerner, 1992, Sameroff, 1995;

Wachs, 2000. Also see chapter 2 by Neiderhiser & Reiss on genetic influences.) Differences in age, gender, competence, attractiveness, and temperament have consistently been shown to evoke different parental
behaviors. Scarr and McCartney (1983) found that as children grow
older and become more competent, they do more to elicit from their environments (parents included) what they want by way of treatment. Although much remains unknown about all the ways children influence
the nature and amount of parental investments, there is little doubt concerning "bidirectional influence" (Bell & Chapman, 1986). The alter-
nating current of parent-to-child/child-to-parent action complicates
interpretation of genetic and environmental effects on children's development (Collins, Maccoby, Steinberg, Hetherington, & Bornstein,
2000). It also makes it difficult to determine what the yield is from parental investments.

When trying to estimate the impact of parental investments, it is particularly important to remember that human beings (including children) actively construct meaning in their own lives and that they have an
emotional investment in their own lives. When children's emotions are in-
tensely engaged, their responses to certain actions can become distorted.
In some instances, the distortion can lead to an intensification of whatever
effect is ordinarily produced by the action; in others, the distortion can
lead to inattention or disconnection; in yet others, the distortion can lead
to a response opposite to that ordinarily produced by the action. Perhaps
the best known examples of these are what sometimes happens during the
"terrible twos" as a function of sibling rivalry and in relation to peers.
Two-year-olds, struggling with issues of autonomy, may respond quite negatively to parental efforts of assistance, however sensitively offered. Likewise, the recent paper on the "equity hypothesis" offers rather convincing
evidence that most children perceive parental treatment of siblings as being better than parental treatment of themselves (Hertwig et al., 2002).
Finally, Harris (1995) presented evidence that peer influences can disrupt
or overshadow parental influences.

EPILOGUE

At the end of almost every review about parenting and child development,
the reviewer is left with two quite contradictory impressions: (a) there seem
to be some identifiable patterns in research findings, but (b) there is something a bit incoherent about the whole. According to systems theory, this
indeterminancy is not likely to be fully resolved even with better measures
and better designs because it is inherent in complex systems that small differences at one point in time may trigger a cascade of events and actions
through time, leading to very different outcomes later.

In parent investments research, there are certainly instances of both the principle that different investments can lead to the same outcome and that the same investment can lead to different outcomes. In interpreting patterns that emerge from future studies of investments, it may be useful to bear in mind the principles of parallel, convergent, and reciprocal causation. The principle of parallel causation stipulates that several different processes or factors may be sufficient but not necessary to produce a particular developmental outcome. The principle of convergent causation stipulates that a particular process may be necessary but not sufficient to produce a particular outcome; its effect depends on another process or factor. The principle of reciprocal causation stipulates that bidirectional influences among several factors interacting across time are required to produce a particular developmental outcome.

One of the greatest challenges in understanding how parent investments matter in the lives of children is that parents do so many things, both big and little, aimed at improving their children's lives. Moreover, what they do varies greatly across time and context. Yet, very little is documented about just what they do, when, and how often. Much could be gained from simple descriptive research that made clearer how often things happen in children's lives. It would provide an important perspective and starting point for better understanding of how it matters.

Finally, it is useful to remember that there was a time not so long ago when social scientists proclaimed that what parents do is almighty in determining the life course of children. Then came behavior genetics and a slew of fine-honed analyses of parenting. Accordingly, we have tempered our beliefs to accommodate newly emergent understandings about relations between parental investments and child well-being. Although research points to some reasonably effective investment strategies, it also suggests the need for patience, continued data gathering, and a willingness to adjust one's strategies as conditions warrant. As we begin the 21st century, there is need for more nuanced and complete studies regarding parental investments in children. Because parents, for the most part, are emotionally invested in their children, better investment advice will lead them to becoming better investors.

REFERENCES

Ainsworth, M. (1973). The development of infant–mother attachment. In B. Caldwell & H. Riccuiti (Eds.), *Review of child development research*, (Vol. 3, pp. 2–94). Chicago: University of Chicago Press.

Alexander, K. L., & Entwisle, D. R. (1988). Achievement in the first two years of school: Patterns and processes. *Monographs of the Society for Research in Child Development, 53* (2, Serial No. 218).

Als, H. (1986). A syactive model of neonatal behavioral organization: Framework for the assessment of neurobehavioral development in the premature infant and for support of infants and parents in the neonatal intensive care environment. *Physical and Occupational Therapy in Pediatrics, 6*, 3–55.

Altman, I. (1977). Privacy regulation: Culturally universal or culturally specific? *Journal of Social Issues, 33*, 66–84.

Ausubel, D. (1968). *Educational psychology: A cognitive view.* New York: Holt, Rinehart & Winston.

Baumrind, D. (1980). New directions in socialization research. *Psychological Bulletin, 35*, 639–652.

Becker, G. S. (1991). *A treatise on the family.* Cambridge, MA: Harvard University Press.

Bell, R., & Chapman, M. (1986). Child effects in studies using experimental or brief longitudinal approaches to socialization. *Developmental Psychology, 22*, 595–603.

Belsky, J. (1984). The determinants of parenting: A process model. *Child Development, 55*, 83–96.

Belsky, J., & Barends, N. (2002). Personality and parenting. In M. H. Bornstein (Ed.), *Handbook of parenting* (2nd ed., Vol. 3, pp. 415–438). Mahwah, NJ: Lawrence Erlbaum Associates.

Bjorklund, D. (Ed.). (1990). Children's strategies: Contemporary views of cognitive development. Hillsdale, NJ: Lawrence Erlbaum Associates.

Bowlby, J. (1969). *Attachment and loss: Attachment* (Vol. 1). New York: Basic Books.

Bradley, R. H. (1994). The HOME Inventory: Review and reflections. In H. Reese (Ed.), *Advances in child development and behavior* (pp. 241–288). San Diego, CA: Academic Press.

Bradley, R. H. (2002). Environment and parenting. In M. H. Bornstein (Ed.), *Handbook of parenting* (2nd ed., Vol. 2, pp. 281–314). Mahwah, NJ: Lawrence Erlbaum Associates.

Bradley, R. H., & Caldwell, B. M. (1976). The relation of infants' home environments to mental test performance at fifty-four months: A follow-up study. *Child Development, 47*, 1172–1174.

Bradley, R. H., & Caldwell, B. M. (1979). Home Observation for Measurement of the Environment: A revision of the preschool scale. *American Journal of Mental Deficiency, 84*, 235–244.

Bradley, R. H., & Caldwell, B. M. (1995). Caregiving and the regulation of child growth and development: Describing proximal aspects of caregiving systems. *Developmental Review, 15*, 38–85.

Bradley, R. H., Caldwell, B. M., & Rock, S. L. (1988). Home environment and school performance: A ten-year follow-up and examination of three models of environmental action. *Child Development, 59*, 852–867.

Bradley, R. H., & Corwyn, R. F. (2002). SES and child development. *Annual Review of Psychology, 53*, 371–399.

Bradley, R. H., & Corwyn, R. F. (2003). Age and ethnic variations in family process mediators of SES. In M. H. Bronstein & R. H. Bradley (Eds.), *Socioeconomic status, parenting, and child development* (pp. 161–188). Mahwah, NJ: Lawrence Erlbaum Associates.

Bradley, R. H., Corwyn, R. F., Burchinal, M., McAdoo, H. P., & Garcia Coll, C. (2001a). The home environments of children in the United States. Part 2: Relations with behavioral development through age 13. *Child Development, 72*, 1868–1886.

Bradley, R. H., Corwyn, R. F., Caldwell, B. M., Whiteside-Mansell, L., Wasserman, G. A., & Mink, I. T. (2000). Measuring the home environments of children in early adolescence. *Journal of Research on Adolescence, 10,* 247–289.

Bradley, R. H., Corwyn, R. F., McAdoo, H. P., & Garcia Coll, C. (2001b). The home environments of children in the United States, Part I: Variations by age, ethnicity, and poverty status. *Child Development, 72,* 1844–1867.

Bradley, R. H., Whiteside, L., Mundfrom, D. J., Casey, P. H., Kelleher, K. J., & Pope, S. K. (1994). Early indications of resilience and their relation to experiences in the home environments of low birthweight, premature children living in poverty. *Child Development, 65,* 246–260.

Bransford, J. D., Brown, A. L., & Cocking, R. R. (Eds.). (2000). *How people learn: Brain, mind, experience, and school.* Washington, DC: National Academy Press.

Bretherton, I., & Waters, E. (1985). *Growing points of attachment theory. Monographs of the Society for Research in Child Development, 50* (No. 209).

Brody, G. H., Stoneman, Z., Flor, D., McCrary, C., Hastings, L., & Conyers, O. (1994). Financial resources, parent psychological functioning, parent co-caregiving and early adolescent competence in rural two-parent African-American families. *Child Development, 65,* 590–605.

Bronfenbrenner, U. (1995). The bioecological model from a life course perspective: Reflections of a participant observer. In P. Moen, G. H. Elder, & K. Luscher (Eds.), *Examining lives in context* (pp. 619–647). Washington, DC: American Psychological Association.

Bronfenbrenner, U., & Crouter, A. (1983). The evolution of environmental models in developmental research. In P. H. Mussen (Series Ed.) & W. Kessen (Vol. Ed.), *Handbook of child psychology: Vol. 1, History, theory, and methods* (4th ed., pp. 357–414). New York: Wiley.

Brown, B., Mounts, N., Lamborn, S., & Steinberg, L. (1993). Parenting practices and peer group affiliation in adolescence. *Child Development, 64,* 467–482.

Bruner, J. (1983). *Child talk: Learning to use language.* Oxford: Oxford University Press.

Caldji, C., Tannenbaum, B., Sharma, D., Francis, D., Plotsky, P. M., & Meaney, M. J. (1998). Maternal care during infancy regulates the development of neural systems mediating the expression of fearfulness in the rat. *Proceedings of the National Academy of Sciences of the United States of America, 95*(9), 5335–5340.

Cassidy, J. (1988). Child–mother attachment and the self in six-year-olds. *Child Development, 59,* 121–134.

Centers for Disease Control (2002). Births: Final data for 2000. *National Vital Statistics Reports, 50,* 1–104.

Christerphersen, E. R. (1989). Injury control. *American Psychologist, 44,* 237–241.

Cohen, L. B., DeLoache, J. S., & Strauss, M. S. (1979). Infant visual perception. In J. D. Osofsky (Ed.), *Handbook of infant development* (pp. 393–438). New York: John Wiley & Sons.

Collins, W. A., Maccoby, E. E., Steinberg, L., Hetherington, E. M., & Bornstein, M. H. (2000). Contemporary research on parenting: The case of nature and nurture. *American Psychologist, 55,* 218–232.

Committee on Health and Behavior, Institute of Medicine. (2001). *Health and behavior: The interplay of biological, behavioral, and societal influences.* Washington, DC: National Academy Press.

Crouter, A., MacDonald, S., McHale, S., & Perry-Jenkins, M. (1990). Parental monitoring and perceptions of children's school performance and conduct in dual- and single-earner families. *Developmental Psychology, 26,* 649–657.

Dennis, W. (1973). *Children of the creche.* New York: Appleton-Century-Crofts.

Darling, N., & Steinberg, L. (1993). Parenting style as context. *Psychological Bulletin, 113,* 487–496.

Dornbusch, S. M., Ritter, P.L., Leiderman, P. H., Roberts, D. F., & Fraleigh, M. J. (1987). The relation of parenting style to adolescent school performance. *Child Development, 58,* 1244–1257.

Dorr, A., Rabin, B. E., & Irlen, S. (2002). Parenting in a multimedia society. In M. H. Bornstein (Ed.), *Handbook of parenting* (2nd ed., Vol. 5, pp. 349–374). Mahwah, NJ: Lawrence Erlbaum Associates .

Deutsch, M., & Associates. (1968). *Social class, race and psychological development.* New York: Holt, Rinehart & Winston.

Drotar, D. (1985). *New directions in failure-to-thrive: Research and clinical practice.* New York: Plenum.

Dubay, L., Joyce, T., Kaestner, R., & Kenney, G. M. (2001). Changes in prenatal care timing and low birth weight by race and socioeconomic status: Implications for the Medicaid expansions for pregnant women. *Health Services Research 36,* 373–398.

Duncan, G. J., Brooks-Gunn, J., & Klebanov, P. (1994). Economic deprivation and early-childhood development. *Child Development, 62,* 296–318.

Ebrahim, S. H., Luman, E. T., Floyd, R. L., Murphy, C. C., Bennett, E. M., & Boyle, C. A. (1998). Alcohol consumption by pregnant women in the United States during 1988–1995. *Obstetrics and Gynecology, 92,* 187–192.

Eccles, J., & Gootman, J. A. (Eds.). (2002) *Community programs to promote youth development.* Washington, DC: National Academy Press.

Eisenberg, N., Cumberland, A., & Spinrad, T. L. (1998). Parental socialization of emotion. *Psychological Inquiry, 9,* 241–273.

Elardo, R., Bradley, R. H., & Caldwell, B. M. (1975). The relation of infants' home environments to mental test performance from six to thirty-six months: A longitudinal analysis. *Child Development, 46,* 71–76.

Evans, G. W., Kliewer, W., & Martin, J. (1991). The role of the physical environment in the health and well-being of children. In H. E. Schroeder (Ed.), *New directions in health psychology assessment* (pp. 127–157). New York: Hemisphere Publishing.

Federal Interagency Forum on Child and Family Statistics (2000). *Trends in the well-being of America's children and youth, 1999.* Washington DC: U.S. Department of Health and Human Services.

Fiese, B. H., Hooker, K. A., Kotary, L., & Schwagler, J. (1993). Family rituals in the early stages of parenthood. *Journal of Marriage and Family, 55,* 663–642.

Finkelhor, D., Mitchell, K. J., & Wolak, J. (2000). *On-line victimization: A report on the nation' s youth.* Alexandria, Virginia: National Center for Missing and Exploited Children.

Fiscella, K. (1995). Does prenatal care improve birth outcomes? A critical review. *Obstetrics and Gynecology, 85,* 468–479.

Fogel, A., Diamond, G. R., Langhorst, B. H., & Demos, V. (1982). Affective and cognitive aspects of the 2-month-old's participation in face-to-face interaction with the mother. In E. Z. Tronick (Ed.), *Social interchange in infancy: Affect, cognition, and communication* (pp. 37–58). Baltimore, MD: University Park Press.

Ford, M. E. (in press). *Motivating humans: Goals, emotions, and personal agency beliefs.* Newbury Park, CA: Sage.

Ford, D. H., & Lerner, R. M. (1992). *Developmental systems theory, an integrative approach.* Newbury Park, CA: Sage.

French, V. (2002). History of parenting: The ancient Mediterranean world. In M. H. Bornstein (Ed.), *Handbook of parenting* (2nd. ed, Vol. 2, pp. 345–376). Mahwah, NJ: Lawrence Erlbaum Associates,

Friedman, S. L., & Sigman, M. D. (Eds.). (1992). *The psychological development of low birthweight children*. Norwood, NJ: Ablex.

Gable, S., & Isabella, R. (1992). Maternal contributions to infant regulation of arousal. *Infant Behavior and Development, 15*, 95–107.

Garbarino, J. (1988). Preventing childhood injury: Developmental and mental health issues. *American Journal of Orthopsychiatry, 58*, 25–45.

Greaves, P., Glik, D. C., Kronenfeld, J. J., & Jackson, K. (1994). Determinants of controllable in-home child safety hazards. *Health Education Research, 9*, 307–315.

Grinker, R. R., Korshin, S. J., Bosowitz, H., Hamburg, D. A., Sabshin, M., Pershy, H., Chevalier, J. A., & Borad, F. A. (1956). A theoretical and experimental approach to problems of anxiety. *AMA Archives of Neurology and Psychiatry, 76*, 420–431.

Guyer, B., Hoyert, D. L., Martin, J. A., Ventura, S., MacDorman, M. F., & Strobino, D. M. (1999). Annual summary of vital statistics—1998. *Pediatrics 104* (6), 1229–46.

Harkness, S., & Super, C. M. (2002). Culture and parenting. In M. H. Bornstein (Ed.), *Handbook of parenting* (2nd ed., Vol. 2, pp. 253–280). Mahwah, NJ: Lawrence Erlbaum Associates.

Harris, J. (1995). Where is the child's environment? A group socialization theory of development. *Psychological Review, 102*, 458–489.

Hart, B., & Risley, T. (1995). *Meaningful differences in the everyday experience of young American children*. Baltimore, MD: Brookes.

Hertwig, R., Davis, J. N., & Sulloway, F. J. (2002). Parental investment: How an equity motive can produce inequality. *Psychological Bulletin, 128*, 728–745.

Hoff, E. (2003). Causes and consequences of SES-related differences in parent-to-child speech. In M. H. Bronstein & R. H. Bradley (Eds.), *Socioeconomic status, parenting, and child development* (pp. 145–160). Mahwah, NJ: Lawrence Erlbaum Associates.

Horowitz. F. D. (1987). *Exploring developmental theories: Toward a structural/behavioral model of development*. Hillsdale, NJ: Lawrence Erlbaum Associates.

Jacobson, J. L., Jacobson, S. W., Padgett, R. J., Brummitt, G. A., & Billings, R. L. (1992). Effects of prenatal PCB exposure on cognitive processing efficiency and sustained attention. *Developmental Psychology, 28*, 297–306.

Johnson, K. L., & Lieberman, A. F. (1999, April). *Protecting 3–5-year-old children from the effects of witnessing domestic violence: The roles of mothers as "emotion coaches.* Paper presented at the biennial meeting of the Society for Research in Child Development. Albuquerque, NM.

Kagan, J. (1984). *The nature of the child*. New York: Basic Books.

Kaplan, H., & Dove, H. (1987). Infant development among the Ache of eastern Paraguay. *Developmental Psychology, 23*, 190–198.

Klingman, A. (2002). Children under stress of war. In A. M. Le Greca, W. K. Silverman, E. M. Vernberg, & M. C. Roberts (Eds.), *Helping children cope with disasters and terrorism* (pp. 359–380). Washington, DC: American Psychological Association.

Kochanska, G. (1993). Toward a synthesis of parental socialization and child temperament in early development of conscience. *Child Development, 64*, 325–347.

Kochanska, G. (1997). Multiple pathways to conscience for children with different temperaments:From toddlerhood to age 5. *Developmental Psychology, 33*, 228–240.

Kuhn, D. (1992). Cognitive development. In M. H. Bornstein & M. E. Lamb (Eds.), *Developmental psychology: An advanced textbook* (3rd ed., pp. 211–272). Hillsdale, NJ: Lawrence Erlbaum Associates.

Ladd, G. W., & Goltner, B. (1988). Parents' management of preschoolers' peer relations: Is it related to children's social competence? *Developmental Psychology, 24,* 109–117.

La Greca, A. M., & Prinstein, M. J. (2002). Hurricanes and earthquakes. In A. M. Le Greca, W. K. Silverman, E. M., Vernberg, & M. C. Roberts (Eds.), *Helping children cope with disasters and terrorism* (pp. 107–138). Washington, DC: American Psychological Association.

Laird, R. D., Pettit, G. S., Mize, J., Brown, E. G., & Lindsey, E. (1994). Mother–child conversations about peers: Contributions to competence. *Family Relations, 43,* 4425–432.

Lazarus, R. S. (1993). From psychological stress to emotions: A history of changing outlooks. *Annual Review of Psychology, 44,* 1–21.

Lewis, M. (1997). *Altering fate.* New York: Guilford.

Lickliter, R. (2000). The role of sensory stimulation in perinatal development: Insights from comparative research for care of the high-risk infant. *Journal of Developmental and Behavioral Pediatrics, 21,* 437–447.

Loeber, R., & Dishion, T. J. (1983). Early predictors of male adolescent delinquency: A review. *Psychological Bulletin, 94,* 68–99.

Lozoff, B., Jiminez, E., & Wolf, A. W. (1991). Long-term developmental outcome of infants with iron deficiency. *New England Journal of Medicine, 325,* 687–694.

Maccoby, E. E. (1992). The role of parents in the socialization of children: An historical perspective. *Developmental Psychology, 28,* 1006–1017.

Maslow, A. H. (1954). *Motivation and personality.* New York, NY: Harper & Row.

Mayes, L. C., & Truman, S. D. (2002). Substance abuse and parenting. In M. H. Bornstein (Ed.), *Handbook of parenting* (2nd ed., Vol. 4, pp. 329–360). Mahwah, NJ: Lawrence Erlbaum Associates.

Melamed, B. G. (2002). Parenting the ill child. In M. H. Bornstein (Ed.), *Handbook of parenting* (2nd ed., Vol. 5, pp. 329–347). Mahwah, NJ: Lawrence Erlbaum Associates.

Moore, G. T. (1988). *Interactions between the spatial organization of the socio-physical environment and cognitive and social behavior.* Unpublished manuscript, University of Wisconsin-Milwaukee.

National Center on Addition and Substance Abuse (2001). *National survey of American attitudes on substance abuse VI: Teens.* New York: Columbia University.

National Center for Education Statistics (2002). *Digest of Education Statistics 2001* (NCES publication no. 2002–130). Washington, DC: Author.

Ogden, C. (1998). *Third national health and nutrition examination survey.* Unpublished analyses. Atlanta, GA: Centers for Disease Control.

Park, K. A., & Waters, E. (1989). Security of attachment and preschool friendships. *Child Development, 60,* 1076–1081.

Patterson, G. R., DeBaryshe, B. D., & Ramsey, E. (1989). A developmental perspective on antisocial behavior. *American Psychologist, 44,* 329–335.

Peterson, L., & Gable, S. (1998). Holistic injury prevention. In J. R. Lutzker (Ed.), *Handbook of child abuse research and treatment* (pp. 291–318). New York, NY: Plenum.

Peterson, L., Ewigman, B., & Kivlahan, C. (1993). Judgments regarding appropriate child supervision to prevent injury: The role of environmental risk and child age. *Child Development, 64,* 934–950.

Pettit, G. S., Dodge, K. A., & Brown, M. M. (1988). Early family experience, social problem solving patterns, and children's social competence. *Child Development, 59,* 107–120.

Pollitt, E. (1988). A critical review of three decades of research on the effect of chronic energy malnutrition on behavioral development. In B. Schureh & M. Scrimshaw (Eds.), *Chronic energy depletion: Consequences and related issues.* Luzanne, Switzerland: IDECC—Nestle Foundation.

Putallaz, M. (1987). Maternal behavior and children's sociometric status. *Child Development, 58,* 324–340.

Rapoport, A. (1985). Thinking about home environment: A conceptual framework. In I. Altman & C. M. Werner (Eds.), *Home environments* (pp. 255–286). New York: Plenum.

Roberts, K. (1983). *Youth and leisure.* London: George Allen and Unwin.

Rohner, R. (1986). *The warmth dimension.* Beverly Hills, CA: Sage.

Rosenweig, M. R., Krech, D., Bennett, E. L., & Diamond, M. C. (1962). Effects of environmental complexity and training on brain chemistry and anatomy: A replication and extensions. *Journal of Comparative and Physiological Psychology, 55,* 429–437.

Rotter, J. B. (1966). Generalized expectancies for internal versus external control of reinforcement. *Psychological Monographs, 80* (Whole No. 609).

Saegert, S., & Winkel, G. H. (1990). Environmental psychology. *Annual Review of Psychology, 41,* 441–477.

Sameroff, A. J. (1995). General systems theory and developmental psychopathology. In D. Chiccheti & D. Cohen (Eds.)., *Developmental psychopathology: Vol. 1. Theory and method* (pp. 659–695). New York: Wiley.

Scales, P., & Leffert, N. (1999). *Developmental assets.* Minneapolis, MN: Search Institute.

Scarr, S., & McCartney, K. (1983). How people make their own environments. *Child Development, 54,* 424–435.

Shonkoff, J. P., & Phillips, D. A. (Eds.). (2000). *From neurons to neighborhoods.* Washington, DC: National Academy Press.

Skeels, H., & Dye, H. (1939). A study of the effects of differential stimulation on mentally retarded children. *American Journal of Mental Deficiency, 44,* 114–136.

Smock, P. (2000). Cohabitation in the United States: An appraisal of research themes, findings, and implications. *Annual Review of Sociology* (pp. 1–20). Washington, DC: American Sociological Association.

Steinberg, L. (1986). Latchkey children and susceptibility to peer pressure: An ecological analysis. *Developmental Psychology, 22,* 433–439.

Thompson, R. A. (1994). Emotion regulation: A theme in search of a definition. In N. A. Fox (Ed.), The development of emotional regulation: Biological and behavioral considerations. *Monographs of the Society for Research in Child Development, 59* (Serial No. 240), 25–52.Boston, MA: Blackwell Publishing.

Tong, S., & McMichael, A. J. (1992). Maternal smoking and neuropsychological development in childhood: A review of the evidence. *Developmental Medicine and Child Neurology, 34,* 191–197.

Trivers, R. L. (1972). Parental investment and sexual selection. In B. Campbell (Eds.), *Sexual selection and the descent of man: 1871–1971* (pp. 136–179). Chicago: Aldine.

U. S. Department of Health and Human Services. (1991). *Healthy people 2000.* (DS publication no. PHS 91-50212). Washington, DC: U.S. Government Printing Office.

Van Izendoorn, M. (2002, July). *What works? Stimulating sensitive parenting through preventive interventions.* Paper presented at the meeting of the International Society for the Study of Behavioral Development, Ottawa, Canada.

Wachs, T. D. (2000). *Necessary but not sufficient.* Washington, DC: American Psychological Association.

Whitehurst, G. J., Arnold, D. S., Epstein, J. N., & Angell, A. L. (1994). A picture book reading intervention in day care and home for children from low-income families. *Developmental Psychology, 30,* 679–689.

Whiteside, L., Pope, S.K., & Bradley, R.H. (1996). Patterns of parenting behavior in young mothers. *Family Relations, 45,* 273–281

Wohlwill, J. F., & Heft, H. (1977). Environments fit for the developing child. In H. McGurk (Ed.), *Ecological factors in human development* (pp. 1–22). Amsterdam: North Holland Publishing.

Yeung, W. J. (1999, April). *How multiple domains of paternal involvement affect children's well-being.* Paper presented at the biennial meeting of the Society for Research in Child Development, Albuquerque, New Mexico.

Zahn-Waxler, C., Duggal, S., & Gruber, R. (2002). Parental psychopathology. In M. H. Bornstein (Ed.), *Handbook of parenting* (2nd ed., Vol. 4. pp. 295–328). Mahwah, NJ: Lawrence Erlbaum Associates.

2

Family Investment and Child and Adolescent Adjustment
The Role of Genetic Research

Jenae M. Neiderhiser
David Reiss
George Washington University

A long-standing focus of developmental research has been to understand how the family affects child and adolescent adjustment. Parent–child relationships, sibling relationships, and marital relationships have all been examined, and in general, warm and supportive relationships within the family have been associated with positive child and adolescent outcomes, whereas coercive and conflictual relationships have been associated with problem development (e.g., Cummings, Goeke-Morey, & Dukewich, 2001; Maccoby, 2002; Markman & Jones-Leonard, 1985; Patterson, Crosby, & Vuchinich, 1992). Because the majority of research has not used genetically sensitive designs, it has been impossible to distinguish the environmental contributions from the genetic. From studies of twins and siblings, however, it is clear that family processes, such as parenting, are not "pure" environmental measures (e.g., Collins, Maccoby, Steinberg, Hetherington, & Bornstein, 2000, 2001).

This chapter reviews the literature on genetic and environmental influences on family process, discusses why such findings are important to understanding child and adolescent adjustment, and suggests future directions that can sharpen an understanding of how genes and the environment work together to influence child and adolescent development.

GENETIC AND ENVIRONMENTAL INFLUENCES ON FAMILY PROCESS

As noted, the role of family process in both producing and maintaining psychopathology during childhood and adolescence has been explored extensively. This chapter examines the role of parenting and marital relationships in child development.

Parenting and Parent–Child Relationships

One of the clearest and most replicated associations is between conflictual parent–child relationships and child and adolescent maladjustment. Harsh, inconsistent, and ineffective discipline has been associated with later antisocial behavior (Loeber & Dishion, 1983; Patterson, DeBaryshe, & Ramsey, 1989); insecure parent–child relationships, including parental rejection and forcefulness, have been traced to later internalizing problems (Rubin, Hymel, Mills, & Rose-Krasnor, 1991). Genetic and environmental contributions to parenting have also been been indicated (Plomin, 1994; Towers, Spotts, & Neiderhiser, in press). Behavioral genetic studies divide the total variance of a measure into genetic influences and two types of environmental influences: shared and nonshared. Genetic influences are indicated by a pattern of correlations between family members that decreases with decreasing genetic similarity. Shared environmental influences include all nongenetic factors that make family members similar to one another, and nonshared environmental influences are all nongenetic factors that result in differences among family members. Measures of parental warmth and support or negativity have typically shown substantial genetic and nonshared environmental influences and modest to negligible shared environmental influences (Elkins, McGue, & Iacono, 1997; Jacobson & Rowe, 1999; Plomin, Reiss, Hetherington, & Howe, 1994; Rowe, 1981, 1983).

In contrast, parental monitoring and control reveal primarily shared and nonshared environmental influences but little genetic influence (Elkins et al., 1997; Plomin et al., 1994; Rowe, 1981, 1983). One exception to this general pattern of findings has been the Nonshared Environment in Adolescent Development project (NEAD, Reiss, Neiderhiser, Hetherington, & Plomin, 2000; Reiss et al., 1994), which used composites across multiple raters and multiple measures. In NEAD, genetic, shared environmental, and nonshared environmental influences contributed significantly to composites of parental positivity, negativity, and monitoring, whereas parental control was more consistent with previous reports, with only modest genetic influences and substantial shared and nonshared environmental influences (Plomin et al., 1994; Reiss et al., 2000).

A reasonable interpretation of these findings is that genetically influenced characteristics of the children appear to affect the way parents treat their children such that identical twins tend to be parented more similarly than fraternal twins, and full siblings are parented more similarly than are half or stepsiblings. Although these findings are interesting, it remains unclear what genetic influences on measures of parenting mean. In other words, how do genetic factors influence parenting; what are the processes involved?

One process that may be involved is genotype-environment correlation, or simply, a correlation between genotype and environment. Three types of genotype–environment (GE) correlation are usually described: passive, active, and evocative (Plomin, Defries, & Loehlin, 1977; Scarr & McCartney, 1983). Passive GE correlation arises because parents and children share both genes and environment. In other words, parents may pass genes related to "difficult temperament" to their children. In parents, these difficult temperament genes may be exhibited as irritable and negative parenting, which is also correlated with the child's difficult temperament.

Evocative GE correlation is the result of others (the environment) responding to genetically influenced characteristics of the child. Using the same example of negative parenting, parents may respond to the child's difficult temperament with harsh and negative parenting. This process is likely to be operating in the coercive cycles of parent–child conflict and antisocial behavior that Patterson and his colleagues described (Patterson, 1982; Patterson DeBaryshe, & Ramsey, 1989).

Finally, active GE correlation occurs when a child's genotype and environment are correlated because the child actively selects his or her environment. This is more difficult to imagine in regard to parenting. A good example, however, is found with adolescents' peer relationships. Adolescents select friends who are like them, and the characteristics that they select are genetically influenced (Manke, McGuire, Reiss, Hetherington, & Plomin, 1995).

Understanding which form of GE correlation is operating can increase our understanding of the processes involved in parent–child relationships. There is an increasing acceptance that children influence the way they are treated by others, including their parents (Belsky & Park, 2000; Deater-Deckard & O'Connor, 2000; Haapasalo & Tremblay, 1994), and that parents tend to respond differently to their children (Brody, Stoneman, & McCoy, 1992; Dunn & Plomin, 1986; McHale & Pawletko, 1992), but in many ways this understanding has been rather broad in nature. Identifying the specific aspects of parenting that appear to be more responsive to the child (evocative GE correlation) and that seem to be more consistently applied by parents (shared environment) is an important step in understanding which parenting behaviors are most likely to be malleable. In other words, if parents are directing their behavior either by a response to their child or through consistently applied behaviors, it may be easier to teach the parents to modify such behaviors. Parenting that is more a function of parents and children sharing genes (passive GE correlation) may be more difficult to modify because this behavior may be, in part, an aspect of the parent's temperament.

Two studies of adoptees have identified evocative GE correlation by examining how characteristics in the birth parents (e.g., psychopathology and substance use disorders) increase the risk of behavior problems in the adopted children, which then influence the parenting behavior of the adoptive parents (Ge et al., 1996; O'Connor, Deater-Deckard, Fulker, Rutter, & Plomin, 1998). Both of these studies found that birth-parent characteristics were associated with the adoptive parents' parenting of the child. Because the adopted children were adopted as infants and the adoptive parents in these studies did not have contact with the birth parents, the most reasonable explanation of these findings is that genetically influenced characteristics of the children were eliciting certain types of parenting. In other words, evocative GE correlation was operating.

A more recent study that examined young twin–parent mutuality in their relationship and then replicated the findings using an adoption design also provides evidence of evocative GE correlation (Deater-Deckard & O'Connor, 2000). The findings from these studies are significant in that they provide some of the best evidence of the importance of evocative GE correlations in influencing parenting, thereby underscoring the importance of the role of the child in parent–child relationships. Unfortunately, passive GE correlations cannot be disentangled using an adoption design, although the report by Deater-Deckard and O'Connor (2000), which paired a twin study with an adoption study, is a step in that direction. By comparing and contrasting these two types of studies, if the measurement used in both is also comparable, it is possible to infer which type of GE correlation is operating.

Another method that can be used to distinguish passive from evocative GE correlation uses matched samples of children who vary in degree of genetic relatedness (child-based) and parents who vary in degree of genetic relatedness (parent-based). If genetic influences are found for measures of parenting in a parent-based design, there is likely some genetically influenced characteristic of the parent that influences parenting. If shared environmental genetic contributions to the same measures of parenting are found using a child-based design, it is likely that the main mode of genetic influence is from parent to child, or through passive GE correlation. If, however, genetic influences on parenting are found in a child-based study, but not in a complementary parent-based study, the mechanism of genetic influence is likely from child to parent, or evocative. Such a finding rules out the possibility that parents' genes were responsible for the observed genetic influence. These expectations are detailed in Table 2.1.

One study systematically compared mothering in a child-based sample of adolescents (NEAD) and a parent-based sample of twin mothers of adolescents (the Twin Moms [TM] sample; Reiss et al., 2001). These samples assessed mothering using the same instruments, and the adolescents were approximately the same age. The study compared adolescent report composites of mother's positivity, negativity, monitoring, and control for each sample. The percentage of variance explained by genetic, shared environmental, and nonshared environmental influences is presented in Fig. 2.1. Based on the interpretations for GE correlation described in Table 2.1, these findings suggest primarily passive GE correlation for mother's positivity and monitoring, and evocative GE correlation for mother's negativity and control (Neiderhiser et al., 2004).

By specifying the type of GE correlation that is influencing parenting, it may be possible to more appropriately target an intervention to the individual or the family. For example, if evocative GE correlations are important factors in conflict between parents and children, as was found in the studies previously described, then training the parents to respond differently to their child may be the most effective strategy for interrupting a potentially coercive cycle. To date, there have been no studies that have attempted to do this within a genetically sensitive design. There are, however, several studies that have focused on parent training in an effort to prevent the development of negative outcomes in at-risk children (e.g., Dishion, Kavanagh, Schneiger, Nelson, & Kaufman, 2002; Reid, Eddy, Fetrow, & Stoolmiller, 1999; Stoolmiller, Eddy, & Reid, 2000). In general, these studies

TABLE 2.1

Expectations for Genetic and Environmental Influences on Parenting Given Different Types of Genotype–Environment (GE) Correlation and Child-Based and Parent-Based Designs

	Child-Based Design	*Parent-Based Design*
Passive GE correlation	Shared environmental	Genetic
Nonpassive GE correlation	Genetic	Shared and/or nonshared environmental
No GE correlation	Shared and/or nonshared environmental	Shared and/or nonshared environmental

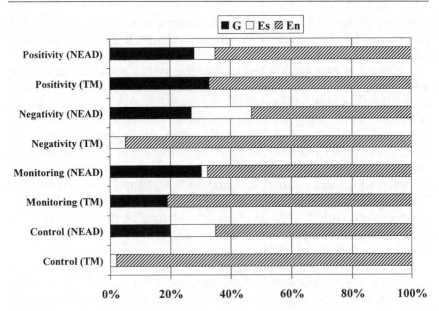

FIG. 2.1. Genetic and environmental contributions to adolescent reports of mother's parenting: NEAD and Twin Moms (TM) samples. Mother's positivity, negativity, monitoring, and control were assessed using the same measures in both studies.

found that training parents to respond effectively to their children reduces the development of negative outcomes, at least in the short term.

Marital Relationships

Several studies have addressed the role of genetic and environmental influences on marriage. The first such study examined genetic and environmental influences on pair-bonding (maintaining a stable heterosexual marriage) and mate diversification (remarriage after divorce) in a sample of male twins (Trumbetta & Gottesman, 2000). Both constructs showed some genetic influence, although most of the variance could be explained by nonshared environmental influences. This finding, of large nonshared environmental influences on marriage and divorce, has been consistent for the few studies that have examined these constructs. A different study found no genetic influence on whether individuals marry, although there was evidence of genetic influence on divorce (Jerskey et al., 2001). Two studies that examined genetic and environmental influences on potential personality predictors of divorce found nearly equal contributions of genetic and nonshared environmental influences on divorce, but a substantial portion of the genetic influence could be explained by the personality characteristics, negative and positive emotionality and constraint (Jockin, McGue, & Lykken, 1996; McGue & Lykken, 1992).

All the studies examined relatively broad indicators of marriage and found evidence of primarily nonshared environmental and genetic effects. Interestingly, the only study that examined a potential correlate, in this case personality characteristics, found that the bulk of the genetic influence on divorce could be explained by personality characteristics. The only study that examined marital quality within a genetically sensitive design found evidence of moderate genetic, but primarily nonshared environmental, influences on marital quality in a sample of twin women (Spotts et al., 2004). In other words, the factor that has the greatest impact on marriage, divorce, and remarriage is nonshared environmental influence. This makes sense given that the partner is genetically unrelated to the co-twin's partner, thereby providing an important nonshared environmental influence on the marriage.

GENETIC INFLUENCES ON FAMILY PROCESS: COVARIATION WITH CHILD AND ADOLESCENT ADJUSTMENT

Parenting and Child and Adolescent Adjustment

As is clear from the many studies in child development, family process, especially parenting, is important to child adjustment (Anderson, Hetherington, Reiss, & Howe, 1994; Dishion, Capaldi, & Yoerger, 1999; Patterson, Cohn, & Kao, 1989; Patterson et al., 1992; Scaramella, Conger, Spoth, & Simons, 2002). However, the impact of parenting on child and adolescent adjustment is not a purely environmental influence. Studies that used genetically sensitive designs to examine this association have found that genetic factors can explain the correlation between parenting and child adjustment, although shared and, occasionally, nonshared environmental influences also play a role (Elkins et al., 1997; Pike, McGuire, Hetherington, Reiss, & Plomin, 1996; Reiss et al., 2000).

Few studies have attempted to understand the processes involved in explaining the genetic and environmental influences on parenting and child adjustment. One such study examined the role of adolescents' perceptions of parenting (Neiderhiser, Pike, Hetherington, & Reiss, 1998). After accounting for adolescents' perceptions of parenting, the remaining association between parenting and adolescent adjustment could be explained by primarily shared environmental influences on mothering and nearly equal shared environmental and genetic influences on fathering. In other words, much of the genetic influence in associations between parenting and adolescent adjustment stems from the adolescent's perceptions of the way he is treated. This suggests that the genetic influences on associations between parenting and adolescent adjustment may be due, at least in part, to the way an adolescent perceives her treatment by her parent, which may be due to a genetically influenced interpretative style that is also correlated with the behavior of the adolescent. Once the genetic influences shared with the adolescents' perceptions of parenting were accounted for, the remaining association between parenting and adolescent adjustment was as much due to common parenting as to common genes.

Taken together, findings from studies on genetic and environmental influences on parenting and child adjustment converge on two messages. First, much of the association stems from genetic factors that influence both parenting and adolescent adjustment. This finding flies in the face of past assumptions of developmentalists that consistency in parenting results in consistency in child outcomes, although it is widely acknowledged that this is no longer the view of the field (Maccoby, 2002). For example, Bradley and Corwyn (chapter 1, this volume) describe parents as regulators of child–environment fit, meaning that parents invest in their children by regulating or providing for their children's basic needs, ranging from safety to socioemotional support. It is important to remember that, in addition to these parental investments being regulated, in part, by things to do with the parent such as personality and mental health, they also may be regulated by characteristics of the children. This possibility is noted by Bradley and Corwyn (this volume) and we argue that the influence of the child extends into other aspects listed under the broader context of investment as well as throughout the family subsystem.

The second message underscores the need to examine the processes involved; various factors, including the perceptions of the adolescent, may explain genetic influences on these associations. There are many possible mediators of genetic influences on parenting and child adjustment, most suggested by developmental research that examined these processes phenotypically. The possible mediators include child and parent personality and psychopathology, social cognition, and relationships with other family members, to name just a few. In other words, there are other factors that may help to explain how genetic factors can influence parenting and its impact on child adjustment. The example provided earlier, of adolescent perceptions, is a good illustration of how these processes may operate (Neiderhiser et al., 1998). What remains to be done is to better explain *how* these processes operate. Understanding whether adolescent perceptions of parenting are a function of their personality would provide information about which individuals are at greater risk of negative outcomes. Specifically, individuals inclined to have a more negative perception are likely to be at greater risk than those who perceive the world in a more positive light.

Marital Relationships and Child and Adolescent Adjustment

Only one study has examined the covariation between marital relationships and child or adolescent adjustment within the context of a genetically informed design (Reiss et al., 2000). That study examined spousal conflict surrounding adolescent adjustment and the genetic and environmental influences on such conflict. Marital conflict was positively associated with adolescent antisocial behavior and depressive symptoms and negatively associated with cognitive agency and social responsibility. In all cases, the majority of this association could be explained by common genetic influences. In other words, the majority of the correlation between marital conflict concerning the adolescent and the adolescent's adjustment could be explained by the teen's genetic influences. It could be that certain characteristics of the teen evoked certain responses from the parents, which in turn influenced the level of conflict between the parents (i.e., evocative GE correlation). Another plausible explanation is that children and parents, who share 50% of their genes, behave in ways that are correlated because of these shared genes (i.e., passive GE correlation). In other words, parents who have an antisocial child, the odds of which are influenced in part by genetic factors, may be more likely to argue with their spouses because they share some of the same genes that influence their child's antisocial behavior. Unfortunately, most studies are unable to examine genetic and environmental influences on the covariance between marital conflict and adolescent adjustment. This leaves yet-unanswered questions about which processes are involved.

CONCLUSIONS

Until recently, much of the research in prevention and intervention took a universal approach. For example, interventions were broadly applied to entire at-risk populations without a focus on the characteristics of the indivuals or families receiving the treatment. Lately, there has been a call for more research that focuses on the family and the individual (Dishion, Andrews, Kavanagh, & Soberman, 1996; Reid, 1993; Webster-Stratton & Taylor, 2001). The importance of genetic factors to both relationships within the family and covariation between family relationships and child and adolescent adjustment underscores the needed focus on the individual. Other research in this area, however, underscores the importance of family relationships in influencing genetic change during adolescence. Specifically, longitudinal studies of parenting and adolescent adjustment suggest that parent–child relationships may serve as protective or exacerbating factors of genetic influences on antisocial behavior (Neiderhiser, Reiss, Hetherington, & Plomin, 1999; Reiss et al., 2000). That is, genetic influences on parenting during middle adolescence have been associated with change in genetic influences on antisocial behavior measured 3 years later, during later adolescence.

Taken together, these findings emphasize the importance of a multilevel approach to prevention and intervention, and of advancing our understanding of the processes involved in explaining genetic and environmental influences on both adjustment and family process. Such a multilevel approach would include a focus on the individual differences in the children and parents as well as on the family process as a whole and the larger context of the environment, such as school or neighborhood. There have been interventions that used similar designs, especially in regard to a focus on the family (e.g., Dishion et al., 2002; Reid et al., 1999; Stoolmiller, Eddy, & Reid, 2000), and the interventions were found to be effective, at least in the short term.

Next Steps in Understanding Genotype–Environment Correlation and Interaction

The studies previously described serve more to suggest the processes that may be operating than to provide any definitive answers about these processes. At least three steps should be taken to gain a firmer grasp on how genotype and environment operate together to influence behavior. The first step is to conduct a study that incorporates child-based and parent-based designs within the same sample. This will enable passive and evocative GE correlations to be untangled within the same sample. This could be accomplished by employing a children-of-twins design, examining parents who are twins, where the parents and the children are both analyzed.

The Twin Moms study is an example, although the sample size is too small to fully realize its potential. The Twin Moms study consists of 326 twin mothers, each with one adolescent child, and their cohabiting partners. The adolescent children of the twin women were matched to be within 4 years of one another and the cohabiting relationship was required to be of 5 years or more in duration. Because identical twins share 100% of their segregating genes, and children share exactly 50% of their genes with each parent, the children of identical twin parents are as similar as half-siblings, sharing 25% of their genes. Children of fraternal twin parents, who share 50% of their genes, are like any other cousin pair, sharing 12.5% of their genes. In addition, the genetic overlap between niece/

nephew and aunt/uncle pairs is 50% for identical twin families and 25% for fraternal twin families.

This complex network of genetic relatedness is especially useful for disentangling genetic and environmental influences because the cousin pairs are being reared in different households with at least one different parent—in the case of Twin Moms, the father.

As mentioned earlier, the sample size of 326 pairs of twin-mother families is not large enough to enable this design to yield reliable results. We are currently expanding this sample, including adding a sample of twin fathers. This increased sample size (450 twin-mother families and 450 twin-father families) will enable the use of children-of-twins analytic models. Because parent-based and child-based designs are nested together in these models, we will be able to better specify the types of genotype–environment correlations that may be operating.

In addition to Twin Moms, three other studies using a children-of-twins design are underway. Expanded twin designs should help to advance our understanding of a wide variety of constructs, including the role of family relationships in influencing child and adolescent adjustment.

A second step in advancing our understanding of GE correlation and interaction is to conduct longitudinal studies using genetically sensitive designs. Of most relevance here are studies that have also included careful measurement of family relationships and of child and adolescent adjustment. Several studies have followed twins or siblings longitudinally, with varying sensitivity in measuring the environment (Plomin, DeFries, & Fulker, 1988; Reiss et al., 2000; Trouton, Spinath, & Plomin, 2003). Some studies of genetically informed samples have now extended into young adulthood, enabling researchers to untangle transition adjustment difficulties from adult disorders (Neiderhiser, 1999; Petrill, Hewitt, Plomin, & DeFries, in press). In general, the findings from studies that examined GE correlations longitudinally suggest that evocative GE correlations are very important factors in child and adolescent development.

Finally, research must pay more attention to genotype–environment interaction. Until recently, few studies focused on such interaction, especially in normative samples of twins or siblings. Numerous studies have since found evidence for such interactions (Caspi et al., 2002; Koeppen-Schomerus, Eley, Woke, Gringras, & Plomin, 2000; Wichers et al., 2002), and others have helped to explicate the methods needed for identifying genotype–environment interactions (Purcell, in press; Purcell & Sham, 2003). The recent activity is encouraging. It is through such consideration of how genetic and environmental factors work together via interaction and correlation that we will be better able to specify how and where to intervene.

ACKNOWLEDGMENTS

The Nonshared Environment in Adolescent Development project (PI: Reiss) was supported by the National Institute of Mental Health (R01-MH43373 and R01-MH48825) and the William T. Grant Foundation. The Young Adult Sibling Study (PI: Neiderhiser) is supported by the National Institute of Mental Health (R01-MH59014). The Twin Moms project (PI: Reiss) and its extension, the Twin and Offspring Study in Sweden (PI: Neiderhiser) is supported by the National Institutes of Mental Health (R01-MH54610).

REFERENCES

Anderson, E. R., Hetherington, E., Reiss, D., & Howe, G. (1994). Parents' nonshared treatment of siblings and the development of social competence during adolescence. *Journal of Family Psychology, 8*(3), 303–320.

Belsky, J., & Park, S. -Y. (2000). Exploring reciprocal parent and child effects in the case of child inhibition in U.S. and Korean samples. *International Journal of Behavioral Development, 24*(3), 338–347.

Brody, G. H., Stoneman, Z., & McCoy, J. K. (1992). Parental differential treatment of siblings and sibling differences in negative emotionality. *Journal of Marriage and the Family, 54*(3), 643–651.

Caspi, A., McClay, J., Moffitt, T. E., Mill, J., Martin, J., Craig, I. W., et al., (2002). Role of genotype in the cycle of violence in maltreated children. *Science, 297,* 851–854.

Collins, W., Maccoby, E. E., Steinberg, L., Hetherington, E. M., & Bornstein, M. H. (2000). Contemporary research on parenting: The case for nature and nurture. *American Psychologist, 55*(2), 218–232.

Collins, W., Maccoby, E. E., Steinberg, L., Hetherington, E., & Bornstein, M. H. (2001). Toward nature WITH nurture. *American Psychologist, 56*(2), 171–173.

Cummings, E., Goeke-Morey, M. C., & Dukewich, T. L. (2001). The study of relations between marital conflict and child adjustment: Challenges and new directions for methodology. In J. H. Grych & F. D. Fincham (Eds.), *Interparental conflict and child development: Theory, research, and applications* (pp. 39–63). New York: Cambridge University Press.

Deater-Deckard, K., & O'Connor, T. G. (2000). Parent–child mutuality in early childhood: Two behavioral genetic studies. *Developmental Psychology, 36*(5), 561–570.

Dishion, T. J., Andrews, D. W., Kavanagh, K., & Soberman, L. H. (1996). Preventive interventions for high-risk youth: The Adolescent Transitions Program. In R. D. Peters & R. J. McMahon (Eds.), *Preventing childhood disorders, substance abuse, and delinquency: Banff international behavioral science series* (Vol. 3, pp. 184–214). Thousand Oaks, CA: Sage.

Dishion, T. J., Capaldi, D. M., & Yoerger, K. (1999). Middle childhood antecedents to progressions in male adolescent substance use: An ecological analysis of risk and protection. *Journal of Adolescent Research, 14*(2), 175–205.

Dishion, T. J., Kavanagh, K., Schneiger, A., Nelson, S., & Kaufman, N. K. (2002). Preventing early adolescent substance use: A family-centered strategy for the public middle school. *Prevention Science, 3*(3), 191–201.

Dunn, J., & Plomin, R. (1986). Determinants of maternal behavior towards three-year-old siblings. *British Journal of Developmental Psychology, 4,* 127–137.

Elkins, I. J., McGue, M., & Iacono, W. G. (1997). Genetic and environmental influences on parent–son relationships: Evidence for increasing genetic influence during adolescence. *Developmental Psychology, 33*(2), 351–363.

Ge, X., Conger, R. D., Cadoret, R. J., Neiderhiser, J. M., Yates, W., & Troughton, E. (1996). The developmental interface between nature and nurture: A mutual influence model of child antisocial behavior and parent behaviors. *Developmental Psychology, 32*(4), 574–589.

Haapasalo, J., & Tremblay, R. E. (1994). Physically aggressive boys from ages 6 to 12: Family background, parenting behavior, and prediction of delinquency. *Journal of Consulting and Clinical Psychology, 62,* 1044–1052.

Jacobson, K. C., & Rowe, D. C. (1999). Genetic and environmental influences on the relationships between family connectedness, school connectedness, and adolescent depressed mood: Sex differences. *Developmental Psychology, 35,* 926–939.

Jerskey, B. A., Lyons, M. J., Lynch, C. E., Hines, D. A., Ascher, S., Nir, T. et al. (2001). *Genetic influence on marital status.* Paper presented at the 10th International Congress of Twin Studies, London, England.

Jockin, V., McGue, M., & Lykken, D. T. (1996). Personality and divorce: A genetic analysis. *Journal of Personality and Social Psychology, 71*(2), 288–299.

Koeppen-Schomerus, G., Eley, T. C., Wolke, D., Gringras, P., & Plomin, R. (2000). The interaction of prematurity with genetic and environmental influences on cognitive development in twins. *Journal of Pediatrics, 137*(4), 527–533.

Loeber, R., & Dishion, T. (1983). Early predictors of male delinquency: A review. *Psychological Bulletin, 94*(1), 68–99.

Maccoby, E. E. (2002). Parenting effects: Issues and controversies. In J. G. Borkowski, S. L. Ramey, & M. Bristol-Power (Eds.), *Parenting and the child's world: Influences on academic, intellectual, and social-emotional development.* Mahwah, NJ: Lawrence Erlbaum Associates.

Manke, B., McGuire, S., Reiss, D., Hetherington, E. M., & Plomin, R. (1995). Genetic contributions to adolescents' extrafamilial social interactions: Teachers, best friends, and peers. *Social Development, 4*(3), 238–256.

Markman, H. J., & Jones-Leonard, D. (1985). Marital discord and children at risk: Implications for research and prevention. In W. Frankenberg & R. Emde (Eds.), *Early identification of children at risk* (pp. 59–77). New York: Plenum Press.

McGue, M., & Lykken, D. T. (1992). Genetic influence on risk of divorce. *Psychological Science, 3*(6), 368–373.

McHale, S., & Pawletko, T. M. (1992). Differential treatment of siblings in two family contexts. *Child Development, 63*(1), 68–81.

Neiderhiser, J. M., Reiss, D., Pedersen, N. L., Lichtenstein, P., Spotts, E. L., Hansson, K., Cederblad, M., & Elthammer, O., (2004). Genetic and environmental influences on mothering of adolescents: A comparison of two samples. *Developmental Psychology, 40*(3).

Neiderhiser, J. M., Pike, A., Hetherington, E., & Reiss, D. (1998). Adolescent perceptions as mediators of parenting: Genetic and environmental contributions. *Developmental Psychology, 34*(6), 1459–1469.

Neiderhiser, J. M., Reiss, D., Hetherington, E., & Plomin, R. (1999). Relationships between parenting and adolescent adjustment over time: Genetic and environmental contributions. *Developmental Psychology, 35*(3), 680–692.

O'Connor, T. G., Deater-Deckard, K., Fulker, D., Rutter, M., & Plomin, R. (1998). Geno-type-environment correlations in late childhood and early adolescence: Antisocial be-havioral problems and coercive parenting. *Developmental Psychology, 34*(5), 970–981.

Patterson, C. J., Cohn, D. A., & Kao, B. T. (1989). Maternal warmth as a protective fac-tor against risks associated with peer rejection among children. *Development & Psychopathology, 1*(1), 21–38.

Patterson, G. (1982). *Coercive family process: A social learning approach.* Eugene, OR: Castalia.

Patterson, G. R., Crosby, L., & Vuchinich, S. (1992). Predicting risk for early police ar-rest. *Journal of Quantitative Criminology, 8,* 333–355.

Patterson, G. R., DeBaryshe, B. D., & Ramsey, E. (1989). A developmental perspective on antisocial behavior. *American Psychologist, 44,* 329–335.

Petrill, S. A., Hewitt, J., Plomin, R., & DeFries, J. C. (2003). *Nature, nurture and the tran-sition to early adolescence.* New York, NY: Oxford University Press.

Pike, A., McGuire, S., Hetherington, E. M., Reiss, D., & Plomin, R. (1996). Family envi-ronment and adolescent depression and antisocial behavior: A multivariate genetic analysis. *Developmental Psychology, 32*(4), 590–603.

Plomin, R. (1994). *Genetics and experience. The interplay between nature and nurture.* Newbury Park, CA: Sage.

Plomin, R., DeFries, J. C., & Fulker, D. W. (1988). *Nature and nurture in infancy and early childhood.* New York: Cambridge University Press.

Plomin, R., DeFries, J. C., & Loehlin, J. C. (1977). Genotype-environment interaction and correlation in the analysis of human behavior. *Psychological Bulletin, 84,* 309–322.

Plomin, R., Reiss, D., Hetherington, E. M., & Howe, G. W. (1994). Nature and nurture: Genetic contributions to measures of the family environment. *Developmental Psy-chology, 30*(1), 32–43.

Purcell, S. (in press). *Variance components models for gene-environment interaction in twin analysis.*

Purcell, S., & Sham, P. (2003). *Variance components models for gene-environment interac-tion in quantitative trait locus linkage analysis.* Manuscript submitted for publication.

Reid, J. B. (1993). Prevention of conduct disorder before and after school entry: Relating interventions to developmental findings. *Development & Psychopathology, 5*(1–2), 243–262.

Reid, J. B., Eddy, J. M., Fetrow, R., & Stoolmiller, M. (1999). Description and immediate impacts of a preventive intervention for conduct problems. *American Journal of Com-munity Psychology, 27,* 483–517.

Reiss, D., Cederblad, M., Pedersen, N. L., Lichtenstein, P., Elthammer, O., Neiderhiser, J. M., & Hansson, K. (2001). Genetic probes of three theories of maternal adjustment: Recent evidence and a model. *Family Process, 40*(3), 247–259.

Reiss, D., Neiderhiser, J. M., Hetherington, E. M., & Plomin, R. (2000). *The relationship code: Deciphering genetic and social influences on adolescent development.* Cambridge, MA: Harvard University Press.

Reiss, D., Plomin, R., Hetherington, E. M., Howe, G. W., Rovine, M. J., Tryon, A. et al. (1994). The separate worlds of teenage siblings: An introduction to the study of the nonshared environment and adolescent development. In E. M. Hetherington, D. Reiss, & R. Plomin (Eds.), *Separate social worlds of siblings: The impact of nonshared en-vironment on development* (pp. 63–109). Hillsdale, NJ: Lawrence Erlbaum Associates.

Rowe, D. C. (1981). Environmental and genetic influences on dimensions of perceived parenting: A twin study. *Developmental Psychology, 17*, 203–208.

Rowe, D. C. (1983). A biometrical analysis of perceptions of family environment: A study of twins and singleton sibling kinships. *Child Development, 54*, 416–423.

Rubin, K. H., Hymel, S., Mills, R. S. L., & Rose-Krasnor, L. (1991). Conceptualizing different developmental pathways to and from social isolation in childhood. In D. Cicchetti & S. L. Toth (Eds.), *Rochester symposium on developmental psychopathology* (Vol. 2, pp. 91–122). Hillsdale, NJ: Lawrence Erlbaum Associates.

Scaramella, L. V., Conger, R. D., Spoth, R., & Simons, R. L. (2002). Evaluation of a social contextual model of delinquency: A cross-study replication. *Child Development, 73*(1), 175–195.

Scarr, S., & McCartney, K. (1983). How people make their own environments: A theory of genotype-environment effects. *Child Development, 54*, 424–435.

Spotts, E. L., Neiderhiser, J. M., Towers, H., Hansson, K., Lichtenstein, P., & Cederblad, M. (2004). Genetic and environmental influences on marital relationships. *Journal of Family Psychology, 18*(1).

Stoolmiller, M., Eddy, J. M., & Reid, J. B. (2000). Detecting and describing preventive intervention effects in a universal school-based randomized trial targeting delinquent and violent behavior. *Journal of Consulting and Clinical Psychology, 68*, 296–306.

Towers, H., Spotts, E. L., & Neiderhiser, J. M. (2001). Genetic and environmental influences on parenting and marital relationships: Current findings and future directions. *Marriage & Family Review, 33*(1), 11–29.

Trouton, A., Spinath, F. M., & Plomin, R. (2003). *Twins Early Development Study (TEDS): A multivariate, longitudinal genetic investigation of language, cognition and behaviour problems in childhood.* Manuscript submitted for publication.

Trumbetta, S., & Gottesman, I. I. (2000). Endophenotypes for marital status in the NAS-NRC twin registry. In J. L. Rogers & D. C. Rowe (Eds.), *Genetic influences on human fertility and sexuality* (pp. 253–269). Boston, MA: Kluwer.

Webster-Stratton, C., & Taylor, T. (2001). Nipping early risk factors in the bud: Preventing substance abuse, delinquency, and violence in adolescence through interventions targeted at young children (0 to 8 Years). *Prevention Science, 2*(3), 165–192.

Wichers, M. C., Purcell, S., Danckaerts, M., Derom, C., Derom, R., Vlietinck, R., & Van Os, J. (2002). Prenatal life and post-natal psychopathology: Evidence for negative gene–birth weight interaction. *Psychological Medicine, 32*, 1165–1174.

3

Family Influences
on Children's Verbal Ability

Robert T. Michael
University of Chicago

Both biology and culture are transmitted from parents to children, one encoded in DNA and the other in a family's culture. Much less is known about the transmission of cultural attributes than of biological ones.

—Becker and Tomes, 1986, p. S4.

Much attention is paid to understanding the determinants of children's cognitive capacities and acquired skills. This seems appropriate, given that the products from these skills will influence the successes of society in the decades ahead. There are many strands of research that address the topic and that contribute to our understanding of how children develop their skills. This chapter employs the perspective of economics and empirically focuses on the child's vocabulary test score to document the considerable influence that the family's resources have on their children's test scores. It also introduces an additional factor, family "culture," conceptualized as a family's willingness or inclination to expend resources on their children. The nested hypothesis is that this willingness differs across families, persists across generations within a family, and influences children's measured cognitive ability. The chapter uses a British data set—the Children of the National Child Development Study—that includes measures of both parental behaviors with the tested child and also grandparental behaviors with one of the child's parents as a child a generation earlier. The study uses as proxy variables for family culture two discretionary parental behaviors and four discretionary grandparental behaviors. The empirical model shows their association with the child's measured vocabulary test score.

BACKGROUND

In modern society, there is no good case to be made that a child would be better off without the skills of reading, a substantial vocabulary, or basic mathematical skills of arithmetic. All parents, it is assumed, wish to encourage in their children a good vocabulary and good reading and math skills, among other attributes. Children differ dramatically in their abilities and their achievements. There is much research that investigates the determinants of these skills. Studies in developmental psychology look at parental processes and practices that are associated with successful "outcomes." Studies in social demography identify associations between family characteristics or structures and children's test scores. Studies in economics emphasize the family resources and relative prices that create incentives for families to invest in their children's cognitive and socioemotional skills. Some emphasize the critical role of genetic endowments; others focus on the importance of the community, of the school, and racial, ethnic or religious cultures to which the child is exposed.

This chapter contributes to the research that emphasizes the role of family resources as a central factor influencing the development of children's measured skills. Prior research identified three broad domains of resources: the parents' education, the family's income level, and the family structure. Evidence of the relation between parents' education and their children's measured ability or cognitive achievement is quite strong and is found in many data sets and reported in practically every analytic perspective. To cite but one example, Smith, Brooks-Gunn, and Klebanov (1997) found strong associations between parent's education level and several measures of children's ability using two distinct data sources.

A second family characteristic that influences the child in many ways, including test scores, is level of income. Here, however, the evidence of influence is more complex and deserves a longer description. Extreme income deprivation or poverty has been shown to severely affect the nutrition and health of the child, and this in turn adversely affects the child's capacity and eagerness to learn. Two excellent collections of studies on this topic are found in Huston, McLoyd, and Coll (1994) and Duncan and Brooks-Gunn (1997), the latter concluding: "Children raised in low-income families score lower than children from more affluent families do on assessments of health, cognitive development, school achievement and emotional well-being" (Brooks-Gunn, Duncan, & Maritato, 1997, p. 1). Income differences well above poverty also affect children's cognitive test scores. Studies use various cognitive tests and report strong relations with family income, some showing a linear effect across wide ranges of incomes, whereas others find stronger effects at lower levels of income (Duncan, Brooks-Gunn, & Klebanov, 1994; Peters & Mullis, 1997; Smith et al., 1997. Also see Hobcraft [1998], who documented for Britain the persistent effects of a different framing of income and resources—"social exclusion"—during childhood on subsequent adult behaviors).

Mayer (2002) provided a comprehensive review of the impact of income on children's outcomes in cognition, health, and later labor market behaviors. Regarding cognitive test scores, she noted that many studies that control for parent's education, or own test scores, or family structure show no sizable effects of family income. Mirroring that point, McCulloch and Joshi (2002) looked at the effects of family income on the child's Peabody Picture Vocabulary Test (PPVT), using the same data set as in this chapter. They measured income by quintile dummy variables and showed strong income effects on PPVT scores controlling for only the child's age and gender. They also showed, however, that these income effects decline in significance as mother's education and aspects of the home environment are included in the statistical models. Clearly, family income is important for children's cognitive development. It is also clear, however, that when the things income can provide or the personal parental attributes that typically generate income are statistically controlled, money itself is no longer as critical an ingredient. This distinction is important in social policy because handing money to a family without those parental attributes will not have the same impact as would handing both the money and the accompanying characteristics to the family, if that were feasible. This distinction is also important for the research strategy adopted in this chapter, as becomes clear below.

There is far less consistency in the evidence on the influence of family structure on children's test scores. Families with only one adult have less parenting capacity and face greater stress in childrearing, so one might expect to find a negative effect of single parenthood. Similarly, stress among families that have experienced the turmoil of marital disruption may also affect the children's measured skills. Yet, empirically, McLanahan (1997) showed that family structure has no strong, persistent effect on children's test scores, although it does have a stronger association with other aspects of their well-being. Similarly, Joshi, Cooksey, Wiggins, McCulloch, Verropoulou, and Clarke (1999, p. 22) reported inconsistent effects of lone parenting on different cognitive tests, and these decline in significance when family attributes such as parent's education are included. Yet, Pierret (2001, p. 36) showed that for adolescents in the National Longitudinal Study of Youth–1997 (NLSY97), their grades in eighth grade are lower by 7%–12% if they were not reared in an intact family, controlling both the family's income and parent's education. DeLeire and Kalil (2002), using National Educational Longitudinal Survey data, also reported effects of family structure on high school graduation rates, with income and parental education controled.

So, family characteristics, including parents' education and income and other indicators of family resources, clearly have an important influence on children's measured cognitive skills. This chapter investigates and confirms these well-established influences on children's test scores and goes beyond these factors to investigate an additional, important cross-generational family influence.

Studies in many disciplines stress the importance of cross-generational family influences on children's healthy development. Scholars from several disciplines are cited briefly to stress the breadth of interest and the range of evidence that children are greatly influenced by family behaviors across generations. Although this chapter suggests a rather novel way in which one generation affects its grandchildren, the basic idea, as is evident in this brief research review, is deeply embedded in thinking about the role of the family: Behaviors and values carry over from one generation to the next.

One type of evidence highlights the similarity between parent and child in terms of behavior patterns or aspects of temperament. For example, Cohen, Kasen, Brook, and Hartmark (1998) used data on two generations (tested as children in each) to document the consistency of what is described as *inhibited behavior* (i.e., shyness and fearfulness or timidity) and *difficult behavior* (i.e., intensity of anger, negative mood, excessive attention-seeking, and low score on a measure of persistence on tasks and being "careful with things"). Of course, the issue of heritability is related to this parent-to-child transmission of attributes and behaviors. It has been suggested that heritability extends beyond physiological or psychological attributes to environmental factors such as "parenting" (see Rowe, 1981). McGuire's (2003) tutorial on "the heritability of parenting" found that several studies, but not all, confirm that parental warmth is heritable, whereas a measure of "parental control" is not. (See the "special section" of *Developmental Psychology*, 1998, p. 1161, for studies of intergenerational continuity suggesting that "parenting practices ... emerge as a gateway for transfer of a variety of characteristics between generations.")

Other evidence suggests that experiences as a child carry over into attitudes and behaviors as an adult. For example, Hauser (1999) following a small group of adolescents with psychological disorders over the past quarter-century, and documented trends in resiliency. It is striking, as he described the open-ended reports by these adolescents, how they associate their behaviors as parents to behaviors they knew as children. Hauser reported one of his subjects describing her husband in later interviews much as she had described her father in earlier years; in essence, "her father and husband converge." It is not surprising that a person carries with them the associations and experiences of childhood as they assume adult roles.

Continuity from the experience as a child to that of a parent is one mechanism for the transmission of family culture.

There are many links, of course, between early experiences of youth and subsequent physical health. To cite but two: The intriguing "Barker hypothesis" offers evidence linking fetal and early childhood growth and coronary heart disease in later life (see Eriksson, Forsen, Tuomilehto, Winter, Osmound, & Barker, 1999; Forsen, Eriksson, Tuomilehto, Osmond, & Barker, 1999). A similar phenomenon is reported by De Stavola, Hardy, Huh, dos Santos Silva, Wadsworth & Swerdlow (2000), who found a robust positive relation between birth weight and the risk of premenopausal breast cancer: "Women who weighed 4kg or more at birth were nearly six times more likely to develop breast cancer prior to menopause than those who weighed less than 3kg" (p. 967). Although far afield from the investigation reported here, these biological connections between exposure at one age and consequences at another are suggestive of the link between experiences as a child and behaviors as an adult and parent.

Vandell (2000) has provided a summary of developmental psychologists' thinking on the importance of parents' behavior and the socialization of their children. She stressed the interactions between the child, the family, and the broader social environment. Parenting, she argued, is undertaken in a complex and conditional way that is "embedded in a framework that is both historical and cultural." What she meant by historical, citing Elder's (1979) work of the effects of the Great Depression on families and their subsequent lifetime behavior, is similar to the notion I wish to stress: the experiences and habits formed during childhood and adolescence influence behavior as parents later in life.

In economics as well, the idea that experience early in life greatly influences later perceptions and actions is well developed. One example is Easterlin's (1973) relative income hypothesis applied to fertility behavior. It suggests that one's recollection of previous economic well-being as an adolescent, when compared to economic circumstance as a young adult, influences the assessment of one's capacity to afford children. The concept of human capital—of investments in skills and attributes at one age that pay dividends later in life—is quintessentially a cross-generational idea given that so much of the early investment in a child reflects the actions and motivations of the parents. As Heckman (2000, p. 8) stressed, "learning begets learning," and so the dynamic of early experiences and efforts to encourage children's learning influences their subsequent capacity and their interest in further learning. Another example is Becker's (1991) discussion of family dynasty, of differences across families in their orientation toward the advancement and perpetuation of the family name or its reputation.

In other contexts as well, the importance of experience as a child on adult behavior is recognized. Sen (2001) noted, "The culture in which one is born

and bred can leave a lasting impact on one's perceptions and predispositions." However, Sen added, "But this does not imply that a person is not
able to modify or even reject antecedent associations" (p. 327). In a context
closer to the subject of this study, Harris (1996, p. 205) observed, "People
seem to have an extremely strong, probably unconscious motivation to replicate their parent's patterns of child rearing even when they end up repeat-
ing the resulting disasters."

Although these citations from several branches of research emphasize
that experiences as a child have profound effects on later behaviors and
perceptions, including as a parent, at least two cautionary notes should be
acknowledged. First, a large portion of the variation among children in
their test scores on any subject is not associated statistically with any measure of family background. The child's personality, innate ability, eagerness to learn, the quality of instruction at home and at school, the social
encouragement and values of peers, characteristics of the child's residential, ethnic, and cultural communities, and signals from the labor market
all have their influence. The child's motivation to do well on the cognitive
tests also has an effect. Many of these varied factors are not measured in
any one study, and they cannot be measured here. Thus, it is known at the
outset that family behavior will not explain a large portion of the variation
in the children's test scores.

A second qualification is that children skilled in one subject are not
necessarily also skilled in another. Huttenlocher, Levine, and Vevea
(1998) showed modest intertest correlations among pairs of skills of language, spatial operations, concept mastery, and associative memory for
kindergarten and first graders (i.e., correlations (ρ) from 0.42 to 0.61).
Sternberg, Grigorenko, and Bundy (2001) documented the relatively
high intertest correlations on different general intelligence tests (i.e.,
Stanford-Binet, WISC, Raven, etc.), with $\rho = 0.50$ to 0.88, but they
show the declining correlation for the same test administered at respec-
tive ages (i.e., for the Stanford-Binet $\rho = 0.87$ between ages 5 and 6, but
$\rho = 0.62$ between ages 5 and 12. Adopted from Sontag, Baker, & Nelson,
1958). As Kagan (1998) eloquently insisted, pointing out that the correlation across children on separate cognitive tests is typically no higher
than 0.4, the notion of a general intelligence is fallacious, if nonetheless
seductive. (Michael [2003a] found confirming evidence that for the
children in the data set used in this chapter, the correlations across cognitive tests are on the order of 0.40.) If measures of cognitive ability are
not highly correlated, then there is no single influence of some family
background factor, or *any* single determinant, on cognitive ability. This
chapter looks only at a measure of vocabulary skills, and thus results may
not reflect influences on other skills.

THE CONCEPTUAL FRAMEWORK

This chapter focuses on the child's verbal ability measured by a test score, T. The inquiry asks how the family influences T. The first in a series of questions is: "Are parental resources positively associated with their child's T?" The research briefly reviewed earlier surely suggests an affirmative answer. From the perspective of an economic approach, the expected answer is also affirmative. If the matter reflects demand for the desired outcome of a healthy and capable child, then as resources such as income increase, demand should rise. If viewed as a matter of household production, then an increase in family resources implies more inputs and an increase in the output T.

Although empirical measures are discussed in the next section, it is helpful to note that the study uses three distinct parental resources: (a) the cognitive ability of one of the parents, assessed when he or she was age 11, (b) that parent's completed education level, and (c) the family's income level. Several additional family controls are included in this vector of "family resources," including the employment of the parents, the sex of the focus parent, the mother's age at first birth, the religion of the family, and the number of siblings of the child. Of these, only the latter is strictly another measure of resources available per child.

The second question is: "Are the grandparents' resources—measured by their socioeconomic status (SES)—additionally associated with the child's T?" Their SES is measured when the child's parent was a young child. The expectation is that this, too, will be positively associated with T. The reason for expecting a positive association is that the measure of the child's parents' resources is probably incomplete, and adding the grandparents' SES should capture some of that unmeasured parental resource.

The third and fourth questions require more extensive framing because they are more novel, and documenting their influence is the main contribution of the chapter. The hypothesis is that there is a quite distinct family attribute that can be described as parental willingness to invest in children, or as parental inclination to sacrifice on behalf of children, or as parental resolve to give nurturance and support and advantage to their children. Designate this family attribute as C; it will be referred to as the family's "culture." C cannot be measured directly. It captures the fact that families differ in their orientation and their efforts on behalf of their children. Indisputably, the family's resource level constrains its capacity to give to the children. But additionally and separately from the level of resources, families also differ in how much they choose to devote to the children, how much to sacrifice their own adult preferences, interests, and activities on behalf of their children. In general, an economic perspective would include prices, in

addition to income, as the key regulator of demand. But in the present context, the argument is that the key differences across families are not differences in prices but are differences in their preference or their commitment
to their children. Furthermore, the argument is that these differences in
commitment are correlated across generations within a family. They are
what the quotation at the beginning of this chapter called "family culture."

If C could be directly measured, the third question would be: "Is the family's C positively associated with their child's T?" Because C is a construct
for which no direct measure is available, let the vector P be a proxy for C,
and again to fix ideas, two measures will be used, both of which are positively
associated with C: a dummy variable indicating that the mother breast-fed
the child, and a continuous variable that measures the child's birth weight,
which partially reflects the mother's efforts to ensure a healthy baby (i.e., by
not smoking or drinking during pregnancy, by early medical care during
pregnancy, etc.). This third question then becomes: "Are breast-feeding and
birth weight (interpreted as proxies for family culture) positively associated
with their child's T?" (A defense of these proxy variables is offered later.)

There is a fourth question that is an extension of the third. Recursively,
the behavior of the parent in the current generation is surely influenced by
the behavior of the grandparent a generation earlier. Another set of proxies
for C, based on the parenting behavior of the grandparents in rearing this
child's parent, can be constructed. Call that vector G, which contains four
elements, each of which is a dummy variable ($1 =$ yes):

1. Did the grandmother breast-feed the parent?
2. Did both the grandmother and grandfather read to the parent as a
    preschooler?
3. Did the parent's teachers consider the grandmother to be uninter-
    ested in her child's schooling at ages 7, 11, and 16?
4. Did those same teachers consider the grandfather to be exception-
    ally (positively) interested in his child's schooling activities at those
    same ages?

Elements 1, 2, and 4 are positively associated with C while element 3 is
negatively associated.

With G defined as these four behaviors by the grandparents in rearing
their child, and serving as a proxy for C, the basic question about the association of the family's C and their child's T, becomes: "Are the breast-feeding
and childrearing practices of the grandparents (interpreted as proxies for
family culture) positively associated with their grandchild's T?"

The symmetry between questions one and two and between questions
three and four is worth discussing. It is not surprising to think that if we measure a few elements of the current family's resources, there are probably

other current resources that are unmeasured that we can capture by including information about the prior generation's resources. That is the rationale for including the grandparent's SES measure in the model of the influence of family resources on T, and we easily accept the notion that there is a cross-generational transmission of financial or material resources.

However, parents pass along not only material assets, they also pass along their attitudes, including their attitude toward children and the way in which they should be nurtured, reared, and provided for. Therefore, if there is an association between C and T, and if there is a cross-generational transmission of C, then the measured vector G should be associated with T. That association should be strongest if P and the parental resources are not included in the estimation because in that model, G captures all the direct and indirect investments of grandparents on their children and, through them, to their grandchildren. The association of G on T should be weaker if the parental resources are included in the estimation because its influence through the parental resources is controlled. In addition, the association of G on T should be weaker still if both the parental resources and P are controlled because only the unmeasured aspects of the cross-generational transmission of C is then reflected in the coefficients on the elements of G. These tests are reported later.

The three measures of family resources need little justification. Family income and parental education and the measured ability of the parent (when a child) all constrain the family's efforts to promote child skills. The intellectual capabilities of the two parents may affect the child's test scores in at least two ways. First, because capability is at least in part inherited, the child is directly influenced by each biological parent's own capability. Second, the more capable the parents in encouraging and teaching their child, the less costly or more productive is that instruction. Thus, more skilled parents probably respond to that lower cost by providing more and better instruction, or by encouraging and participating in their child's learning. There is surely an interaction as well, with a more capable child finding it easier to learn and, therefore, being more eager to focus on learning.

It is useful to reflect on the notion of family "culture," and to consider the proxy variables used to measure it. What are the ways in which family attributes and behaviors can influence a child's cognitive ability, specifically their verbal skills? Part of that influence, surely, is genetic: The parents' choices of one another as a partner are a primary influence on their child. Subsequently, the biological mother carries the fetus and influences the child physiologically and perhaps in other ways that may affect later skills. From birth onward, the parental influence reflects a direct engagement with their child and indirect guidance including their choices about the child's care during infancy and preschool ages, and their efforts to affect the child's experiences in neighborhoods, schools, and with peers.

Considered across the child's developmental stages—in utero, in infancy, and then in the preschool and school-aged years—the parents' direct influence probably declines as the child spends more time away from home. Yet the correlation of parental attributes with the child's cognitive skills may not decline with the child's age because of the cumulative effect of learning on new learning. As with other types of human capital formation, we can think of the production of additional units of T in year i, call them K_i (i.e., new verbal skills acquired in year i), as produced in part using the accumulated stock T_i. Because parental influence on the production of T at early ages is substantial, it may be that the influence is as clearly identified at later ages as it would be at young ages. Indeed, it would be odd if the parental efforts diminished to obscurity as the child aged. For one thing, if it did, the parents would have far less incentive to make large investments early in the child's life.

It may be tempting to conceptualize and to estimate a production function that relates the "inputs" of the parents, the child, the community, and subsequently the schools to the "output" of the child's measured test score. This is not attempted here for three reasons. First, the theory of children's skill development tells us how complex that relation seems to be (see, e.g., Vandell, 2000). For example, the influence of the parents on the child's skills is not a one-to-one relation: The same parental action will not have the same outcome for every child. At best, parental actions are influencing, not determining. Therefore, although conceptually there may be an input-to-output relation, it is probably not an engineering production function relation. That framework is too deterministic, too mechanical as a representation of the process of interest.

Second, although "parenting" is a primary focus within developmental psychology, research does not provide much guidance in statistically formulating the way parents influence their children's skill acquisition. It provides no guidance about what particular parental behavior or action might yield a higher score on a particular achievement test. Therefore, even if a data set had extensive information about childrearing practices—for example, the number of hours a mother read to her child or the detailed nature of her play with the child—it is unclear how to link those actions to any particular skill development through an empirically estimated production function. Third, the data set used here does not have enough detail about the childrearing practices or time spent instructing or motivating the child to estimate an input–output relation.

It is, however, a helpful heuristic to frame the activity of the parents expending effort and resources on their child as production that yields skills in the child. The heuristic guides the analysis even though no structural estimation is attempted. The analysis here assumes that parents want to promote their child's verbal ability, measured by T, and assumes that two types of characteristics influence its production. The first characteristic is the level of resources, and the second is parents' willingness or resolve to use these resources on behalf of the child.

Families with greater resources are expected to invest more in their children's skill development. They can provide greater stimulation and encouragement to their child, they can protect their child from detrimental external insults, or they can help their child overcome adverse events. Although they cannot ensure successful skill development, they have the capacity to promote it and protect it, relative to less well-endowed families. Just as one's own "learning begets learning," a parent's skill facilitates similar skill acquisition in the child. Thus, the family's income, and the capabilities of the parents as measured by the formal schooling and by the ability test scores of the parent (measured as a youth), reflect the family resources.

The second of the two constraints, the parents' willingness, resolve, or commitment to nurture their child, is family culture. One attribute of a family is that it has a history; the adults who manage it and establish its patterns and activities were themselves children in their own families of origin. The experiences they had as children influence their perceptions about attractive and appropriate family life and about the appropriate ways to rear and nurture children. The child-oriented nature of the family of origin may or may not be motivated primarily by a concern about human capital development in the children. The motivation may have more to do with direct preferences for having, engaging, and rearing children, or it may be a preference or a habit of family activities, such as making big events of birthdays and holidays, and this naturally includes the family's children. In other cases, the motivation may be a conviction of an ethnicity, shared by families from that culture. Examples include the conviction that schooling is the key to economic success, or that a strong work ethic is critical for social success, or that service to others is the highest calling. These help define what being a member of this family means, as emphasized by the adults, and absorbed if not always accepted by the children. Be it habit or purposive strategic behavior, there are family cultures or family capital that become part of one's sense of an appropriate family style or way of living, and these are carried into the next generation of the family. Some of these practices or values constitute what is meant by the culture of an ethnicity, community, or a family dynasty.

Of course, this is not a linear, one-to-one translation of doing what one's parents did. One complication is that there are experiences of childhood that, as an adult, one may reject or rebel against and purposely avoid in the interest of a successful family experience. Another complication is that there are at least two family cultures that merge when forming a new family; one partner may be dominant, or his or her family culture may be dominant in some social or economic way. The new family may reside in a neighborhood that reinforces one of the family cultures at the expense of the other. One religious culture may, for example, have an express policy of promoting its beliefs among the next generation, whereas the other does not. How the two family cultures develop into the new family's style of action is not explored here.

The family's resolve or commitment to devote resources to childrearing is separate from and additional to the level of available family resources: Both additional resources or a greater commitment to use available resources on the child's behalf are expected to have a positive effect on the child's skill acquisition.

This chapter uses two direct measures of behavior by parents that are considered good indicators, or proxies, of this family resolve. These are behaviors that are discretionary; they suggest the degree of commitment by the parents on behalf of their child. The first is whether the mother breast-fed the child. Although there may be many reasons why a mother does or does not choose to breast-feed her new infant, the contention here is that partitioning mothers into two groups of those who do and those who do not breast-feed effectively partitions the mothers into a first group who are more engaged and inclined to invest in their child, and a second group who are on balance less so. In the data set used here, 63% of the mothers breast-fed their child. This dummy variable serves as a proxy variable; its coefficient is interpreted as indicating the influence on the child's test score of the parents being more willing, resolved, or committed to investing in the child.

The second proxy, the baby's birth weight, reflects the mother's efforts to protect the healthy development of her baby while she was pregnant. It is described more extensively later. These two proxy variables, referred to earlier as the vector P, are included in the empirical model.

In addition, the study uses four indicators of the grandparents' culture or style of childrearing when the parent was a child. These four indicators of commitment to the children in the family are introduced into the model to provide further evidence on this family-specific attribute. The empirical strategy is first to control for family characteristics that have been shown to affect children's cognitive development, and then, with those controls in place, to determine any incremental influence on the child's test scores of the family's resolve to invest in their child. This resolve is measured, first, by two indicative discretionary behaviors by the parents, and then also by four discretionary behaviors by the grandparents when they reared their child.

THE NCDS DATA

This study uses survey data from a longitudinal 1958 British birth cohort study, the National Child Development Study (NCDS). The study began as a perinatal mortality study of births in the week of March 3–9, 1958. Nearly all (98%) of the women who gave birth in England, Scotland, and Wales that week were interviewed and the child born that week became the subject of the follow-up surveys conducted in 1965, 1969, 1974, 1981, and 1991 when the child was aged 7, 11, 16, 23, and 33. The size of the sample was 18,558 subjects, with information from at least one of the surveys. The 1991 interview was undertaken for a sampled subset of 15,666, with a survey response rate of 85%.

That 1991 interview included a supplemental survey of the biological children of a randomly subsampled one third of the male and female cohort members (the response rate on this child survey was a remarkable 96%). That sample of "Children of the NCDS," sponsored principally by National Institute of Child Health and Human Development (NICHD), is used here, together with information on the cohort-member-parent (cm-parent) and information from an interview with the child's mother (she may or may not have been the cohort member). There are 4,229 children in the data set. The verbal ability test was administered to 2,847 children aged 4 and older. It is the dependent variable in most of the analyses reported here.

The 1991 survey administered several cognitive tests to the youth; the one used here is the Peabody Picture Vocabulary Test, Revised (PPVT-R). It assesses the hearing vocabulary for standard English and is described as "a quick estimate of the verbal ability of scholastic aptitude" (Dunn & Dunn, 1981). The test consists of a set of 175 words spoken to the child, who is asked to point to a picture of the word spoken, selecting one of four pictures shown on an easel, word by word. The test is scored according to a strict protocol dictating the starting and ending of the test, initiated according to the age of the test taker. The test has been extensively used in the United States and was Anglicized by the test authors for administration in England. The children's raw scores have been transformed to adjust for the age of the child normalized on this British sample. (See Michael, 2003a, for a comparison of test scores for these British children and a comparable sample of U.S. children from the "Children of the NLSY.")

The models estimated in this chapter use as control variables only a few attributes of the child—age, gender, and race. One does not want to control for malleable attributes of the child through which the family's influence on cognitive skills may operate. The attributes of the child's parents used in the analysis are more extensive. These are mostly attributes of the cohort member (cm-parent), about two thirds of whom are the mother. A few facts pertain to the child's mother, whether she is the cohort member or the spouse.

Three sets of variables directly measure current family resources. One is the cm-parent's education level, defined in categories from the lowest if no certification was earned, through the O-levels and A-levels (about equivalent to U.S. high school graduation), and higher education. The second is the cm-parent's reading and mathematics test score at age 11, in 1969. The third is family income. It can be measured in five different ways, described here, but the empirical results rely on only one, with a few sensitivity checks described in the text.

One measure is the family's gross income, expressed in natural logs. Although it is the most conventional measure, it is missing for about 16% of the cases. A second measure is the log of the value of the family's home, which is an indicator of longer run income, but it is missing for more than half the cases. The third measure is derived from the 1991 survey, which asked whether the family met each of seven conditions that typically vary with family income; this measure is featured here because it is defined for all cases and reflects longer run income. The conditions, in descending order of commonality (showing the percentage of families that meet each condition), indicate whether the family: has a bathroom in their home (98% do), has a phone (90%), was currently not on welfare in 1991 (89%), owned or was buying their home (73%), has some savings account (68%), has never been on welfare (68%), and has some financial investments (23%). In the empirical model reported here, income is measured as the simple sum of these seven dummies, called "income index." It ranges in values from zero to seven. A fourth income measure uses all seven of these dummies separately as a step function in income. A fifth income indicator is the total number of rooms in the family home.

Several additional family attributes are controlled in the statistical models, and several of these can be interpreted as further measures of resources available for the child. One is the age at which the mother had her first child. Women who are very young at their first birth may lack the maturity and psychological resources suited to childrearing. The second attribute is the total number of children in the family. As it increases, holding constant the family's income and other resources, there is a simple negative relation to the resources available per child. Other controls include the employment status of each parent and the religion practiced in the family. A dummy variable is included indicating whether the family "often" attends religious services. The cm-parent's marital history was also used, but showed no influence in the regressions, and was therefore dropped.

As discussed earlier, the SES of the cm-parent's parents is included and is measured in four categories (1 = lowest; 4 = highest) in 1958 and the early 1960s and averaged over the two time points. (I thank Kath Kiernan for sharing this variable.)

These measures of the child, parents, and grandparents are the basic family characteristics and resources used in the regression model reported here. The child's test score is expected to be positively associated with the family resources—the focal parent's education, cognitive skills, income, and maturity (age at first birth)—and with grandparents' SES. It is expected to be negatively associated with number of siblings, given that more siblings lower the parental resources available per child.

As previously noted, two proxy variables reflect the mother's resolve or commitment to her child. One, discussed earlier, is a dummy variable indicating whether the mother breast-fed her child. The other is the child's birth weight. Birth weight is frequently used as an indicator of the initial well-being or health of the child. Although the variable involves much stochastic variation, it also has an inherited component and may reflect certain maternal behaviors, such as whether she smoked and drank alcohol during the pregnancy. It is these maternal behaviors—her attentiveness to her pregnancy—that are of interest here. They are interpreted as an in utero investment by the mother on behalf of the child and are an indication of parental commitment to the child's nurturance.

To strengthen this interpretation of the variable, it is used in several separate statistical strategies. One simply includes the child's birth weight as a regressor, along with the mother's breast-feeding practice as a proxy for the unmeasured commitment, C. The second strategy purges the variable of its stochastic component and includes only that portion of the child's birth weight that is associated with the parent's own attributes and behaviors during the pregnancy. This purging is accomplished in two separate manners. One uses a two-stage, least squares regression, with birth weight as an endogenous variable identified by certain maternal behaviors during pregnancy. These behaviors include the amount she smoked and drank during that pregnancy, the month in which the pregnancy was confirmed and the month of her first prenatal medical visit, whether the pregnancy was planned, and, as controls, the cm-parent's own birth weight, and the race and gender of the baby.

The other strategy involves a side regression that estimates the child's birth weight as a function of these several parental attributes and behaviors during pregnancy (this is essentially the first stage regression in the 2SLS but without the other exogenous variables from the second stage). That side regression's predicted value is used as a proxy variable measuring the commitment to the child. However, because the mother's actions explain only a small portion of the variation in the child's birth weight, and because the additional variation in birth weight may also contribute to the child's cognitive development, a second variable, the side regression's residual, is also included. This residual, orthogonal to the predicted birth weight by construction, is interpreted as a child-specific stochastic influence on the child's development. The model with the side regression and the use of both the predicted and the residual birth weight variables is considered superior to the more standard, two-stage least squares model. Therefore, it is featured in this discussion. These two sets of variables, breast-feeding and the two birth-weight measures, are the proxy variables in the vector P.

The other set of four proxy variables for the unmeasured family culture, C—those referred to in the vector G—are measures of the grandparents' behaviors toward the cm-parent as a child. The argument is not that these four grandparent behaviors directly influence the child's cognitive skills, but rather that they reflect the culture or style of that family, and thereby act as proxy variables for unmeasured family investments that influence the child's cognitive skills. These four variables indicate the grandparents' willingness, resolve, or commitment to their child in the late 1950s and early 1960s. That behavior helped develop the cm-parent's own expectation about appropriate childrearing behavior. Thus, the argument is that the child-turned-parent was influenced by how her (or his) parent behaved as a parent and this affected the willingness to invest in her own children. If she grew up in a family that exhibited a great resolve to use available resources on behalf of the children, then it is much more likely that she did so herself as a parent in the 1980s and early 1990s. This is, admittedly, a subtle and indirect test of the importance of family culture. Among other limitations, even at its best, the information captures only one of the two sets of grandparents' behaviors.

The four grandparent variables are these. One is a dummy variable indicating whether the grandmother breast-fed her child, the cm-parent, in 1958. A second is a dummy variable indicating that both grandparents reported that they spent time reading to their child before the child was age 7 (in 1965). The third and fourth measure the grandparents' engagement in their child's schooling at ages 7, 11, and 16 (in the 1960s and early 1970s). Although the grandparents reading to the child is a self-reported fact, these measures of engagement in the schooling of their child are assessments reported by the child's teachers in the three classes, asked in the 3 years and then averaged. One is a dummy variable indicating that the teachers considered the grandmother to be among the least interested mothers, and the other is a dummy variable indicating that those teachers reported that the grandfather was among the most interested fathers. (These two variables are constructed from composites of the three teacher reports. See Hobcraft, 1998.)

The empirical strategy is to estimate a regression of the child's verbal test score on the set of family resources to determine whether the resources have the positive association found in other studies and to affirm the notion that resources contribute to the healthy cognitive development of the child. Then the vector P is introduced and subsequently the vector G is added as well. Later, models are estimated with other combinations of P and G, with and without including parental resources. In this series of regressions, we see the direct and the indirect effects of both P and G.

REGRESSION MODELS

Table 3.1 shows the summary statistics for the variables used in this analysis. The children range in age from 4 to 18 (11 are a month or so under age 4 and were eligible for the PPVT), about half are girls, and nearly all of these British children whose parent is in the NCDS are White.

The PPVT score, normed on these British children, has a mean of 100 and a standard deviation of 15. About two thirds of the cm-parents are the mother of the child; the many descriptive statistics are self-explanatory. For the grandparent (the parent of the cm-parent), the SES is shown, missing for about one in five grandparents. The variables listed as child experiences include the child's birth weight (in pounds), dummies for those born at "low" and "very low" birth weight, a dummy indicating if the child was breast-fed (nearly two thirds were), and the number of siblings. For the parent's behavior, all variables refer to aspects of this child's prenatal life. About three quarters of these pregnancies were reported to be "planned" by the couple; the pregnancy was confirmed, on average, in the eighth week; the first antenatal doctor's visit occurred, on average, in the 10th week of the pregnancy; and during the pregnancy, the mother drank, on average, about four drinks per month and smoked about 0.6 cigarettes per day. (During the pregnancy, about 34% of the mothers drank no alcohol and 90% did not smoke.)

Regarding the grandparents' behaviors, 58% breast-fed their child. (This information is from the 1965 survey.) About one quarter of both grandparents read to their young child. Teachers identified 10% of the grandmothers as having low interest and 16% of the grandfathers as having high interest; Table 3.1 also shows the entire distribution of these assessments, those with low, some, more, and great interest in their children's schooling.

The regression analysis is shown in Table 3.2. Model 1 reports the relation of the child's test score to the child's, parent's, and grandparents' attributes and resources. This regression confirms results from many other studies. Although the child's age is not statistically related to the PPVT score when it is regressed alone or with only gender and race, it is positively related to the test score in this model. White children do substantially better on this vocabulary test than the non-White children. This is an interesting finding because in the United States, the PPVT has been somewhat controversial in its use of words that are more likely known by White children. However, non-Whites in Britain also score lower, although a much smaller fraction is Black, and at least one of the child's parents was born in Britain in 1958.

Many of the cm-parent's, or mother's, attributes are strongly associated with the child's test scores. The cm-parent's own reading test score (measured at age 11) is significantly related to the child's PPVT score, but the age 11 score in mathematics is not. The cm-parent's education level is quite

TABLE 3.1
Descriptive Statistics for Child of NCDS Variables

Variable Description	Variable Name	Mean	SD	Min.–Max.
Child Test Score				
PPVT	PPVTB	100.10	14.98	1–187
Child Attributes				
Age (years)	AGE	8.16	3.07	3–18
Gender	GIRL=1	0.51	0.50	0–1
Race	WHITE=1	0.98	0.13	0–1
CM-Parent Attributes and Resources				
Gender	CMMOM=1	0.63	0.48	0–1
Age at first birth	AGEPAR	22.98	3.23	15–33
Education: no edu.	NOEDUC	0.16	0.37	0–1
Low (cse 4/5)	NOQUAL	0.15	0.36	0–1
O-levels	OQUAL	0.37	0.48	0–1
A-levels	AQUAL	0.11	0.32	0–1
Higher edu.	HIGHQUAL	0.18	0.38	0–1
Missing*	MISCMED	0.02	0.13	0–1
Ln(Incomegr)	LNINCG	4.52	0.76	1.39–5.96
Missing*	MISINCG	0.16	0.36	0–1
Ln(homeprice)	LNHOMEPR	9.60	0.30	6.26–11.51
Missing*	MISLNHPR	0.64	0.48	0–1
Income index	INCINDEX	5.11	1.48	0–7
Number rooms	ROOM	4.80	1.38	0–19
Religion: Church of England	RELENGL	0.32	0.47	0–1
Catholic	RELCATH	0.10	0.30	0–1
None	RELNONE	0.47	0.50	0–1
Attend relig serv. Often	RELOFTEN	0.16	0.37	0–1

CM full-time employed	CMFTEMPL	0.45	0.50	0–1
CMFTemploy*cm-mom	EMPLOYDM	0.13	0.34	0–1
CM's general ability	CMGNABLE	42.73	14.49	0–79
CM's reading comp.	CMREADTS	15.57	5.40	0–32
CM's math score	CMMATHTS	16.05	9.28	0–39
Missing	MISCMABL	0.12	0.33	0–1
CM's birth weight	CMBRTWT	7.30	1.15	2.25–12.75
CMbwt*cm-mom	MOMBWT	4.55[1]	3.57	0–12.75
Missing*	MISCMWT	0.05	0.22	0–1
Grandparent Attributes				
SES lowest	GRPSES1	0.53	0.50	0–1
SES second	GRPSES2	0.18	0.38	0–1
SES third	GRPSES3	0.07	0.26	0–1
SES highest	GRPSES4	0.04	0.21	0–1
Missing*	MISGRSES	0.18	0.38	0–1
Child Experiences				
Number of siblings	TOTCHLD	2.41	0.88	0–7
Birth weight	BRTWT	7.27	1.20	1.75–11.56
Very low b-wt (<1.5kg)	VLOWBWT	0.01	0.10	0–1
Low b-wt (1.5–2.5kg)	LOWBWT	0.06	0.24	0–1
Missing*	MISBRTWT	0.02	0.14	0–1
Was child breast-fed?	BREAST=1	0.63	0.48	0–1
Missing*	MISBREAS	0.02	0.14	0–1
Parents' Behavior				
The child's pregnancy:				
Was it planned?	PGPLAN	0.72	0.45	0–1
When confirmed	CMPGCONF	8.00	3.66	1–39

(continued on next page)

TABLE 3.1 (continued)

Variable Description	Variable Name	Mean	SD	Min.–Max.
First antenatal visit	CMPG1V	10.21	4.02	1–36
Missing*	MISPG1V	0.06	0.24	0–1
Number drinks/mo during pregnancy	CMPGALCN	3.96	6.21	0–31
Missing*	MISPGALN	0.02	0.14	0–1
Number cigs/day during pregnancy	PGSMOCN	0.59	2.56	0–60
Grandparent Behavior (with CM-parent)				
Grmom breast-fed CM	GRPBREAS	0.58	0.49	0–1
Both gp's read to CM	BOTHREAD	0.24	0.43	0–1
Gm's school interest				
Low	MOMINTL	0.10	0.30	0–1
Some	MOMINTS	0.20	0.40	0–1
More	MOMINTM	0.42	0.49	0–1
Great	MOMINTG	0.25	0.43	0–1
Gf's school interest:				
Low	DADINTL	0.11	0.31	0–1
Some	DADINTS	0.24	0.43	0–1
More	DADINTM	0.39	0.49	0–1
Great	DADINTG	0.16	0.37	0–1

*If the variable's value was missing, its mean value was substituted for the missing value. A missing-variable dummy variable was created; its mean indicates the percent of cases missing information. For all variables, $N = 2,775$.

[1]The mean (SD) birth weight of fathers and mothers are, respectively: 7.53 (1.10) and 7.16 (1.15) in pounds.

TABLE 3.2
Regression Models: Child's PPVT Test Score

MODEL	#1	#2	#3	#4
Child's attributes				
Age	1.09 (8.62)	1.11 (8.71) (9.24)*	1.10 (8.67)	1.10 (8.67)
Gender (girl = 1)	–0.68 (–1.31)	–0.51 (–0.98) (–0.96)	–0.48 (–0.91)	0.08 (0.13
Race (white = 1)	8.01 (2.47)	7.78 (2.41) (2.21)	7.80 (2.43)	5.66 (1.72)
CM–parent attributes				
CM is female	5.09 (3.23)	5.13 (3.27) (3.12)	5.15 (3.30)	5.07 (3.24)
CM's reading test	0.43 (5.95)	0.41 (5.55) (5.11)	0.39 (5.28)	0.39 (5.31)
CM's math test	0.08 (1.80)	0.08 (1.97) (1.78)	0.07 (1.73)	0.07 (1.57)
Missing cmtests	–1.03 (–1.17)	–0.98 (–1.12) (–1.05)	–0.88 (–1.01)	–0.87 (–0.99)
Education: no quals	1.82 (1.96)	1.68 (1.79) (1.57)	1.45 (1.53)	1.36 (1.44)
O–levels	3.61 (4.12)	3.36 (3.84) (3.51)	3.09 (3.48)	3.05 (3.44)
A–levels	5.04 (4.28)	4.51 (3.83) (3.51)	4.09 (3.42)	3.99 (3.35)
Higher educ	5.34 (4.92)	4.71 (4.33) (3.94)	4.29 (3.89)	4.19 (3.80)
Missing*	6.84 (2.60)	6.58 (2.47) (2.55)	6.40 (2.41)	6.39 (2.41)
Income index	0.96 (4.28)	0.84 (3.75) (3.45)	0.79 (3.51)	0.76 (3.42)
CM full–time emply	3.83 (2.35)	4.04 (2.50) (2.39)	4.10 (2.55)	4.03 (2.50)
Cmftempl*cmmom	–4.89 (–2.76)	–5.07 (–2.90) (–2.72)	–5.12 (–2.93)	–5.03 (–2.87)
Religion: often	1.94 (2.41)	1.69 (2.10) (1.89)	1.56 (1.94)	1.52 (1.89)
Church of Engl	–0.45 (–0.75)	–0.36 (–0.61) (–0.56)	–0.51 (–0.85)	–0.56 (–0.94)
Catholic	–1.73 (–1.69)	–1.49 (–1.47) (–1.32)	–1.51 (–1.48)	–1.52 (–1.49)
Age at first birth	0.60 (4.45)	0.58 (4.32) (4.24)	0.56 (4.14)	0.55 (4.03)
Number sibs	–0.69 (–2.01)	–0.71 (–2.11) (–1.85)	–0.73 (–2.16)	–0.76 (–2.28)

TABLE 3.2 (continued)

MODEL	#1	#2	#3	#4
Grandparent attributes				
Grpar's SES2	0.91 (1.24)	0.79 (1.08) (0.99)	0.63 (0.86)	0.63 (0.86)
Grpar's SES3	2.85 (2.60)	2.79 (2.57) (2.44)	2.23 (2.02)	2.27 (2.04)
Grpar's SES4	3.39 (2.19)	3.22 (2.09) (1.91)	2.32 (1.46)	2.27 (1.43)
Missing*	−0.11 (−0.15)	−0.08 (−0.11) (−0.10)	0.52 (0.68)	0.48 (0.62)
Mother's Investment (Vector P)				
Breast-fed (yes = 1)		2.33 (4.03) (3.79)	2.24 (3.89)	2.29 (3.97)
Missing*		4.47 (2.03) (2.02)	4.55 (2.07)	4.36 (1.99)
Birth weight		0.64 (2.64) (2.57)	0.64 (2.66)	
Predicted				3.18 (2.92)
Residual				0.55 (2.21)
Missing*		−4.37 (−2.10) (−1.77)	−4.39 (−2.12)	−4.34 (−2.10)
Grandparents' Investments (Vector G)				
Gm breast-fed			0.76 (1.37)	0.68 (1.23)
Both grpts read			0.92 (1.45)	0.88 (1.39)
Gm low interest			−1.22 (−1.44)	−1.19 (−1.41)
Gf great interest			1.59 (2.10)	1.69 (2.22)
Intercept	50.60 (9.06)	46.12 (7.83) (7.71)	46.90 (7.90)	30.89 (3.40)
Adj-R^2	.171	.180	.184	.185
N	2775	2775	2775	2775

* See text for explanation: the second set of t-statistics adjust for within-family clustering.

strongly related to the child's test score. The family's income level is strongly associated with the test scores, and continues to be strongly related when the other income variables are substituted in the model. For example, when the income index is replaced by the log of income (and missing variable dummy), the coefficient on the log of income is 0.87 ($t = 2.41$) and the missing variable coefficient is not near statistical significance ($t = 0.26$). ROOM as the income variable is also significant: the coefficient is 0.52 ($t = 2.33$). (ROOM is a reasonable indicator of longer run income. About 10% of the cases have 0–3 rooms, about 80% have 4–6 rooms, and the remaining 10% have 8–12, with a very few having 14–19 rooms.)

The current employment status of the cm-father is positively associated with the child's test score, whereas that of the cm-mother is consistently negative. Religious affiliation is not significant, but "often" attending religious services is. (Tepper's [2001] suggestive essay that parents influence their children by the structure they introduce into the family life may help explain this finding.) The older the mother was at the birth of her first child, the higher the child's test score. The more siblings the child has, the lower is the test score. In addition, SES of the grandparents when the cm-parent was a child is positively associated with the child's PPVT score.

Overall, the results in model 1 are quite impressive in several respects. First, nearly all of these estimated relations conform to expectations. Second, these results are quite similar to those reported for U.S. children. Third, the strength of the relations to the PPVT test score is substantial. Interpreting family resources as a constraint on the parents' capacity to influence their child's cognitive test scores offers a compelling interpretation of these findings: As these constraints are relaxed, the test scores increase. The similarity of the British and U.S. results suggests that the same factors are at work in both societies.

Model 2 introduces the two proxy variables for the family's resolve or commitment to invest in its children. This model includes all the variables in model 1 plus the two additional ones: the child's birth weight (in pounds) and the breast-feeding dummy variable. Both variables show relatively strong, positive relations to the child's cognitive test scores measured several years hence, even though all the other descriptive characteristics of the cm-parent are held constant in this regression. (When the model was rerun replacing the continuous birth weight variable with two dummies, one indicating that the child was born at "very low birth weight" [less than 1.5 kilograms, or 3.31 pounds] or at "low birth weight" [less than 2.5 kilograms, or 5.51 pounds], only the very low birth weight coefficient was significant; its coefficient was –8.09, $t = -2.87$.) Model 2 is consistent with the interpretation suggested earlier that, holding the level of resources fixed, another dimension of parental investment in children is a commitment or willingness to make those investments.

The regression can be interpreted in other ways as well, of course, but it does offer support to this interpretation.

Model 3 adds the four measures of the grandparents' behaviors when the cm-parent was a child; they are the elements in the vector G. These, too, are indicators of family resolve or commitment to invest in the family's children. As previously described, each is a dummy variable. Although all four show the expected direction of effect, only one—the dummy that the grandfather was exceptionally interested in his child's schooling—shows statistical significance in this highly controlled regression. The model holds fixed many parental attributes and behaviors that influence the child's skills. Consequently, much of the influence of grandparents on their child's behaviors and skills as parents are already controlled here, and yet these grandparent behaviors still show some influence. Investigating their association with the child's test score in a less highly controlled regression is discussed later, but first, alternative strategies for handling the measure of the child's birth weight are addressed.

Model 4 decomposes the child's birth weight into two components; the regression is otherwise the same as model 3. As already described, given that the child's birth weight in part reflects the behavior of the mother during the child's prenatal growth but is, in part, also independent of the mother's behavior, this regression partitions the influence of these two elements. The birth weight variable is decomposed by a first-stage regression of the child's birth weight on gender, race, cm-parent's own birth weight, the planning status of the conception, the duration of the pregnancy (in weeks) when confirmed, the week of the first prenatal medical visit, and the amount of drinking and smoking during the pregnancy. That side regression is shown in Table 3.3. For each child, a predicted birth weight is calculated from this regression; it is interpreted as reflecting the parent's investment in the child's well-being during pregnancy. It, far better than the birth weight measure used in models 2 and 3, captures the parental investment or efforts on behalf of their child. However, because birth weight from whatever source, including luck, may influence the child's cognitive development, model 4 also includes the residual from that side regression. It measures the birth weight that is unrelated to the mother's behavior. The second variable has a zero mean but a much larger variance than the predicted component of the child's birth weight (see Table 3.3).

Model 4 of Table 3.2 shows that both birth-weight variables are indeed relevant. As expected, the predicted birth weight has a strong and quite large coefficient—more than five times as large as the coefficient on the residual. Expressed in terms of the effect of one additional pound of weight at birth, the parent-related pound is associated with a 3.2 point increase in the PPVT test score, whereas an additional pound of weight at birth unrelated to the parent is associated with about a half-point in the test score. (If we

TABLE 3.3
Regression on Child's Birth Weight

	All Children–NCDS*		PPVT–Children	
	Coef (std. err.)		Coef (std. err.)	
Girl (yes = 1)	–0.20	(–5.44)	–0.19	(–4.23)
White (yes = 1)	0.84	(6.05)	0.76	(3.64)
Pregnancy planned?	0.11	(2.49)	0.11	(2.09)
Week preg confirmed	–0.01	(–1.06)	–0.02	(–2.31)
Week first prenatal visit	–0.002	(–0.32)	0.010	(1.35)
Number alcohol drinks during preg.	–0.002	(–0.58)	–0.004	(–1.08)
Number cigarettes during preg.	–0.020	(–2.95)	–0.012	(–1.50)
CM–parent's birth weight	0.19	(11.45)	0.18	(8.96)
Mom's birth weight	0.012	(2.27)	0.008	(1.33)
Intercept	5.13	(28.16)	5.24	(19.94)
Prob>F	.000		.000	
Adj–R2	.06		.05	
N	4228		2775	

Summary Statistics: Actual, Predicted and Residual Birth Weight, Based on All Children Model

	Mean	SD	Min.–Max.
Actual birth weight	7.27	1.20	1.75 – 11.56
Predicted birth weight	7.31	0.29	5.96 – 8.64
Residual	–0.03	1.17	–5.50 – 4.46

* All analyses use this regression with 4,228 observations. The second regression includes only the 2,775 children with a PPVT score. For that subset, the mean predicted birth weight is 7.27.

consider instead the standardized coefficient reflecting the larger standard deviation in the residual birth weight variable, the parent-related pound of birth weight is associated with a little less than one point on the test score [0.92 = 3.18*0.29], whereas the residual effect is about two thirds of a point [0.64 = 0.55*1.17]) The suggested interpretation of the difference in these two measures of birth weight is that the first proxies the many parental efforts that typically go unmeasured in regressions of this nature and that affect the child's skill development, whereas the second shows the influence of a stochastic pound of birth weight.

Model 4 contains the central finding in this chapter, but before discussing the implied magnitudes or interpreting its results, several sensitivity checks and extensions deserve mention. A two-stage, least squares model was estimated, with the identical structures for the endogenous child's birth weight and the child's test score as in model 4. There were few notable differences in the coefficients or their significance. The coefficient on breast-feeding is 2.02 (3.40), and the birth weight coefficient is 3.17 (2.54). Of course, the residual from the birth weight regression is not included in the two-stage, least squares model.

The sampling strategy for the children in this data set included all biological children of the cm-parent, so there are many siblings in the sample. Consequently, the observations are not all independently sampled. In fact, the distribution of the 2,755 children by the number from each family is: 31%, one child; 38%, two children; 23%, three children; 7%, four children; 1.4%, five children; and 0.4%, six children from the same family. Model 2 in Table 3.2 was re-estimated, adjusting the standard errors for the family clustering. The coefficients are unaffected, and the t–statistic based on the adjusted standard errors is shown in Table 3.2 model 2 as the second number in parentheses. The adjustments are not major.

Because the data structure includes more than one child per family, this allows an investigation of the within-family influence of different breast-feeding practices and different pregnancy behaviors as reflected in the children's birth weights. The data set has information about breast-feeding and the smoking, drinking, and prenatal behavior of the mother for each child. Consider breast-feeding practice. By the logic of the interpretation suggested in this chapter, one would not expect a within-family effect on the children's test scores. The interpretation is that breast-feeding is a proxy for a family-specific effect—the family's commitment to childrearing and nurturing—not a child-by-child effect of breast-feeding per se. In fact, in this interpretation, one would have trouble explaining different breast-feeding practices within the family. The within- and between-family differences, however, offer a test of the suggested interpretation.

First, the regression model can be run looking for the effect of a within-family breast-feeding difference on the children's test scores. We should expect to find no effect if the breast-feeding is a family-fixed effect. That is just what is found. Using the families with exactly two children (N = 1,045), the within-family breast-feeding coefficient is -0.20, $t = -0.11$, a wholly insignificant effect. When all pairs, threes, fours, fives, and six-sibling groups from a given family are included in a family-fixed effect model (N = 1,921), again the coefficient on breast-feeding is wholly insignificant: -0.18, $t = -0.14$. By contrast, as expected from the interpretation offered here, when the model is estimated with only the one-child families (N = 854), the coefficient on breast-feeding shows the effect across families, not within families, and here the effect is very strong and large: 3.30, $t = 3.30$. These results reinforce the interpretation here. The fact of breast-feeding per se is not what is being captured in the basic model; instead, the breast-feeding practice is a proxy that partitions the families. The suggested interpretation is that it partitions families into those with a tradition and commitment of nurturing their children (those who do breast-feed), and those lacking that tradition (those who do not breast-feed).

As another check on the robustness of model 4, the model was re-estimated on four subsets of the children: those whose mother, or separately the father, was the cohort member, and again separately for those children younger or older than age 8. These comparative models show a few interesting facts. For many of the covariates, the estimated coefficients are similar, with somewhat larger standard errors because of the smaller number of cases. For example, the child's age, the parent's own test scores, and family income have about the same coefficient for all four subsets of children. Race, however, has a very large and significant coefficient in the cm-father regression and for children aged 8 and under, but it is not significant for the cm-mothers or the children older than age 8. The cm-parent's education level shows somewhat different patterns across the four subsets, but it is uniformly positive. Father's employment is consistently positive whereas mother's employment is always negative, but strongly significant only for the younger children. The degree of structure in the family life, as indicated by "often" attending religious services, is stronger for the cm-mothers and the younger children, and the number of siblings is not a factor for the children of cm-fathers or the older children.

It is the older children who are, by the construction of the data set, much more likely to be born to a teenage mother, and so it is quite reasonable that for that subset, the mother's age at first birth is a key factor reflecting the resource of her own maturity. The two proxy variables measuring family commitment and involvement—breast-feeding and predicted birth weight—are stronger for the younger children and stronger also for the cm-fathers but are not statistically significant for the cm-mothers. Perhaps this latter fact indicates that the several variables about the cm-parent better capture the investment in children when it measures the mother's attributes, so there is less remaining variation to capture by the mother's breast-feeding and prenatal behavior. The grandparents' interest in their child's schooling a generation earlier shows its largest influence on the older, not the younger, children, which is reasonable if these variables are indicators of family differences in habits of investing in their children; these effects would show up more clearly over the longer life of the older children given that the regression has no directly measured parental actions beyond the first year of life. In all, the pattern of the estimated coefficients on these subsets appears to reinforce the interpretations previously suggested.

Returning to the issue of the elements in the vector G, Table 3.4 shows their influence on the child's test score under five different sets of controls. Column 1 simply repeats the results from model 3 of Table 3.2 for convenience. Column 2 discards all the variables describing the parent's behaviors and the SES of the grandparents and shows the effects of the elements of G and of P without those other intervening variables. Both the magnitude and

TABLE 3.4
Regressions Featuring the Vectors G and P

	#1	#2	#3	#4	#5
Vector P					
Breast–fed	2.24 (3.89)	4.66 (8.10)	5.81 (9.99)	—	—
Birth weight	0.64 (2.66)	0.85 (3.44)	0.96 (3.77)	—	—
Vector G					
Grdmother breast–fed	0.76 (1.37)	1.07 (1.95)	—	1.48 (2.64)	0.90 (1.61)
Both grpts read	0.92 (1.45)	1.66 (2.57)	—	1.84 (2.80)	0.93 (1.47)
Gm low interest	–1.22 (–1.44)	–4.90 (–5.79)	—	–5.77 (–6.73)	–1.34 (–1.58)
Gf great interest	1.59 (2.10)	6.17 (8.60)	—	6.74 (9.28)	1.54 (2.01)
The regression includes the					
21 variables grpt–SES and					
Parent's resources	Yes	No	No	No	Yes

Note: All regressions include the child's age, gender, race.

statistical significance of all four variables in G and the two variables in P increase in this model. Column 3 shows the effects of the two variables in P when G is discarded, and symmetrically column 4 shows the coefficients on the G variables when the two P variables are discarded. Column 4, therefore, shows the direct and indirect influence of the grandparents' behaviors on the grandchild's test scores, and they are quite large and statistically significant in all four cases. Adding in the cm-parent's resources and attributes (column 5) dramatically reduces these G associations, as does, alternatively, adding in the cm-parent's own proxies P (column 2). (The reader interested in seeing the full models can find them in Michael, 2003b.)

Featuring the estimated model 4 of Table 3.2, the implied magnitude of the relation between the parent's behaviors and the child's test scores is illustrated in Table 3.5 for three key variables. Panel A shows the actual differences in PPVT scores by parent's education level and the effect implied by the regression model 4, holding all the other variables at their mean. There are quite large differences in the actual test scores by parent's education level—nearly a full standard deviation (i.e., $105.67 - 92.88 = 12.79$, and $\sigma = 14.99$)—and the muted, yet strong, effect of education with all other variables held constant—about one-third of a standard deviation ($101.92 - 97.73 = 4.19$). The interpretation of the partial effects would be that either those with more education are more effective in influencing their child's ability in vocabulary skills within the behaviors controlled in the regression, or they also act differently with their children in ways not measured by the regression covariates.

Panel B of Table 3.5 shows the relation of PPVT score to family income. Here the sample is divided into three groups by the log of measured income: those below, at, or above a standard deviation from the mean of log-income. The actual PPVT scores differ by about 7 points, or one half a standard deviation, whereas the regression-predicted values differ by nearly 4 points. Holding all other variables in the model fixed, the estimated coefficient on income implies only a 1 point difference among these three groups. This is an example of a variable that has its effects through the several other covariates in the model. Interpreting the equation as structural would suggest, as often discovered, that handing the family more income and none of the other attributes that typically accompany income in the real world would result in only a very slight effect on the child's PPVT score, at least in the range of the average level of income in these families.

Most important for the theme of this chapter is Table 3.5, panel C, with its four subpanels, each showing the joint and separate influence of both breast-feeding and the mother's efforts regarding birth weight. Subpanel 1 shows the average actual PPVT scores for the children, simply sorted by whether their mother breast-fed them and by their predicted birth weight. The findings show that the children with the least

TABLE 3.5
PPVT Actual and Estimated from Model #4, Table 3.2, by Selected Variables

Panel A: CM-Parent's Education Level

	Actual PPVT	Estimated with all other variables at their means	(N)
CM-Parent's Education			
No education	92.88	97.73	(453)
No qualifications	97.00	99.09	(427)
O-Levels	100.66	100.78	(1033)
A-Levels	103.55	101.72	(317)
Higher education	105.67	101.92	(496)

Panel B: Family Income {measured by ln(income)}

Family Income[1]	Actual PPVT	Regression Predicted Value	Estimated at mean Incindex with other vars. at their means	(N)
Lower than $\mu - \sigma$	97.31	98.77	99.64	(281)
Between $\mu - \sigma$ & $\mu + \sigma$	100.03	100.01	100.10	(2265)
Above $\mu + \sigma$	104.17	102.61	100.63	(229)

Panel C: Breast-Feeding and Mother's Efforts toward Birth Weight

Breast-Feeding	Predicted Birth Weight[2]			
	Low ($\mu - \sigma$)	Mid ($\mu +/- \sigma$)	High $\mu + \sigma$	Total
	Subpanel 1. All Children: Average Actual PPVT			
No	92.93 (123)	96.63 (736)	97.71 (138)	96.32 (997)
Yes	99.95 (203)	102.11 (1281)	105.27 (239)	102.29 (1723)
Total	97.28 (327)	100.09 (2063)	102.53 (385)	100.10 (2775)

TABLE 3.5 (continued)

Subpanel 2. All Children: Average Predicted PPVT

No	92.73 (123)	96.50 (736)	98.58 (138)	96.32 (997)
Yes	99.02 (203)	102.45 (1281)	104.23 (239)	102.29 (1723)
Total	96.60 (327)	100.27 (2063)	102.18 (385)	100.10 (2775)

Subpanel 3. CM-parent has O-level education qualifications: Average Predicted PPVT

No	95.96 (34)	98.04 (269)	99.57 (51)	98.06 (354)
Yes	100.03 (89)	102.05 (480)	103.89 (93)	101.85 (662)
Total	98.91 (123)	100.60 (763)	102.41 (147)	100.66 (1033)

Subpanel 4. Regression-estimated PPVT with all other variables at their means

No	97.00	98.65	100.04	98.65
Yes	99.28	100.94	102.33	100.94
Total	98.44	100.10	101.49	100.10

[1] The μ & σ of ln(income) are 4.518 & 0.757, so the values used are < 3.76; 3.76-5.27; > 5.27.
[2] The μ & σ of predicted birth weight are 7.307 & 0.289, so the values used are < 7.0; 7.0-7.6;> 7.6.

involved parents (those who did not breast-feed and with the lowest pre-dicted birth weight) have a PPVT of 92.93, whereas those with the most involved parents have a PPVT of 105.27, an unadjusted difference of 12.3 points, nearly one standard deviation.

When the average predicted PPVT scores are compared (subpanel 2), again the difference between those same two groups is quite large: 11.5 points. These two comparisons, however, do not hold constant any of the attributes or variables that covary with the breast-feeding and prenatal be-havior. Subpanel 3 partially does that by showing the average of the pre-dicted PPVT score for each cell for only those children whose cm-parents had completed their O-level qualifications in school. There, the influence of both breast-feeding and prenatal behavior is muted, yet there remains about an 8-point difference between the two extreme groups of mothers, with low or high involvement measured by both behaviors. Finally, subpanel 4 shows the implied effects from the regression while controlling all the covariates at their means. In this circumstance, the least involved group has an estimated PPVT of 97.00, and the most involved has an estimate of 102.33, a difference of more than 5 points, or about one third of a standard deviation in the test score.

This, then, is the order of magnitude of the estimated influence of the parents' efforts or commitment to childrearing, over and above the influence of their economic and social attributes or characteristics. One third of a standard deviation in measured ability is not a breathtaking magnitude, but it is about the same size as the standardized influence estimated in comparisons of higher education and no formal education (seen in panel A), and it is in addition to that influence. Moreover, the effect here is based on only two behavioral proxies that reflect the mother's behavior prenatally and in the first few months of the child's life. The interpretation offered is that these behaviors of sacrificing on behalf of the child by forgoing alcohol or cigarettes during pregnancy, by early medical attention to the pregnancy, and by breast-feeding and enduring its limitations on the mother's mobility reflect a commitment that probably continues as the child grows, although this regression uses no further information about that subsequent behavior.

CONCLUSION

Family behavior is certainly not the only factor influencing the cognitive development of children; the low explained variance in the regression models reported here reminds us of that fact. Yet, the model also supports the hypothesis that the family's available resources of money, skills, and time help promote their child's measured vocabulary skills. This evidence confirms much evidence in the literature. In addition to the influence of parental characteristics and behaviors, the grandparents' attributes also have influence. Therefore, the answers to the first two questions posed earlier are both yes: Parental resources and grandparental resources are both positively associated with the child's T, measured by the PPVT score.

The answer to the third question is also yes: Breast-feeding the child and the child's birth weight are positively associated with the test score, controlling for parental attributes and resources and the grandparents' SES. The interpretation of this evidence, however, is more debatable. By the logic of the argument presented here, these two behaviors proxy the family's "culture" in terms of the parent's willingness to invest in children and their resolve to give the child nurturance, support, and advantage. If one sees these two discretionary practices as indicative of, or as proxies for, this willingness, then the interpretation is that, yes, this aspect of family culture is positively associated with the child's test score. Even if the interpretation is not accepted, the empirical result remains: Breast-feeding and the child's birth weight are strongly and positively associated with the PPVT score.

A more qualified "yes" is found for the fourth question. The breast-feeding and childrearing practices of the grandparents are weakly but positively associated with their grandchild's test score when added to the previous model. However, as Table 3.4 shows, the influence of these four proxies is stronger when the parental proxies are not included, and are quite strong when the parental attributes are also removed (column 4 of Table 3.4). The pattern shown in Table 3.4 supports the notion that these grandparental behaviors both have indirect influence through the child's parent, as well as a discernible direct influence even when the measured parental attributes and behaviors are controlled. This is evidence, in this interpretation, of the influence of family culture across generations.

Because we cannot fully measure the family's commitment to investing in their children, these proxy variables reflect that commitment and capture some of its influence. What, if anything, might better define the nature of a family than its commitment to its children? Family dynasties are built only in part on the transferable accumulation of economic wealth, and relatively few families have the economic capacity to pass along to their children much accumulated financial wealth. A far larger proportion of families invest in the human capital, the skills, of their children through formal schooling. (See Becker's, [1991], well-known Woytinsky Lecture for a theoretical explanation of this fact which is also discussed in Becker & Tomes, 1986.) Even more families, indeed nearly all, have the capacity to invest in their young children by sacrificing time, enduring much tedium and repetition, and engaging with their young children. Those efforts and investments by parents influence both their child's cognitive development and also how those children act, as parents, a generation later.

ACKNOWLEDGMENTS

The funding of the data used in this study was provided by NICHD, grant R-01-HD27150. The British survey that made the child data collection feasible, the NCDS-5, was overseen initially by John Fox and subsequently by John Bynner and I thank them, and Peter Shepherd in Britain, and Jeff Evans at NICHD, for their efforts and support. The analysis was supported by a grant to the Harris School from the McCormick Tribune Foundation, for which I express my thanks. Kath Kiernan and John Hobcraft have contributed composite variables used in this analysis as well as valuable suggestions and I thank them. I have benefited from comments at workshops at Princeton University; The Institute of Education, London; Chapin Hall Center for Children; and the Harris School, and particularly from comments from John Bynner, Tom DeLeire, Harvey Goldstein, Ariel Kalil, Tom Kane, Helen Levy, Cybele Raver, and Yoram Weiss.

REFERENCES

Becker, G. S. (1991). *A treatise on the family*. Cambridge MA: Harvard University Press.
Becker, G. S., & Tomes, N. (1986). Human capital and the rise and fall of families. *Journal of Labor Economics, 4*(3), Part 2, S1-S39.
Brooks-Gunn, J., Duncan, G. J., & Maritato, N. (1997). Poor families, poor outcomes: The well-being of children and youth. In G. J. Duncan & J. Brooks-Gunn (Eds.), *Consequences of growing up poor* (pp.1–17). New York: Russell Sage.
Cohen, P., Kasen, S., Brook, J. S., & Hartmark. C. (1998). Behavior patterns of young children and their offspring: A two-generation study. *Developmental Psychology, 34*(6), 1202–1208.
DeLeire, T., & Kalil, A. (2002). Good things come in threes. *Demography, 39*(2), 393–413.
De Stavola, B. L., Hardy, R., Huh, D., dos Santos Silva, I., Wadsworth, M., & Swerdlow, A. J. (2000). Birth weight, childhood growth and risk of breast cancer in a British cohort. *British Journal of Cancer, 83*(7), 964–968.
Developmental Psychology. (1998). Special section: Longitudinal studies of intergenerational continuity and the transfer of psychological risk. Author, *34*(6),1159–1273.
Duncan, G. J., & Brooks-Gunn, J. (Eds.). (1997). *Consequences of growing up poor.* New York: Russell Sage.
Duncan, G. J., Brooks-Gunn, J., & Klebanov, P. K. (1994). Economic deprivation and early childhood development. *Child Development, 64*, 296–318.
Dunn, L. M., & Dunn, L. M. (1981). *PPVT-revised manual*. Circle Pines, MN: American Guidance Service.
Easterlin, R. A. (1973). Relative economic status and the American fertility swing. In E. B. Sheldon (Ed.), *Family economic behavior*. Philadelphia: J.B. Lippincott.
Elder, G. H. (1979). Historical change in life patterns and personality. In P. B. Baltes & O. G. Brim, Jr. (Eds.), *Life span development and behavior, Vol. 2, (pp. 117–159)*. New York: Academic Press.
Eriksson, J. G., Forsen, T., Tuomilehto, J., Winter, P. D., Osmond, C., & Barker, D. J. P. (1999). Catch-up growth in childhood and death from coronary heart disease: Longitudinal study. *British Medical Journal, 318*(7181), 427–431.
Forsen, T., Eriksson, J. G., Tuomilehto, J., Osmond, C., & Barker, D. J. P. (1999). Growth in utero and during childhood among women who develop coronary heart disease: Longitudinal study. *British Medical Journal, 319* (27), 1403–1407.
Harris, I. B. (1996). *Children in jeopardy: Can we break the cycle of poverty?* New Haven: Yale University Press.
Hauser, S. T. (1999). Understanding resilient outcomes: Adolescent lives across time and generations. *Journal of Research on Adolescence, 9*(1), 1–24.
Heckman, J. J. (2000). Policies to foster human capital. *Research in Economics, 54*, 3–56.
Hobcraft, J. (1998). Intergenerational and life-course transmission of social exclusion: Influences of childhood poverty, family disruption, and contact with the police. CASE paper no. 15. London: London School of Economics.
Huston, A. C., McLoyd, V. C., & Coll, C. G. (Eds.). (1994). Special issue: Children and poverty. *Child Development, 65*(2).
Huttenlocher, J., Levine, S., & Vevea, J. (1998). Environmental input and cognitive growth: A study using time-period comparisons. *Child Development, 69*(4), 1012–1029.

Joshi, H. E., Cooksey, E. C., Wiggins, R. D., McCulloch, A., Verropoulou, G., & Clarke, L. (1999). Diverse family living situations and child development: A multilevel analysis comparing longitudinal evidence from Britain and the United States. *International Journal of Law, Policy and the Family, 13*(2), 292–314.

Kagan, J. (1998). *Three seductive ideas.* Cambridge MA: Harvard University Press.

Mayer, S. E. (2002). *The influence of parental income on children's outcomes.* Wellington, NZ: Ministry of Social Development. Available at: msd.govt.nz.

McCulloch, A., & Joshi, H. E. (2002). Child development and family resources: Evidence from the second generation of the 1958 British birth cohort. *Journal of Population Economics, 15*, 283–304.

McGuire, S. (2003). The heritability of parenting. *Parenting: Science and Practice, 3*(1), 73–94.

McLanahan, S. S. (1997). Parent absence or poverty: Which matters more? In G. H. Duncan & J. Brooks-Gunn (Eds.), *Consequences of growing up poor* (pp.35–48). New York: Russell Sage.

Michael, R. T. (2003a). Children's cognitive skill development in Britain and the United States. *International Journal of Behavioral Development, 27*(5), 396–408.

Michael, R. T. (2003b). *Family Influences on Children's Verbal Ability.* Harris School Working Paper #03.07 (March 2003).

Peters, H. E., & Mullis, N. C. (1997). The role of family income and sources of income in adolescent achievement. In G. H. Duncan & J. Brooks-Gunn (Eds.), *Consequences of growing up poor* (pp. 340–381). New York: Russell Sage.

Pierret, C. R. (2001). The effect of family structure on youth outcomes in the NLSY97. In R. T. Michael (Ed.), *Social awakening* (pp. 25–48). New York: Russell Sage.

Rowe, D. C. (1981). Environmental and genetic influences on dimensions of perceived parenting: A twin study. *Developmental Psychology, 17*, 203–208.

Sen, A. (2001). Other people. *Proceedings of the British Academy, 111*, 319–335.

Smith, J. R., Brooks-Gunn, J., & Klebanov, P. K. (1997). Consequences of living in poverty for young children's cognitive and verbal ability and early school achievement. In G. H. Duncan & J. Brooks-Gunn (Eds.), *Consequences of growing up poor* (pp.132–189). New York: Russell Sage.

Sontag, L. W., Baker, C. T., & Nelson, V. L. (1958). Mental growth and personality development: A longitudinal study. *Monographs of the Society for Research in Child Development, 23*(2).

Sternberg, R. J., Grigorenko, E. L.,& Bundy, D. A. (2001). The predictive value of IQ. *Merrill-Palmer Quarterly, 47*(1), 1–41.

Tepper, R. L. (2001). Parental regulation and adolescent discretionary time-use decisions: Findings from the NLSY97. In R. T. Michael (Ed.), *Social awakening* (pp. 79–105). New York: Russell Sage.

Vandell, D. L. (2000). Parents, peer groups, and other socializing influences. *Developmental Psychology, 36*(6), 699–710.

4

The Long-Term Impact of Parental Organization and Efficiency

Rachel Dunifon
Cornell University

Greg J. Duncan
Northwestern University

Jeanne Brooks-Gunn
Columbia University

A large body of research examines the influence of parental investments in children, focusing on structural factors such as marital status (McLanahan & Sandefur, 1994), income (Duncan & Brooks-Gunn, 1997), and education (Michael, 1972). Other research measures parental investments by examining the influence of the home environment on children's attainments (Bradley & Caldwell, 1984). This study seeks to broaden the research on children's home environments in two ways. First, when measuring the home environment, researchers often combine measures that are constrained by parental resources (such as the provision of toys or quality of housing) with those that are not resource-constrained (such as praising the child and showing affection). The measure used here of the home environment, cleanliness, is largely not constrained by parental resources and, instead, can be seen as reflecting parental personality or motivation. Second, unlike most studies in this area, which examine impacts of the home environment on childhood outcomes, this study considers the impact of the home environment on children's attainments in adulthood, as measured by education and earnings, which allows the examination of whether parental investments have long-term impacts on children.

The analysis draws on approximately 30 years of data from the Panel Study of Income Dynamics (PSID). The measure of cleanliness is purged of the amount of time parents and others (including hired help) spent doing housework, and as such, it represents a parental characteristic of organization and efficiency. As with other personality measures, this measure may affect children's achievement in different ways. For example, organization and efficiency (captured by home cleanliness) may be a trait that is inherited and passed directly from parents to children. Alternatively, parents who are more organized and efficient may invest in children in ways that serve to foster children's attainments.

The analysis tests alternative hypotheses about the pathways through which parental home cleanliness influences children's attainments, examining specifically whether it operates through the cleanliness of the child's own home in adulthood. That is, the study examines whether the parental trait of organization and efficiency is passed directly to children, testing whether it is the inheritance of this trait, reflected in the cleanliness of the children's own homes, that influences later child success. The chapter begins with a literature review, followed by a description of the data, measures, and results. A concluding discussion summarizes the results.

BACKGROUND

Bowles and Gintis (2001) recently called on researchers to broaden their study of parental factors that may influence children's success, noting that research thus far has been unable to explain most of the intergenerational transmission of economic status with measures of parental cognitive ability, wealth, or educational attainment. Using rich longitudinal data from the PSID, previous research moved in this direction by examining a wide range of parental measures that may influence children's attainments. This work (Dunifon & Duncan, 1998; Duncan & Dunifon, 1998; Dunifon, Duncan, & Brooks-Gunn, 2001) examined behaviors, such as expenditures on alcohol and eating meals together as a family, and attitudes, such as fear of failure or sense of efficacy, as predictors of intra- and intergenerational success. A consistent, and somewhat surprising, finding was the robust association between the cleanliness of the parental home and later attainments of children, net a wide range of family background and socioeconomic factors. Specifically, this research found that a higher average score on the clean home measure was associated with increased average earnings measured between 1994 and 1996 for the parents themselves and for their children, and with increased educational attainments of their children.

We know of no other research that has examined the intergenerational impact of home cleanliness in particular. However, a rich body of research does examine the ways in which parental characteristics, personality traits, and the home environment come together to influence children's attainments. By examining this research, and testing alternative hypotheses about the pathways through which home cleanliness may influence children's attainments, this chapter seeks to shed light on prior findings. Although it is impossible to identify the precise mechanism through which home cleanliness influences children, it is possible to rule out some pathways and develop theories about others that will guide future research in this area.

As described later, the measure of home cleanliness is adjusted for the amount of time parents and others spend cleaning the house. Thus, this measure is a proxy for a parental personality trait of organization and efficiency. Net the amount of time spent cleaning, a cleaner home represents a more efficient use of time and a greater ability to organize one's use of time. Psychologists have long sought to understand links between personality characteristics and future indicators of success, such as schooling, income, occupational status, mental health, morbidity, mortality, and life satisfaction. One tradition, dating back to Cattell (1934) and Thurstone (1951), is to look for categories that include some of the hundreds of known personality characteristics (McCrae & Costa, 1989; Wiggins & Pincus, 1992). Perhaps best known of the domains are extraversion (gregariousness, assertiveness); openness to experience (openness to feelings and values, an aesthetic sense); and neuroticism (anxiety, hostility) (Goldberg, 1990; Wiggins & Pincus, 1992).

Two other domains—agreeableness and conscientiousness—have since been added and, when combined with the other three, constitute what is called the "five factor approach model." Of the five, conscientiousness is most relevant for our purposes, given that it is thought to encompass orderliness, will, constraint, dependability, and prudence (Digman, 1990; Goldberg 1990). The measure of cleanliness, described later and after adjustments for housework time, captures aspects of parental conscientiousness.

If conscientiousness is defined as discipline, orderliness, and effort, then it is likely to be associated with education and occupation outcomes. In the few longitudinal studies spanning adulthood, conscientiousness is indeed linked with educational and career success. A notable example is the 45-year follow-up of the Harvard College students in the Grant Study (Soldz & Vaillant, 1999). Conscientiousness, measured during the college years, was correlated positively with adult adjustment (correlations ranged from the high teens to the mid-20s); including income and career advancement, and negatively to smoking, alcohol abuse, and psychiatric treatment. Research relating supervisor ratings to "big five" personality traits also identifies conscientiousness as predictive of employment success (Hunter, 1986; Schmidt & Hunter, 1998).

The research mentioned links the personality trait of conscientiousness with intragenerational success. However, it is likely that a parental characteristic such as organization and efficiency would be associated with intergenerational success as well. There are two potential pathways through which parental organization and efficiency may influence children's attainments. The ability to maintain order and cleanliness may be an inherited trait, benefiting both parent and child directly. That is, children with more organized parents (those growing up in cleaner homes) may fare well as adults because they, too, are more organized and efficient. Alternatively, parents who are more organized and efficient may not only have a clean home, but may also create other, unmeasured, aspects of the home environment that are predictive of children's achievement. Such parents may also be better able to take advantage of opportunities outside of the home that could benefit their children. That is, something about growing up with more organized and efficient parents could have long-term benefits for children, regardless of the children's own organization and efficiency.

There is an extensive body of psychological research connecting the quality of the home environment to child development. Much of this research uses the Home Observation for Measurement of the Environment (HOME), a measure of the quality of the home environment that combines mothers' reports and interviewer observations on language stimulation, toys and reading materials, and the physical environment (Bradley & Caldwell, 1984). For children over age 2, the HOME contains an interviewer observation of the cleanliness of the child's home, but in previous research this individual item has not been used in isolation, but rather has been used as part of a multi-item measure of the cognitive stimulation provided to children in the home. (The correlation between the clean home assessment in the HOME and the cognitive stimulation subscale of the HOME is .38, $p <$ .001; authors' calculation using 1986 data from the Child Supplement of the National Longitudinal Survey of Youth.) The HOME has been effectively used to identify home environments associated with impaired mental development and poor school performance (Bradley, 1985). Higher HOME scores are associated with improved cognitive ability among children (Smith, Brooks-Gunn, & Klebanov, 1997).

A potential criticism of the HOME is that it is confounds resource-based parental investments with nonresource-based measures, such as personality or motivation to invest in children. Some of the HOME items, such as the provision of toys and books, taking a child to a museum, or taking a child on a trip, are directly related to a family's ability to pay for such things. Because these items are used in combination with nonresource-based measures of parental behavior, such as warmth or frequency of reading to the child, it is difficult to separate the influence of income from that of parental motivation to invest in the home environment. A key innovation of the analysis presented here is that it focuses solely on one aspect of the home environment that is largely not constrained by family economic resources. (A family resource that may constrain the ability to provide a clean home is time; some parents may have less time than others to spend cleaning. However, as described later, the clean home measure used here is adjusted for time spent on housework, meaning that it represents the cleanliness of the home per hour spent cleaning. This addresses the issue of the amount of time parents have available to clean their homes, and removes parental time as a factor that may influence home cleanliness.)

Other research on the home environment has moved away from assessing parenting behaviors to focus on space and other physical measures of children's homes. As noted by Evans and English (2002), most research on child development has largely ignored the role of the physical environment. As with a clean home measure, measures of the physical environment can be viewed as reflections of parental personality traits and indicators of parenting behaviors in the home. However, unlike the clean home measure, the physical environment also reflects parents' material resources.

One scale developed to measure the physical home environment is the Confusion, Hubbub, and Order Scale (CHAOS), which is based on parents' reports and focuses on environmental confusion, such as noise, crowding, and traffic patterns. The scale does not include items related to slovenly or unsanitary homes (Matheny, Wachs, Ludwig, & Phillips, 1995). The CHAOS measure has been validated by research showing that the parental reports gathered with the scale correspond with interviewer ratings of noise, crowding, and traffic patterns (Matheny et al., 1995). Findings show that confusion, crowding, and noise in the home are associated with lower quality parenting, specifically, it is associated with parenting that is less responsive and less vocally stimulating (Corapci & Wachs, 2002).

Other work uses a measure of children's physical home environment developed by Evans, Wells, Chan, and Saltzman (2000), consisting of 88 interviewer-rated items in six domains—child resources, cleanliness/clutter, climate, privacy, hazards, and structural quality. Although home cleanliness is one component of the scale, it has not yet been used separately in analyses. In a study of predominantly White families living in rural upstate New York, a lower quality home environment was associated with greater behavior problems among children. In addition, children living in lower quality home environments performed worse than other children on a measure of task persistence, controlling for family income. Task persistence is often thought of as a measure of motivation, or conversely, learned helplessness. The authors, in a later article, hypothesize that "chronic exposure to aversive housing conditions may lead to a sense that one cannot alter one's surroundings ... a central tenet of learned helpless-ness" (Evans, Saltzman, & Cooperman, 2001, p. 395).

The research just described uses multi-item scales to capture the physi-cal home environment of children. Other research, including the current analysis, has focused on only one measure of the home environment. The factor that has received the most attention is home crowding. Using a cross-sectional sample of school children in India, Evans, Lepore, Shejwal, and Palsane (1998) found that, controlling for income (but not for family size), greater crowding (defined as the number of people in the home di-vided by the number of rooms) is associated with higher behavior prob-lems, lower academic achievement, and greater conflict with parents. In addition, for boys only, crowding was associated with elevated blood pres-sure. Further analyses revealed that the influence of crowding on children is mediated through increased conflict with parents. In another study of U.S. children aged 6 months to 3 years, Evans, Maxwell, and Hart (1999) found that crowding is associated with less verbal responsiveness among parents, which in turn is associated with less diverse and sophisticated pa-rental speech toward children.

Much of the existing research examining the influence of the physical en-vironment on children is based on cross-sectional samples, and very few studies examine the impact of the childhood home environment on adult attainments. One exception is Conley (2001), who used longitudinal PSID data to relate characteristics of children's home environments measured be-tween 1968 and 1972 to their educational attainments as adults. Focusing on three measures of housing—homeownership, crowding, and housing quality (i.e., whether the home is structurally sound or in need of re-pairs)—Conley found that both homeownership and crowding influence the later educational attainment of children, controlling for a wide range of family factors such as sibling size, family structure, parental education, and income. Growing up in a household that did not own its own home over the 5-year period is associated with a decrease in educational attainment of about one quarter of a year. Growing up in a household that averaged more than one person per room over the 5 years is associated with a similar de-crease in years of education. Although Conley controlled for family eco-nomic factors that may be associated with children's home environments, measures such as home ownership, crowding, and housing quality still likely capture aspects of parental wealth.

Taken together, the research described here indicates that aspects of the home environment can exert important influences on child well-being. The research also suggests that the physical home environment is corre-lated with other parenting behaviors. As noted, Dunifon, Duncan, and Brooks-Gunn (2001) found that higher average scores on the clean home measure were associated with increased average earnings for the parents themselves and for their children, and with increased educational attainments of their children. The current study extends these analyses by focusing on the cleanliness of both the parental home and child's adult home in order to measure the correlation between the two cleanliness measures, examining the extent to which cleanliness is a trait that is passed directly from parents to children (either through inheritance or role modeling). The study is also able to test whether the cleanliness of the child's home accounts for any associations between parental home cleanliness and child attainments.

DATA AND MEASURES

The analysis is based on 29 years of data from the Panel Study of Income Dynamics (Hill, 1992). Since 1968, the PSID has followed and interviewed annually a nationally representative sample of about 5,000 families. Split-off families are followed when children leave home, when couples divorce, and when more complicated changes break families apart. Except for problems of immigration, this procedure produces an unbiased population sample each year (Fitzgerald, Gottschalk, & Moffitt, 1998).

Sample

The analysis relates the clean home measure, assessed for PSID parents between 1968 and 1972, to the completed schooling and labor market outcomes of their children. Because a key interest is in the cleanliness of these children's homes when they reach adulthood, the sample includes only those children who, as adults, were included in the Child Development Supplement to the PSID (PSID-CDS), which also contained an interviewer rating of the cleanliness of the home. The PSID-CDS occurred in 1997, when the PSID supplemented its core data collection with data on parents and a maximum of two of their children ages 12 or younger. The supplement includes assessments of the cognitive, behavioral, and health status of 3,500 children. Therefore, the sample in this analysis ($N = 927$) consists of children of PSID heads and wives who resided with them at least 1 year between 1968 and 1972 (when the parental clean home measure was assessed), who were the parent of at least one child between the ages of 0 and 12 years in 1997 who was selected to participate in the PSID-CDS, and who do not have missing information on any of the variables analyzed.

Members of this child-based sample are referred to as G3, their parents (for whom we have the clean home measure) as G2, and their grandfather (for whom we have some background information) as G1. The restriction of the sample to G3s who were included in the 1997 PSID-CDS significantly reduces the sample ($N = 927$). Without this restriction, we would have a sample of 2,895. However, the impact of our measure of interest (G2 clean home) on the G3 outcomes of education and earnings are virtually identical when comparing results using this larger sample with those from the restricted sample of 927.

The analyses regress average 1994–1996 hourly earnings of this sample (taken from the PSID main file and measured from the 1995–1997 surveys) on a 1968–1972 measure of the cleanliness of their parental homes. The analyses also regress children's completed schooling (measured in 1993) on the 1968–1972 clean home measure of their parents. Because this sample is so restricted and unique, PSID sampling weights are not used. This sample is not nationally representative but is simply a convenient sample that allows for the examination of some interesting questions.

Measures

Clean House.   The key independent variable is a measure of the cleanliness of the G2 respondents' homes taken at the time of the 1968–1972 annual interviews. Each year, interviewers were asked to rate "How clean was the interior of the DU [dwelling unit]?" Responses were coded on a scale of 1–5, with 5 being *very clean*; 4 being *clean*; 3 being *so-so*; 2 being *not very clean*; and 1 being *dirty*. Mean values for the annual scores are relatively high; correlations across years are substantial but far from perfect (Table 4.1). The cross-year reliability of the five annual measures is quite high (alpha = .86).

For all analyses presented, the 5-year average clean home score is divided by its whole-sample standard deviation. Thus, the regression coefficients reflect the estimated impact of one standard deviation change in the average clean house scores. Experimentation with dummy variables established that this scale had roughly linear associations with the earnings and schooling outcomes. Furthermore, tests for whether the effects of a clean home differed for race, gender, or for single- versus two-parent households revealed no differences; therefore, the results reflect the entire sample of adult children.

Our G3 clean house measure is taken from the in-person interviews associated with the 1997 PSID Child Development Supplement. Interviewers were asked to rate "all visible rooms in the house/apartment" on a scale of (1) *not at all clean* to (5) *very clean*, and from (1) *very cluttered* to (5) *not at all cluttered*. These two measures were averaged, and as with its G2 counterpart, this G3 clean house measure was divided by its whole-sample standard deviation for all analyses.

Outcomes.   The G2 clean home measure is first used to predict the G3 clean home measure, allowing for an examination of the bivariate relation

TABLE 4.1
Correlations

	Clean68	Clean69	Clean70	Clean71	Clean72	68–72 Clean	G3 Clean	94–96 wage	G3 Edu.	Mean	SD
Clean68	1									3.77	1.15
Clean69	.62	1								3.81	1.12
Clean70	.60	.64	1							3.93	1.06
Clean71	.49	.53	.61	1						3.92	1.04
Clean72	.46	.54	.54	.59	1					3.94	.99
G2 Clean 68–72	.78	.81	.80	.65	.79	1				4.01	.85
G3 clean (1997)	.16	.15	.23	.19	.14	.19	1			4.05	.96
94–96 G3 wage	.17	.21	.20	.15	.18	.22	.14	1		2.14	1.00
G3 education	.36	.36	.36	.32	.31	.40	.17	.37	1	13.14	2.18

Note: Clean68 refers to the standardized rating of the cleanliness of the home in 1968; Clean69 refers to the same measure in 1969, etc. G2 Clean 68–72 refers to the average of all clean home assessments between 1968 and 1972.

93

between the G2 and G3 clean home measures, as well as any attenuation of this relation from adding other important controls.

The second dependent variable is G3 completed schooling. Schooling data come from the 1993 wave of the PSID and reflect total years of completed schooling. For cases in which 1993 educational attainment was unavailable, we used the 1992 measure. For G3s who were still missing the educational attainment measure, we used the 1997 measure of education contained in the Child Development Supplement.

The next dependent variable is the natural logarithm of G3 average hourly earnings between 1994 and 1996, measured between 1995 and 1997 and inflated to 1996 price levels using the CPI-UX1. In all cases, wage rates in 1996 dollars below $1.00 were set equal to $1.00; wage rates above $100 were set to $100. Wage-rate data in a given year of this 3-year span were counted as valid only if the respondent reported working at least 250 hours during that year. Our sample consists of people who had valid wage data in any of these years. Only four sample members were dropped because, although they had valid wage data, they did not work at least 250 hours in any given year.

The analyses follow a step-wise pattern in which categories of controls are added sequentially to examine their impact on the association between the G2 clean home measure and the outcomes examined. The categories of control variables are described next.

Family of Origin and Demographic Controls.   The first set of controls includes important characteristics of the G2 family of origin, as well as some sociodemographic measures. These controls include: G1's years of education and number of siblings; dummy variables for whether the G1 was a laborer, farmer, clerical worker, craftsman, operative, self-employed, or (the omitted group) a professional or manager; whether G2 grew up in a city, a town, or farm/other location (the omitted group); whether G2 grew up in the South; whether G2 reported his or her family of origin as being poor, average (the omitted group), or well-off; G2's race (Black = 1, other = 0); and whether G2 (i.e., the head of household in 1968–1972) was a male or female. We also control for the G3 age in 1997 and whether the G3 is male.

Parental and Family Characteristics.   We next control for a set of measures representing characteristics of the parents (G2s) themselves as well as the household in 1968–1972. House cleanliness may reflect a parent's organization and efficiency, but it may also be a product of a host of other household characteristics. A key task of the analysis is to eliminate as many sources of omitted-variable bias as possible. An obvious confound is the amount of time spent cleaning the house. Households more inclined to devote time to or better able to afford domestic help for housework may have varied success in rearing children for reasons unrelated to their organization and efficiency.

Thus, we sought a measure of the productivity of household production, as reflected in the housework-hours-adjusted assessment of house cleanliness. The PSID assessed housework with: (a) a question asked about the person doing the most housework: "How much time does (he/she) spend on this housework in an average week—I mean time spent cooking, cleaning, and other work around the house?"; (b) questions asked about all others in the household performing housework: "About how much time does (he/she) spend on housework in an average week?"; and (c) questions about unpaid and paid housework performed by anyone outside the household: "About how many hours would you say they helped in [year]?" This final measure was only available in 1969–1972; all others are available for all 5 years.

Housework hours were summed across all of these categories, averaged across the 5 years between 1968 and 1972, and converted to weekly housework hours. Nonlinear relations between housework hours and the outcomes demand that housework hours be represented with a set of four dummy variables based on quintiles of the housework hour distributions.

The analysis next considered ways of purging the housework-adjusted cleanliness of other sources of bias, such as compulsiveness, sensitivity to the judgments of others, formal schooling and mental ability, health limitations on daily activities, the ability to afford paid domestic workers, or more basic factors such as the size of the dwelling, the number and ages of children who might mess it up, and the number of adults who might be enlisted to help clean it up. The PSID provides G2 measures of many of these possible sources of bias.

The analyses also control for the schooling levels of both parents taken in 1985. In cases in which the parents did not survive in the PSID sample until 1985, we used the most recent report of completed schooling gathered between 1968 and 1972. Missing data dummies were created for maternal education (missing dummies for paternal education were collinear with the measure indicating the sex of G2 and therefore were not used).

The measure of G2 cognitive skills was the PSID respondent's sentence-completion test score from the 1972 interview. As documented in Veroff, McClelland, and Marquis (1971), this test was adapted from the Lorge-Thorndike intelligence test. The sample distribution of test scores indicates a much greater degree of differentiation at the low end of the distribution than at the high end. Missing data cases were assigned the sample mean. Both the sentence completion test and the measure of fear of failure were asked only in 1972, which causes missing data problems for individuals who were not observed as heads of their own households in that year. Experimentation with various ways of treating missing data

showed that key results were not affected, and we opted for mean assignment for these two measures.

G2 family structure was controlled with the 1968–1972 average number of years that the head was married; the average number of adults (>
age 18) and children in G2's household between 1968 and 1972; and the
average number of years in which the household contained very young
children (< 6 years old).

Family economic status is controlled with 1968–1972 averages of the percent of time the family owned their home and the percentage of time spent
in public housing. Controls for total family income or wages during the
1968–1972 period were not included. However, additional analyses revealed that including such controls does not change the association between G2 clean home and the outcome measures.

Difficulties in maintaining a clean house are indicated by the 1968–1972
average number of: rooms in the dwelling; percentage years in which the
household purchased cigarettes; years the respondent reported a health limitation; and percentage of years in which others in the family were reported
to have health limitations.

Psychological characteristics of G2 respondents were measured by scores
on a 1968–1972 index of sense of personal control (sample item: "When you
make plans ahead, do you usually get to carry out things the way you expected, or do things usually come up to make you change your plans?") and a
1972 index of fear of failure (sample item: "When taking tests some people
have an uneasy, upset feeling. When you took tests would you say you were
very upset, somewhat upset, or not upset at all?").

G3 Educational Attainment.   When predicting G3 clean home and G3
earnings, we add a control for G3 educational attainment, measured as described earlier.

G3 Clean Home.   When predicting G3 education and G3 earnings, we
include a measure of the cleanliness of the G3 home, taken in 1997. This
control allows us to examine whether the impact of the G2 clean home on
G3 outcomes operates through the cleanliness of the G3 home. This measure was already described.

1997 Controls.   Finally, we add controls for characteristics of the G3
family in 1997 that may be confounded with the cleanliness of the home in
1997, including whether the G3 is married, the number of children in the
household, and the average family income between 1994 and 1996, measured between 1995 and 1997 and converted to 1996 dollars (family income
is not added in the G3 wage regressions). Means and standard deviations for

all measures are presented in Table 4.2. As noted, PSID sampling weights are not used; therefore, these data are not nationally representative.

RESULTS

Table 4.1 presents correlations among the individual items composing the clean house measure, the 5-year clean house index, and the two dependent variables examined. Noteworthy in this table is the modest correlation of .22 between the 1968–1972 average G2 clean home measure and the 1997 G3 clean home measure. This suggests far from perfect overlap between the parental and child clean home assessments. Table 4.1 also shows large correlations between the yearly clean home assessments between 1968 and 1972. The correlation between G3 education and the 1968–1972 clean home measure is .40, whereas the correlation between G3 education and the G3 clean home measure is less than half, at .17. The correlation between G3 earnings and the parental clean home measure is .22, and the correlation between G3 earnings and G3 clean home is again lower, at .14. This suggests that G2 home cleanliness has a stronger association with G3 outcomes than does G3 home cleanliness, and that G2 home cleanliness is more strongly correlated with G3 education than with G3 earnings. The next set of analyses will test whether these associations remain in a multivariate context.

Tables 4.3, 4.4, and 4.5 present the results of regression analyses in which the dependent variables are the cleanliness of the sample child's home in 1997 (G3 clean home), the child's level of education (G3 education), and the child's log hourly wage (G3 wage), respectively. In each set of analyses, control variables are added sequentially to determine whether and how their addition affects the influence of G2 clean home on the dependent variables. In addition, after each new set of regressors is added, results from an F test of the joint significance of the added variables are presented; a significant result indicates that the added set of variables contributes significantly to the overall explanatory power of the model. In all analyses, the sample is restricted to G3s with complete information on all of the dependent variables. This means that we only estimate impacts of G2 clean home on G3 education, for example, for those G3s who also had valid wage measures in any year between 1994 and 1996. For the G3 education analysis, this reduces the sample size by 39, or about 4%. However, additional analyses revealed that the reduction in sample size does not affect our coefficient of interest—G2 clean home. Because some G3s in the PSID may come from the same family of origin, we calculate robust standard errors clustered by family of origin for all regression analyses.

TABLE 4.2
Unweighted Means and Standard Deviations

	Mean	SD
G3 years of education	13.14	2.18
G3 1994–1996 average log hourly wage in 1997 dollars	2.14	1.00
G2 clean house 1968–1972	4.01	0.95
G1 education	7.74	3.25
G1 number of siblings	4.45	2.60
G1 self-employed	0.04	0.19
G1 occupation clerical	0.04	0.21
G1 occupation craft	0.13	0.34
G1 occupation operative	0.15	0.36
G1 occupation labor	0.15	0.36
G1 occupation farmer	0.30	0.46
G1 occupation missing	0.11	0.31
G2 grew up in city	0.35	0.48
G2 grew up in town	0.29	0.45
G2 grew up poor	0.54	0.50
G2 grew up well-off	0.16	0.37
G2 grew up in South	0.47	0.50
G2 Black	0.40	0.49
G2 is male	0.82	0.39
G3 age 1997	36.41	5.83
G3 is male	0.40	0.49
Health limit G2 ability to work	0.14	0.25
G2 1972 sentence completion test	9.30	2.33
G3's mother's education (1972)	9.38	4.90

G3 mother's education missing	0.16	0.37
G3's father's education (1972)	9.32	5.49
G2 housework in second quintile (22–30 hours)	0.30	0.46
G2 housework in third quintile (31–37 hours)	0.24	0.42
G2 housework in fourth quintile (38–46 hours)	0.30	0.46
G2 housework in fifth quintile (> 46 hours)	0.24	0.43
G2 average. Number add't adults in HH	0.46	0.70
G2 average. Years married	4.07	1.73
G2 average. Number of children	3.52	2.04
G2 average. Number of children lt 5	0.48	0.42
G2 average. Number of rooms	5.77	1.28
G2 average. % Time someone smoked	0.59	0.43
G2 average. % Time someone needed care	0.08	0.18
G2 fear of failure	−0.27	0.49
G2 efficacy	1.90	0.86
G2 average. % Time in public housing	0.07	0.20
G2 average. % Time owned home	0.62	0.43
G3 clean home 1997	4.05	0.96
Whether G3 married in 1997	0.71	0.45
Number of children G3 has in 1997	2.12	1.10
Average G3 family income 1994–1996 (10000s)	5.37	5.18
N	927	

Note: G3 refers to the child who grew up in the home for which cleanliness was assessed in 1968–1972, G1 refers to this person's grandfather, G2 to this person's parents.

TABLE 4.3
G3 Clean House as Dependant Variable

	Coeff.	S.E.		Coeff.	S.E.		Coeff.	S.E.		Coeff.	S.E.	
G2 family of origin and demographic controls													
G2 clean home	0.16	0.04	***	0.14	0.05	***	0.12	0.05	**	0.10	0.05	**
G1 education	0.00	0.01		-0.005	0.01		-0.005	0.01		-0.01	0.01	
G1 number of siblings	-0.02	0.02		-0.02	0.02		-0.02	0.02		-0.01	0.01	
G1 self–employed	0.23	0.19		0.13	0.21		0.16	0.21		0.16	0.21	
G1 occupation clerical	0.13	0.23		0.26	0.20		0.26	0.21		0.20	0.20	
G1 occupation craft	0.17	0.16		0.19	0.16		0.22	0.16		0.15	0.15	
G1 occupation operative	0.04	0.16		0.07	0.16		0.10	0.16		0.06	0.16	
G1 occupation labor	-0.01	0.17		0.03	0.17		0.07	0.17		0.03	0.16	
G1 occupation farmer	0.15	0.17		0.16	0.17		0.18	0.17		0.13	0.16	
G1 missing occupation	0.21	0.17		0.20	0.18		0.23	0.18		0.20	0.17	
G2 grew up in city	-0.09	0.10		-0.07	0.10		-0.08	0.10		-0.08	0.10	
G2 grew up in town	-0.01	0.11		0.003	0.12		-0.01	0.12		-0.01	0.11	

	(1)		(2)		(3)		(4)	
G2 grew up poor	−0.01	0.08	−0.01	0.08	−0.02	0.08	−0.05	0.08
G2 grew up well-off	0.18	0.10 *	0.17	0.11	0.16	0.11	0.15	0.10
G2 grew up in South	−0.09	0.11	−0.04	0.11	−0.05	0.11	−0.05	0.11
G2 Black	−0.04	0.11	0.09	0.12	0.09	0.12	0.18	0.12
G2 male	−0.03	0.10	0.01	0.20	0.07	0.20	0.12	0.19
G3 age in 1997	−0.01	0.01	−0.01	0.01	−0.01	0.01	−0.01	0.01
G3 is male	0.10	0.07	0.11	0.07	0.11	0.07	0.05	0.07
Parental and family characteristics								
Health limits G2 ability to work	−0.24		−0.25	0.15	0.02	0.15	0.15	−0.19
G2 1972 sentence completion test			−0.003	0.02	0.01	0.02	−0.003	0.02
G3 mother's education			0.02	0.02	0.25	0.23	0.01	0.02
G3 mother's education missing			0.34	0.23	−0.01	0.01	0.24	0.22
G3 father's education			−0.01	0.01	0.13	0.11	−0.01	0.01
G2 housework in seond quintile (22–30 hrs/week)			0.12	0.11	0.02	0.12	0.12	0.10
G2 housework in third quintile (31–37 hrs/week)			−0.01	0.12	0.48	0.15	0.03	0.12

(continued on next page)

TABLE 4.3 (continued)

	Coeff.	S.E.	Coeff.	S.E.	Coeff.	S.E.	Coeff.	S.E.
G2 housework in fourth quintile (38–46 hrs/week)			0.46	0.15 ***		***	0.48	0.15 ***
G2 housework in fifth quintile (>46 hr/week)			-0.30	0.13 **	-0.31	0.13 **	-0.26	0.13 **
G2 avg. number of add't adults in hh			-0.02	0.05	-0.01	0.05	-0.03	0.05
G2 total years married			-0.03	0.03	-0.04	0.03	-0.04	0.03
G2 avg. number of children			-0.04	0.03	-0.04	0.03	-0.04	0.03
G2 avg. number children lt 5			0.06	0.11	0.09	0.11	0.10	0.11
G2 avg. number of rooms			0.05	0.03	0.04	0.03	0.03	0.03
G2 avg. % time someone smoked			0.16	0.09 *	0.17	0.09 *	0.13	0.08
G2 avg. time someone needed care			-0.06	0.20	-0.06	0.20	-0.02	0.19
G2 fear of failure			-0.11	0.07	-0.10	0.07	-0.12	0.07
G2 efficacy			0.02	0.05	0.01	0.05	-0.01	0.05
G2 avg. % time in public housing			-0.35	0.21	-0.33	0.22	-0.29	0.21
G2 avg. % time owned home			0.10	0.10	0.08	0.10	0.09	0.09
G3 Education								

	(1)	(2)	(3)	(4)
G3 educational attainment	0.05 0.02 *			0.02 0.02
1997 controls				
Whether G3 married in 1997				0.20 0.08 **
Number of children G3 has in 1997				-0.15 0.03 ***
Average G3 family income 1994–1996 (10000s)				0.03 0.01 ***
N	927	927	927	927
R-square	.06	.10	.10	.15
F-test of joint significance of added variables		1.88 **	6.75 **	14.65 ***

TABLE 4.4
Predicting G3 Years of Education

	Coeff.	S.E.		Coeff.	S.E.		Coeff.	S.E.		Coeff.	S.E.	
G2 Family of origin and demographic controls												
G2 clean house 1968–1972	0.67	0.08	***	0.44	0.08	***	0.42	0.08	***	0.37	0.08	***
G1 education	0.03	0.02		-0.0004	0.03		0.001	0.03		-0.01	0.02	
G1 number of siblings	-0.07	0.03	**	-0.02	0.03		-0.02	0.03		-0.01	0.03	
G1 self-employed	-0.73	0.42	*	-0.70	0.36	*	-0.72	0.36	**	-0.80	0.33	**
G1 occupation clerical	0.06	0.42		0.02	0.43		-0.02	0.44		-0.20	0.40	
G1 occupation craft	-0.90	0.32	***	-0.63	0.30	**	-0.66	0.30	**	-0.84	0.28	***
G1 occupation operative	-0.90	0.30	***	-0.66	0.29	**	-0.67	0.29	**	-0.73	0.28	***
G1 occupation labor	-1.06	0.34	***	-0.90	0.32	***	-0.90	0.32	***	-0.93	0.30	***
G1 occupation farmer	-0.57	0.35		-0.30	0.33		-0.33	0.32		-0.45	0.31	
G1 occupation missing	-0.81	0.34	**	-0.62	0.32	*	-0.66	0.32	**	-0.70	0.31	**
G2 grew up in city	0.04	0.21		0.07	0.20		0.09	0.20		0.11	0.19	
G2 grew up in town	0.35	0.22		0.25	0.22		0.25	0.22		0.25	0.21	

Parental and family characteristics	Model 1		Model 2		Model 3		Model 4	
G2 grew up poor	0.14	0.17	0.26	0.16	0.26	0.16*	0.13	0.16
G2 grew up well–off	0.21	0.20	0.19	0.19	0.16	0.19	0.17	0.18
G2 grew up in South	-0.06	0.19	0.06	0.18	0.07	0.18	0.07	0.17
G2 is Black	-0.54	0.20 ***	0.14	0.22	0.13	0.22	0.34	0.22
G2 is male	-0.08	0.18	-1.31	0.37 ***	-1.31	0.37 **	-1.10	0.35 ***
G3 age 1997	0.05	0.01 ***	0.04	0.02 **	0.04	0.02	0.02	0.02
G3 is male	-0.12	0.13	-0.05	0.13	-0.07	0.13	-0.13	0.13
Health limit G2 ability to work			0.15	0.28	0.19	0.28	0.21	0.27
G2 1972 sentence completion test			0.02	0.04	0.02	0.04	0.02	0.03
G3's mother's education (1972)			0.13	0.03 ***	0.12	0.03 ***	0.11	0.03 ***
G3 mother's education missing			1.83	0.41 ***	1.77	0.41 **	1.70	0.40 ***
G3's father's education (1972)			0.08	0.03 ***	0.08	0.03 ***	0.06	0.02 **
G2 housework in second quintile (22–30 hours)			-0.28	0.20	-0.30	0.20 **	-0.28	0.19
G2 housework in third quintile (31–37 hours)			-0.48	0.24 **	-0.48	0.24 **	-0.39	0.23 *

(continued on next page)

TABLE 4.4 (continued)

	Coeff.	S.E.	Coeff.	S.E.	Coeff.	S.E.	Coeff.	S.E.
G2 housework in fourth quintile (38–46 hours)			-0.55	0.31 *	-0.63	0.31	-0.47	0.29
G2 housework in fifth quintile (> 46 hours)			0.21	0.30	0.26	0.30	0.24	0.29
G2 average. Number add't adults in hh			-0.19	0.11 *	-0.18	0.11	-0.18	0.10 *
G2 average. Years married			0.13	0.05 **	0.13	0.06	0.12	0.05 **
G2 average. Number of children			0.01	0.04	0.01	0.04	0.01	0.04
G2 average. Number of children lt 5			-0.70	0.23 ***	-0.71	0.22	-0.62	0.21 ***
G2 average. Number of rooms			0.07	0.07	0.07	0.07	0.01	0.07
G2 average. % Time someone smoked			-0.17	0.16	-0.20	0.16	-0.18	0.16
G2 average. % Time someone needed care			-0.05	0.39	-0.04	0.38 **	0.01	0.36
G2 fear of failure			-0.10	0.14	-0.08	0.14	-0.11	0.13
G2 efficacy			0.10	0.10	0.10	0.10	0.08	0.10

	(1)		(2)		(3)		(4)	
G2 average. % Time in public housing			−0.42	0.43	−0.36	0.44	−0.30	0.44
G2 average. % Time owned home			0.24	0.21	0.23	0.20	0.21	0.19
G3 Clean home								
G3 clean home 1997					0.18	0.07 ***	0.08	0.07
1997 controls								
Whether G3 married in 1997							0.29	0.17 *
Number of children G3 has in 1997							−0.04	0.06
Average G3 family income 1994–1996 (10000s)							0.11	0.02 ***
N	927		927		927		927	
R-square	.25		.33		.33		.39	
F-test of joint significance of added variables			4.82 ***		6.60 **		11.02 ***	

Note: * indicates p. < .10, ** indicates p. < .05, *** indicates p. < .01.
G3 refers to the child who grew up in the home for which cleanliness was assessed in 1968–1972, G1 refers to this person's grandfather, G2 to this person's parents.

TABLE 4.5
Predicting G3 Earnings (1994–1996 average log hourly wage in 1997 dollars)

	Coeff.	S.E.	Coeff.	S.E.	Coeff.	S.E.	Coeff.	S.E.	Coeff.	S.E.
G2 Family of origin and demographic controls										
G2 clean house 1968–1972	0.16	0.04 ***	0.09	0.04 **	0.03	0.04	0.03	0.04	0.02	0.04
G1 education	0.01	0.01 *	0.001	0.01	0.001	0.01	0.001	0.01	0.002	0.01
G1 number of siblings	-0.02	0.01	-0.01	0.01	-0.01	0.01	-0.01	0.01	-0.01	0.01
G1 self-employed	0.03	0.19	-0.02	0.20	0.07	0.20	0.06	0.20	0.08	0.20
G1 occupation clerical	-0.21	0.21	-0.19	0.21	-0.19	0.21	-0.20	0.21	-0.20	0.21
G1 occupation craft	0.00	0.14	0.08	0.14	0.16	0.14	0.15	0.14	0.15	0.14
G1 occupation operative	0.03	0.14	0.08	0.14	0.17	0.14	0.17	0.14	0.16	0.14
G1 occupation labor	-0.01	0.15	0.02	0.15	0.14	0.14	0.14	0.14	0.13	0.14
G1 occupation farmer	0.01	0.15	0.08	0.15	0.12	0.15	0.11	0.15	0.11	0.14
G1 occupation missing	-0.28	0.17	-0.23	0.17	-0.15	0.16	-0.16	0.17	-0.16	0.16
G2 grew up in city	0.08	0.08	0.09	0.08	0.08	0.08	0.09	0.08	0.08	0.09

	Model 1		Model 2		Model 3		Model 4		Model 5	
G2 grew up in town	0.14	0.09	0.09	0.09	0.06	0.09	0.06	0.09	0.06	0.09
G2 grew up poor	0.01	0.07	0.02	0.07	-0.01	0.07	-0.01	0.07	-0.01	0.07
G2 grew up well–off	-0.01	0.09	-0.03	0.09	-0.05	0.09	-0.06	0.09	-0.06	0.09
G2 grew up in South	0.16 **	0.08	0.23 ***	0.08	0.22 ***	0.08	0.22 ***	0.08	0.22 ***	0.08
G2 Black	-0.27 ***	0.09	-0.21	0.10	-0.23 **	0.10	-0.24 **	0.10	-0.21 **	0.10
G2 is male	-0.08	0.09	-0.45 ***	0.17	-0.27 *	0.16	-0.28 *	0.16	-0.27 *	0.16
G3 age 1997	0.02 ***	0.01	0.02 ***	0.01	0.01 **	0.01	0.01 **	0.01	0.01 ***	0.01
G3 is male	0.71 ***	0.06	0.72 ***	0.06	0.73 ***	0.06	0.72 ***	0.06	0.70 ***	0.06
Parental and family characteristics										
Health limit G2 ability to work			-0.34 **	0.13	-0.36 ***	0.12	-0.35 ***	0.12	-0.33 ***	0.12
G2 1972 sentence completion test			0.01	0.01	0.003	0.01	0.003	0.01	0.004	0.01
G3's mother's education (1972)			0.02	0.01	0.01	0.01	0.01	0.01	0.004	0.01
G3 mother's education missing			0.27	0.18	0.02	0.18	0.01	0.18	0.001	0.18
G3's father's education (1972)			0.03 **	0.01	0.02	0.01	0.02	0.01	0.02	0.01
G2 housework in 2nd quintile (22–30 hrs)			0.09	0.10	0.13	0.10	0.12	0.10	0.13	0.10

(continued on next page)

TABLE 4.5 (continued)

	Coeff.	S.E.	Coeff.	S.E.	Coeff.	S.E.	Coeff.	S.E.	Coeff.	S.E.
G2 housework in 3rd quintile (31–37 hrs)			0.09	0.11	0.16	0.11	0.16	0.10	0.16	0.10
G2 housework in 4th quintile (38–46 hrs)			-0.08	0.16	-0.01	0.16	-0.03	0.16	-0.04	0.16
G2 housework in 5th quintile (> 46 hrs)			0.00	0.14	-0.03	0.14	-0.01	0.14	0.000	0.014
G2 average. Number add't adults in HH			0.04	0.05	0.07	0.05	0.07	0.04	0.06	0.04
G2 average years married			0.005	0.03	-0.01	0.03	-0.01	0.03	-0.01	0.03
G2 average number of kids			0.02	0.02	0.02	0.02	0.02	0.02	0.02	0.02
G2 average number of kids lt 5			-0.19 **	0.10	-0.10	0.09	-0.11	0.09	-0.10	0.09
G2 average number of rooms			0.03	0.03	0.02	0.03	0.01	0.03	0.01	0.03
G2 average. % Time someone smoked			0.03	0.07	0.05	0.07	0.04	0.07	0.03	0.07
G2 average. % Time someone needed care			-0.06	0.18	-0.05	0.17	-0.05	0.17	-0.04	0.17
G2 fear of failure			-0.001	0.07	0.01	0.06	0.02	0.06	0.01	0.06

	Model 1		Model 2		Model 3		Model 4	
G2 efficacy	-0.002	0.04	-0.02	0.04	-0.02	0.04	-0.02	0.04
G2 average. % Time in public housing	0.08	0.15	0.14	0.15	0.15	0.15	0.16	0.15
G2 average. % Time owned home	0.14	0.09	0.11	0.08	0.10	0.08	0.11	0.08
G3 Education								
G3 education			0.13	0.02 ***	0.13	0.02 ***	0.13	0.02 ***
G3 Clean home								
G3 Clean home 1997					0.05	0.03 *	0.04	0.03
1997 Controls								
Whether G3 married in 1997							0.07	0.08
Number of children G3 has in 1997							-0.06	0.03 **
N	927		927		927		927	
R–square	.25		.34		.34		.35	
F–test of joint significance of added variables	2.35		69.13	***	3.18	*	2.63	*

Note: * indicates p <.10, ** indicates p <.05, *** indicates p <.01

G3 refers to the child who grew up in the home for which cleanliness was assessed in 1968<@1501972, G1 refers to this person's grandfather, G2 to this person's parents.

Table 4.3 shows results of a series of regression analyses in which the dependent variable is the cleanliness of the G3 home in 1997. The first column shows the relation between the G2 and G3 cleanliness ratings, controlling for the G2 family of origin and demographic controls; this relation is surprisingly weak with a coefficient of .16. Adding controls for the parental and family characteristics reduces the coefficient of G2 clean house to .14. A substantial reduction in the association between G2 and G3 clean home is found when adding G3 education, which reduces the coefficient from column 1 by 25%, to .12 (column 3, Table 4.3). Here, G3 educational attainment is a relatively strong predictor of G3 house cleanliness. Finally, in column 4, the addition of the 1997 G3 controls further reduces the coefficient on G2 clean home to .10. Positive second-generation impacts on house cleanliness are observed for children whose parents' housework hours were in the fourth or fifth highest quintile. This might suggest that parents model housework behavior for their children, leading children of parents who spend more time on housework to have cleaner homes themselves. The number of children in 1997 is negatively associated with the G3 clean home, whereas years married and income both have positive associations.

The results of the analyses in which the 1968–1972 G2 clean house measure is used to predict G3 education and earnings are presented in Tables 4.4 and 4.5. In Table 4.4, the dependent variable is years of G3 educational attainment. A bivariate regression (not shown) indicates that a one-standard-deviation increase in the clean home measure is associated with an increase in education of a little less than 1 year (coefficient of .92, which amounts to roughly 40% of a standard deviation). The coefficient is reduced to .67 with the inclusion of the G2 and G3 background and demographic control measures (column 1, Table 4.4), and to .44 when the parental and family controls are added. This coefficient (.44) is highly significant, (DF = 665, t = 5.3, p = .0000), and suggests that a one-standard-deviation increase in G2 clean house is associated with nearly one half of a year more G3 schooling, representing about 20% of a standard deviation. In the next column, the coefficient on the G2 clean home measure drops only slightly (to .42) with the inclusion of the G3 clean home measure, suggesting that the pathway through which the G2 clean home measure influences G3 education is not through G3 cleanliness. Finally, in the last column, the coefficient on G2 clean home remains highly significant with the inclusion of the other 1997 family controls. In this final model, a one-standard-deviation increase in the G2 clean home measure is associated with an increase in G3 years of education of more than one third of a year (coefficient of .37). In contrast, the G3 clean home measure is not associated with G3 education (coefficient of .08). Other measures associated with G3 education in the final model are G1 occupation, G3 parental education, family structure in 1968–72, and G3 family income from

1994–1996. (It should be noted that G3 family income is assessed after the measurement of the dependent variable of years of education, which was taken in 1993. The G3 income measure is included merely to attempt to control for other factors that may be associated with the cleanliness of the G3 home, not to test a predictive relation between income and an earlier measure of education.)

Additionally, the indicator that the head of the household in 1968–1972 was male is negatively associated with G3 education, suggesting that, controlling for all other covariates, children from female-headed households obtain more years of schooling than do other children. This counterintuitive association is likely due to the fact that so many other factors also associated with family structure in 1968–1972 are controlled in the analysis.

Table 4.5 presents results of analyses predicting G3 log average hourly earnings. In the presence of background controls, a standard deviation increase in the parental clean home measure is associated with a 17% increase in earnings ($e^{.16}-1$; column 1, Table 4.5). The addition of the parental and family characteristics reduces the coefficient to .09, although it retains significance. However, in the third model, which adds a control for G3 educational attainment, the coefficient on the G2 clean home measure drops below significance, dropping by more than two thirds to .03, whereas the coefficient on G3 education is highly significant at .13. This suggests that the influence of growing up in a clean home on G3 earnings operates through G3 education. In the last columns, the addition of the G3 clean home measure and the 1997 family controls does not further reduce the impact of the 1968–1972 clean home measure. The G3 clean home measure is not a significant predictor of G3 earnings. Measures associated with G3 earnings are G3 age, sex, and race, whether G2 grew up in the South, and G2 health limitations; G3 education remains the strongest predictor.

EXTENSIONS

Stability Analysis

Using a 5-year average measure of the ratings of the cleanliness of the G2 home raises questions about the stability of these ratings over time. We investigated the stability of this measure and found that 84% of the sample changed by at least 1 point on the 5-point rating scale over the 1968–1972 period. Those with dirtier homes in 1968 were more likely to change in subsequent rating periods than those with cleaner homes. Although a large majority of the sample sees its rating change at some point during the 5 years, the vast majority (86%) of those whose ratings change experience a change of only 1 point on the 5-point scale. Thus, the clean home ratings of the sample as a whole are quite stable over time.

Cluster Analyses

The analysis uses a measure of the G2 clean home that averages all available information from the 1968–1972 assessments. However, it is possible that the pattern of assessments matters more than the average across multiple years. Results of cluster analyses (not shown here) suggested that the sample was divided into four groups: those whose home is consistently rated clean or very clean, those whose home is consistently rated less clean, those whose cleanliness ratings are rising over time, and those whose cleanliness ratings are declining over time. Results (not shown) of the influence of being in one of these four categories on the G3 outcomes of earnings and educational attainment indicate that patterns of change over time do not predict G3 outcomes in a consistent way and that the average level of home cleanliness is the most important predictor. For example, the impact of being in the "rising" category was not significantly different from that in the "declining" group, whereas being in the "always clean" group was consistently associated with better G3 outcomes, compared with all other groups.

Interviewer Effects

Given that the PSID tried to build respondent rapport by using the same interviewers across years, and given that an interviewer often interviews several dozen respondents in a year, it is possible that the clean house results might change with adjustments for interviewer fixed effects. Such adjustments are complicated because some respondents had the same interviewer across the 1968–1972 period whereas others did not. Analyses (not shown here) that adjusted for 1970 interviewer fixed effects using 1970 data on the cleanliness of the home had virtually no effect on the results. Specifically, the 1970 clean home measure was a significant predictor of G3 education both with and without the fixed-effects adjustment; it was not a significant predictor of G3 earnings, either with or without the fixed-effects adjustment.

Interactions Between Education and Organization

Goldsmith, Veum, and Darity (2000) developed a model in which higher levels of a personality characteristic—in their case, sense of personal control—increase the wage payoff to schooling. One could readily imagine a similar scenario with the measure of parental efficiency and organization used here, with the combination of growing up in a more organized household and attaining higher levels of education having a bigger impact on earnings than the additive effects of the two factors taken separately. However, interactions between the clean home measure and G3 educational attainment did not attain statistical significance when predicting G3 wages.

House Cleanliness and the Wage Payoff to Schooling

Bowles, Gintis, and Osborne (2000) reviewed studies showing that, on average, less than one fifth of the impact of education on earnings can be accounted for by differences in cognitive skills. We investigated this issue by estimating the earnings models with and without controls for the clean house measure, first by predicting 1994–1996 earnings that included only the full set of G1 and G2 controls and G3 education. Included next was the 1968–1972 measure of the cleanliness of the G2 home. The addition of the clean home measure did not change the impact of G3 education on G3 earnings (coefficient of .14 in both models; analyses not shown here). Thus, it does not appear that the measure of parental organization plays a large role in accounting for wage payoffs to schooling.

DISCUSSION

This research suggests some positive intergenerational effects of growing up with parents who are more organized and efficient. The clean home assessment is predictive, net of housework, education, cognitive skills and other correlates, of the subsequent educational attainment and earnings of the children of these respondents, with earnings measured 25 years after the assessment of parental household cleanliness. In addition, the association between growing up in a clean home and earnings is accounted for by higher rates of educational attainment.

These results raise questions of *why* children benefit from growing up in an organized household. Is a penchant for organization and efficiency an inherited trait, or is parents' organization and efficiency associated with enhanced parenting behaviors, leading to improved child outcomes (specifically, education), but leaving no impact on the child's actual tendencies toward organization and efficiency?

Although far from definitive, the evidence suggests a limited role for inheritance. Intergenerational correlations between the clean house ratings are modest and can partially be accounted for with controls for other parental background factors. Moreover, most of the apparent long-run earnings impact of growing up in an organized household is explained by the higher levels of completed schooling that children bring to the labor market. The cleanliness of the parents' home was more strongly associated with children's earnings and education than was the cleanliness of the child's own home.

Thus, it appears that the impact of growing up in a clean home on children does not operate through the cleanliness of their own home; that is, through their own tendency toward organization and efficiency. Instead, the evidence suggests that parents who are more organized and efficient (as measured by the cleanliness of their home) may invest in children in ways that promote children's later achievement and success. Although unable to measure the specific aspects of the more organized and efficient home environment that are associated with children's success, the current study suggests that the measure of home cleanliness may serve as a proxy for an underlying personality trait associated with providing an enriching home environment that fosters higher levels of children's educational attainment. In addition, parents who are more organized and efficient may provide more beneficial out-of-home environments for their children. Future work can seek to better understand this relation by examining the correlation between home cleanliness and other parental personality characteristics, and by investigating the correlations between home cleanliness and other more commonly considered aspects of the home environment, such as crowding, cognitive stimulation, or parental warmth. Finally, future research could examine the associations between home cleanliness and child behaviors that may influence education attainment, such as problem behavior.

Obvious limitations to this study should be noted. The measure of organization and efficiency is indirect and based on a housework-hours-adjusted rating of the cleanliness of a respondent's dwelling. Although the adjustments for possible sources of bias are extensive, they may not have been able to account for all the ways other than organization in which families who are rated as having a clean home may differ from those who are not.

This analysis has sought to broaden the research on parental investments in children by considering a unique measure of the home environment that is not constrained by parental resources. The study goes beyond most research on the home environment by examining long-term impacts of the environment on children's attainments in adulthood. The findings suggest that a specific measure of the home environment often included in traditional home assessments, cleanliness, may be a proxy for a set of parenting behaviors that lead to higher levels of children's educational attainment and, through education, greater earnings among children up to 25 years later.

ACKNOWLEDGMENTS

We are grateful for financial support from the National Institute on Aging (George Kaplan, PI, grant P50-HD38986 Michigan Interdisciplinary

Center on Social Inequalities, Mind, and Body). We are also grateful for helpful comments from Samuel Bowles, John Cawley, Tom DeLeire, Dorothy Duncan, Gary Evans, Arthur Goldsmith, Ariel Kalil, Abigail Stewart, and graduate student fellows at Northwestern University's Joint Center for Poverty Research.

REFERENCES

Bowles, S., & Gintis, H. (2001). The intergenerational transmission of economic status: Education, class, and genetics. In M. Feldman (Ed.), *Genetics, behavior, and society* (Vol. 6, pp. 4132–4141) in N. Smelser & P. Baltes (Eds), *International Encyclopedia of the Social and Behavioral Sciences*, Oxford: Elsevier.

Bowles, S., Gintis, H., & Osborne, M. (2000, August 28–29). *The determinants of earnings: skills, preferences, and schooling.* Paper presented at the Northwestern University/University of Chicago Joint Center for Poverty Research Conference on Noncognitive Skills and Labor Market Outcomes, Chicago.

Bradley, R. (1985). The HOME inventory: Rationale and research. In J. Lachenmeyer & M. Gibbs (Eds.), *Recent research in developmental psychopathology, book supplement to the Journal of Child Psychology and Psychiatry* (pp. 191–210). New York: Gardner.

Bradley, R., & Caldwell, B. (1984). 174 children: A study of the relationship between home environment and cognitive development during the first 5 years. In A. W. Gottfried (Ed.), *Home environment and early cognitive development* (pp. 5–56). Orlando, FL: Academic Press.

Cattell, R. B. (1943). The description of personality: Basic traits resolved into clusters. *Journal of Abnormal and Social Psychology 38*, 476–506.

Conley, D. (2001). A room with a view or a room of one's own? Housing and social stratification. *Sociological Forum, 16*(2), 263–280.

Corapci, F., & Wachs, T. D. (2002). Does parental mood or efficacy mediate the influence of environmental chaos upon parenting behavior? *Merrill-Palmer Quarterly, 48*(2), 182–201.

Digman, J. M. (1990). Personality structure: Emergence of the five-factor model. *Annual Review of Psychology, 41*, 417–440.

Duncan, G. J., & Brooks-Gunn, J. (1997). *Consequences of growing up poor.* New York: Russell Sage Foundation.

Duncan, G. J., & Dunifon, R. (1998). Soft skills and long-run labor market success. In Solomon W. Polacheck & John Robst (Eds.), *Research in labor economics* (Vol. 17, pp. 123–150). London: JAI Press.

Dunifon, R., & Duncan, G. J. (1998). Long-run effects of motivation on labor-market success. *Social Psychology Quarterly, 61*(1), 33–48.

Dunifon, R., Duncan, G. J, & Brooks-Gunn, J. (2001). As ye sweep, so shall ye reap. *American Economic Review: Papers and Proceedings, 91*(2), 150–154.

Evans, G. W., & English, K. (2002). The environment of poverty: Multiple stressor exposure, psychophysiological distress, and socioemotional adjustment. *Child Development, 73*(4), 1238–1248.

Evans, G. W., Lepore, S. J., Shejwal, B. R., & Palsane, M. N. (1998). Chronic residential crowding and children's well-being: An ecological perspective. *Child Development, 69*(6), 1514–1523.

Evans, G. W., Maxwell, L., & Hart, B. (1999). Parental language and verbal responsiveness to children in crowded homes. *Developmental Psychology*, 35(4), 1020–1023.

Evans, G. W., Saltzman, H., & Cooperman, J. L. (2001). Housing quality and children's socioemotional health. *Environment and Behavior*, 33(3), 389–399.

Evans, G. W., Wells, N. M., Chan, H. E., & Saltzman, H. (2000). Housing quality and mental health. *Journal of Consulting and Clinical Psychology*, 68(3), 526–530.

Fitzgerald, J., Gottschalk, P., & Moffitt, R. (1998). An analysis of the impact of sample attrition on the second generation of respondents in the Michigan Panel Study of Income Dynamics. *Journal of Human Resources*, 33(2), 300–343.

Goldberg, L. R. (1990). An alternative "description of personality": The big-five factor structure. *Journal of Personality and Social Psychology*, 59, 1216–1222.

Goldsmith, A., Veum, J., & Darity, W. (2000, August 28–29). Motivation and labor market outcomes. Paper presented at the Northwestern University/University of Chicago Joint Center for Poverty Research Conference on Noncognitive Skills and Labor Market Outcomes, Chicago.

Hill, M. (1992). *The panel study of income dynamics*. Newbury Park, CA: Sage.

Hunter, J. (1986). Cognitive ability, cognitive aptitudes, job knowledge, and job performance. *Journal of Vocational Behavior*, 29, 340–362.

Matheny, A. P., Wachs, T. D., Ludwig, J. L., & Phillips, K. (1995). Bringing order out of chaos: Psychometric characteristics of the confusion, hubbub, and order scale. *Journal of Applied Developmental Psychology*, 16, 429–444.

McCrae, R. R., & Costa, P. T. Jr. (1989). The structure of interpersonal traits: Wiggins circuplex and the five-factor model. *Journal of Personality and Social Psychology*, 56, 430–446.

McLanahan, S., & Sandefur, G. (1994). *Growing up with a single parent: What hurts, what helps?* Cambridge, MA: Harvard University Press.

Michael, R. (1972). *The effect of education on efficiency in consumption*. New York: Columbia University Press.

Schmidt, F., & Hunter, J. (1998). The validity and utility of selection methods in personnel psychology. *Psychological Bulletin*, 124(2), 262–274.

Soldz, S., & Vaillant, G. E. (1999). The big five personality traits and the life course: A 45-year longitudinal study. *Journal of Research on Personality*, 33, 208–232.

Smith, J., Brooks-Gunn, J., & Klebanov, P. (1997). Consequences of living in poverty for young children's cognitive and verbal ability and early school achievement. In G. J. Duncan & J. Brooks-Gunn (Eds.), *Consequences of growing up poor* (pp. 132-189). New York: Russell Sage Foundation.

Thurstone, L. L. (1951). The dimensions of temperament: Analysis of Guilfords' thirteen personality scales. *Psychometrika*, 16, 11–20.

Veroff, J., McClelland, L., & Marquis, K. (1971). *Measuring intelligence and achievement motivation in surveys*. Final Report to the Department of Health, Education, and Welfare, Office of Economic Opportunity. Ann Arbor, University of Michigan, Contract No. OCO–4180.

Wiggins, J. S., & Pincus, A. L. (1992). Personality: Structure and assessment. In M. R. Rosenzweig & L. W. Porter (Eds.), *Annual review of psychology*, 43, (pp. 473–504). Palo Alto, CA: Annual Reviews.

5

Family Investments in Response to the Developmental Challenges of Young Children with Disabilities

Michael J. Guralnick

University of Washington

Virtually all parents have concerns about their child's development at some point. Major developmental milestones are keenly anticipated, and parents are acutely sensitive to the reports by friends and relatives of the course of development of other children. Indeed, parents often compare their own child to those reports, to observations of their child's peers, and to memories or records of their child's siblings' growth and development. Moreover, their child's adjustments or reactions to novel or challenging circumstances are often scrutinized for signs of precocity, as a window to help them understand emerging personality, or as a signal that not all may be well.

For the most part, any developmental concerns that arise constitute only minor tensions compared with the sheer pleasure of the parent-child bond and parents' appreciation of their child's emerging capabilities. However, sometimes concerns warrant professional consultation, a process that can forever alter the life course of all family members.

This process generally begins with professional assessment and diagnosis, with evaluations focusing on the various domains of a child's health and development. To varying degrees, children's cognitive, language, socioemotional, motor, and sensory development are examined. If developmental problems are detected during early childhood in one or more do-mains, categorical labels may be applied, such as cerebral palsy, developmental (cognitive) delay, specific language impairment, autism disorder, or deafness. Occasionally, etiologic information also is generated as genetic or infectious causes may be identified, but more often than not etiologic information is problematic and speculative. The assigned labels carry important information but, of course, fail to describe the complexity of the child's characteristics and how relationships and parenting tasks will be irrevocably altered.

For young children with an established developmental disability—that is, when the developmental problems identified are likely to be substantial and life-long—varying levels of services and supports over time, that generally involve professionals from multiple disciplines, will be required. The family must now adjust to a set of unexpected and uncertain issues that will affect all family members and virtually all aspects of home and community life.

This chapter offers a developmental framework to help understand the ad-justments families must make to accommodate a young child with an estab-lished developmental disability. This discussion reveals the tasks and demands facing parents who are seeking to optimize their child's develop-ment. The extent of the adjustments parents must make to maximize their child's development is also discussed. The reallocation of time, energy, and re-sources to accommodate their child requires careful analysis within the broader family context. Finally, the willingness of parents to take advantage of early interventions is examined in conjunction with a commentary on how government-sponsored early interventions can be designed to support appro-priate parental adjustments and thereby optimize children's development.

DEVELOPMENTAL FRAMEWORK
AND PARENTING INVESTMENTS

Most parents display an intrinsic interest in and natural instinct for support-ing and promoting their child's development. For optimal results, however, parents must invest considerable and sustained psychological and material resources (see Bornstein, 2003). Much is known about which resources are important and how to organize those resources to promote children's devel-opment (e.g., Belsky, 1984; Bronfenbrenner; 1979; Dunst, 1985; Sameroff, 1993). However this occurs, it is clear that investments must relate to spe-cific family patterns of interaction. There are three categories of family in-teraction that can be applied generally to both typical development and conditions related to risk and disability: (a) the quality of parent–child transactions; (b) family-orchestrated child experiences; and (c) health and safety provided by the family (Guralnick, 1998; see Fig. 5.1).

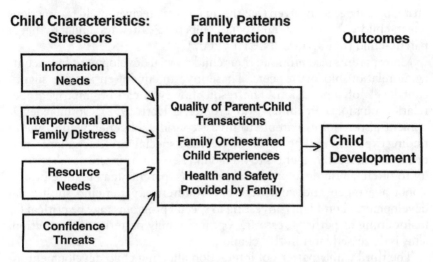

FIG. 5.1. Figure slightly modified from "Early Childhood Intervention: Evolution of a System" by M. J. Guralnick, 2000, in M. Wehmeyer and J. R. Patton (Eds.), *Mental retardation in the 21st century*. Copyright © 2000 by PRO-ED, Inc. Reprinted with permission.

The first category, parent–child transactions, consists of interactions that appear to govern critical aspects of children's cognitive and social competence (Bornstein & Tamis-Lemonda, 1989; Landry, Smith, Swank, Assel, & Vellet, 2001; Landry, Smith, Swank, & Miller-Loncar, 2000; National Research Council, 2000; Wachs, 1992). These interactions include the sensitivity and responsiveness of the parent, the ability to scaffold tasks in an affectively warm and nonintrusive manner, and the ability to engage in discourse-based interactions.

Recent research on responsive parenting provides insight into both the complexity of these interactions and the persistence and vigilance required of parents to maximize their child's development (e.g., Landry et al., 2001). Perhaps most important, these recent findings provide strong evidence that the work of supportive and responsive parenting must occur in many contexts as part of the various daily routines and be consistent over time. Given the demands of everyday contemporary life, this can be quite a challenge.

The second family pattern of interaction that directly influences child development is family-orchestrated child experiences. These include providing developmentally appropriate toys and materials and organizing social experiences that are stimulating and that extend the advantageous parent–child transactions previously noted. Introducing the child to the parents' social network is an example. It may also mean selecting an appropriate childcare environment if both parents are working. Appropriate childcare is an important decision, given that the quality of caregiver–child transactions affects children's cognitive and social competencies in ways similar to that of parent–child transactions (NICHD, 2001).

Many parents also promote their child's social development by encouraging relationships with peers. These investments often involve significant levels of supervision. The result, however, can be improved peer relationships for their child (Ladd, Profilet, & Hart, 1992). Optimal development also requires parents to invest considerable energy and time in finding experiences that match their child's special interests, talents, and needs. Beyond attentiveness to their child's emerging interests or sensitivity to often subtle developmental concerns, parents may require professional assistance and guidance. For children experiencing substantial developmental problems, investing in special programs may be critical for maintaining or perhaps restoring optimal family patterns of interaction. This is discussed later in this chapter.

The third family pattern of interaction affecting child development involves the ability of the family to ensure the health and safety of their child. For example, protecting their child from experiencing or even witnessing violence, although difficult to accomplish in many circumstances, constitutes a fundamental task with important developmental consequences (e.g., Osofsky, 1995). Other parent actions include obtaining proper immunizations, accessing health care as needed, and providing adequate nutrition. Although the mechanisms involved governing the relation between nutrition and child development are complex, failure to provide proper nutrition to young children is likely to result in less than optimal development (Georgieff & Rao, 1999; Gorman, 1995).

Taken together, these three family interaction patterns are viewed as essential to optimal social and cognitive competence of young children. The resultant social and cognitive competencies can then be employed in fostering children's individual and culturally relevant goals. It must be admitted, however, that a full understanding of how these family patterns of interaction exert their influence, including how they interact with one another and the number and extent of family activities and routines in which they must be implemented to achieve the anticipated developmental benefits, remains to be achieved. Similarly, there is a need to refine our measures of these constructs, particularly as development unfolds, and to determine whether other higher order dimensions may emerge as more valid constructs of these three family patterns of interaction. Nevertheless, the proximal patterns identified to date appear to matter. Evident as well is the fact that, despite parents' natural tendencies and inclinations to do so, gathering and deploying resources in connection with these family patterns of interaction is a complex and demanding task for all families.

PARENTAL CHALLENGES WHEN CHILDREN
HAVE A DISABILITY

The developmental and behavioral patterns of children with disabilities create unusual and often perplexing difficulties for families at every level. Not only do typical and expected interaction patterns between parents and children often fail to be realized, but families also begin to consider the broader and longer term implications of having a family member with a developmental disability. It soon becomes apparent that they must consider special issues with respect to the nature of parent–child transactions, the types of family-orchestrated child experiences, and the health and safety concerns of their child with an established disability.

The developmental science of risk and disability has carefully documented these challenges to optimal family patterns of interaction (Guralnick, 1997; Shonkoff & Meisels, 2000). Viewed within the developmental framework outlined earlier, children with established disabilities have the potential to create a set of stressors that can perturb family patterns of interaction and further compromise child development. These potential stressors of family patterns of interaction generally take four forms (see Fig. 5.1).

First, parents require considerable information, the absence of which can easily adversely affect all three family patterns of interaction. Parents usually initially grapple with the diagnostic and assessment process, a complex sequence of events that can be frustrating and distressing (Carmichael, Pembry, Turner, & Barnicoat, 1999). Failure to adequately come to terms with a diagnosis can result in relationship difficulties with long-term negative implications for a child's development (Pianta, Marvin, Britner, & Borowitz, 1996).

On a day-to-day basis, the quality of parent–child transactions is stressed by numerous child characteristics. Discrepancies between children's receptive and expressive language, unusual affective patterns, or their child's under- or overactivity leave many parents wondering how best to promote their child's development. Children with established disabilities often have problems with emotional expressiveness, joint attention and social referencing skills, initiating social interactions, responsiveness to others, and they can exhibit unusual behavior problems (Spiker, Boyce, & Boyce, 2002). These patterns are complex and vary widely by individual, even among children with the same identified disability (Guralnick, 2002). Moreover, certain subgroups of children, such as those with autism, pose special relationship challenges, whereas those with sensory impairments require families to become knowledgeable about technical supports for their children. Certainly, not all of the developmental challenges to parental interaction are fully recognized by families, but parents are well aware that substantial information and corresponding adjustments are needed to optimize parent–child transactions.

Information needs can seem never-ending, extending well beyond day-to-day parent–child interactions. Perhaps most significant is the need to orchestrate an array of coordinated supports and services that families now face. Seeking out the best professionals and programs, including daycare, is a task that can consume the considerable energies of most families. Information is also needed as families involve their child in their own social network. For example, the family must consider which details of their child's disability should be provided to friends and family members. Similarly, information is needed about the numerous health and safety issues that are certain to arise.

A second category of potential stressors is interpersonal and family distress. Family members, including siblings, soon realize that changes in family routines are necessary, and parents may not entirely agree on how to address fundamental issues that arise (e.g., whether to enroll their child in an inclusive or specialized early intervention program). Social isolation from friends and family can easily occur for many reasons, not the least of which is the family's feeling that somehow they share the stigma related to their child with a disability (Goffman, 1963).

Characteristics of children with disabilities are clearly associated with perceived parental stress (e.g., depression, role restriction, competence threats; Roach, Orsmond, & Barratt, 1999), with child behavior problems often being the most disruptive (Baker, Blacher, Crnic, & Edelbrock, 2002). Contemplating the long-term implications of the child's quality of life can be distressing as well. Taken together, increased interpersonal and family distress can be debilitating, distracting, and isolating, resulting in less than optimal family patterns of interaction.

Resources needs, the third category of potential stressors, emerge in many forms. Increased expenses for health care or certain types of professional services can rapidly become overwhelming even for families with reasonable financial resources. The disrupted daily routines and the additional time demands needed for therapeutic services also can become a constant source of problems for families. The search for respite care becomes a high priority.

Finally, all of these stressors can combine to threaten the confidence parents have in their ability to effectively parent. This shaken confidence (the fourth category of potential stressors) can undermine all aspects of family patterns of interaction, creating a sense of helplessness. A family's sense of mastery and control remains a critical element in the development of all children (Affleck & Tennen, 1993).

RESPONSES AND INVESTMENTS BY FAMILIES
TO ADDRESS STRESSORS

The cumulative effect of these four types of stressors on children's development is to produce or contribute to a decline in cognitive and social competence during the first few years of life (Guralnick, 1998; Sameroff, Seifer,
Barocas, Zax, & Greenspan, 1987). That is, without addressing these stressors, one or more of the family patterns of interaction will be perturbed
enough to alter the optimal course of child development. Of course, children's developmental delays and disabilities have substantial effects on all
aspects of competence, reflected in their lower developmental trajectories.
Nevertheless, stressors affecting family patterns of interaction appear to
contribute to additional developmental delays. Fortunately, most parents
soon become aware of the potential impact of these stressors, and generally
recognize the need to seek additional resources, to solidify or expand social
supports for the family, and to obtain information and services about their
child's unique developmental needs.

At the same time, however, parents must consider how these new activities related to their child's disability affect family life in general. Indeed, it
has been argued that a major goal of families is to create or maintain "a sus-
tainable and meaningful daily routine of family life" (Gallimore, Weisner,
Bernheimer, Guthrie, & Nihira, 1993, p. 186). Within this framework, it is
these routines that create the context for family activities relevant to development and, more generally, for expressing family goals and values
(Gallimore, Keogh, & Bernheimer, 1999). It is the types of new activities
families choose to engage in (or accommodations they may or may not
make) in connection with stressors that reflect these larger family goals and
values; many of which may be competing with one another (Gallimore,
Weisner, Kaufman, & Bernheimer, 1989).

Analyses of interview data with 102 families of young children with
nonspecific developmental delays reveal the responses or accommodations families make. Based on previous work (Gallimore et al., 1989;
Weisner, 1984), the following 10 domains of accommodation were identified: (a) family subsistence and financial base; (b) accessibility of
health and educational services; (c) home and neighborhood safety and
convenience; (d) domestic tasks and chore workload for the family; (e)
childcare tasks; (f) child playgroups and peers; (g) marital role relationships; (h) social support; (i) father's role; and (j) sources of parental information and effort to obtain this information. The coding system
required that accommodations be specifically linked to a response to
their child with a disability. Examples of these accommodations are presented in Table 5.1.

TABLE 5.1
Domain Example

Domain	Example
Family subsistence	Hours worked; flexibility of work schedule; adequacy of financial resources; amount of coverage provided by medical insurance
Services	Availability of services; eligibility for services; sources of transportation; amount of parent involvement required
Home/neighborhood safety and convenience	Safety and accessibility of play area; alterations in home (installation of locks, fences related to safety concerns); choice of particular neighborhood
Domestic workload	Amount of work that needs to be done; persons available to do it; amount of time spent by different family members
Childcare tasks	Complexity of childcare tasks; presence of extraordinary childcare demands (medical problems, behavior problems); number and availability of caregivers
Child peer group	Child's play groups (children with disabilities vs. typically developing children); amount of parent supervision needed; role of siblings as playmates
Marital roles	Amount of shared decision making regarding child with delays; degree to which childcare and household tasks are shared
Instrumental/emotional support	Availability and use of formal (church, parent groups) and informal (friends, relatives) sources of support; costs of using support
Father/spouse role	Amount of involvement with child with delays; amount of emotional support provided
Parent information	Reliance on professional versus nonprofessional sources of information; amount of time and effort spent accessing information

Note. From "Weaving Interventions Into the Fabric of Everyday Life: An Approach to Family Assessment" by L. P. Bernheimer and B. K. Keogh, 1995, *Topics in Early Childhood Special Education, 15,* 415–433. Copyright © 1995 by PRO-ED, Inc. Reprinted with permission.

Overall, the research identified an average of nearly seven accommodations per family (Gallimore et al., 1993). As might be expected, there was substantial variability in the accommodations, but all 10 domains were affected. Of considerable importance is that social support, childcare tasks, and sources of information were identified by approximately 75% of the families as producing either moderate or high levels of accommodation.

RESOURCE SUPPORTS, SOCIAL SUPPORTS, AND INFORMATION AND SERVICES

The three most common domains that emerged from the analysis of these families seem to confirm that families accord high priority to expanding or maintaining social supports, to obtaining resource supports, and to gathering information and obtaining services. The critical point is that all of these accommodations constitute investments that have at least the potential to reduce the stressors that can alter optimal family patterns of interaction (Guralnick, 1998).

More specifically, participation in parent-support groups for families of children with disabilities can be extremely valuable but is often time consuming and psychologically demanding (Krauss, Upshur, Shonkoff, & Hauser-Cram, 1993; Santelli, Turnbull, Sergeant, Lerner, & Marquis, 1996). This more formal form of social support complements the informal accommodations involving family members and friends to provide both instrumental and emotional forms of support (Crnic & Stormshak, 1997; Dunst, Trivette, & Jodry, 1997). Information regarding child-rearing advice can also be considered a form of social support. Indeed, many parent-to-parent groups are a source of highly technical information about disability issues.

Childcare tasks increase in complexity, generally requiring additional caregivers or caregiver time. Sometimes such help can be found within families (e.g., accommodations by siblings or grandparents, flextime at work), but more consistent and extensive caregiver assistance is needed when both parents are employed outside the home. Locating high-quality, affordable, and competent childcare is a major task for most parents given that it ultimately affects both the financial status and career plans of family members. But as Kelly and Booth (2002) pointed out:

> Parents of children with disabilities face additional challenges of finding care that is accommodating to their child's special needs, overcoming barriers to inclusive practices in child care settings, finding trained care providers to care for their children, and coordinating other special services with their children's child care arrangements. (p. 71)

As might be expected, parents report substantial difficulties finding satis-factory childcare arrangements for young children with disabilities (Booth & Kelly, 1998). The commitment of time and energy to select an appropri-ate caregiver and coordinating special services is considerable. Many fami-lies make a different type of accommodation with respect to the domain of childcare as more mothers of infants with disabilities choose to postpone work or not return to school. This constitutes a clear investment toward the child with a disability and away from themselves and, indirectly, other family members (Booth & Kelly, 1998). During the child's first year of life, caregiving primarily occurs in the home by mothers, fathers, relatives, or nonrelatives. The quality of care is usually higher in these home settings than in childcare homes or childcare centers (Booth & Kelly, 1998; Kelly & Booth, 2002). Even as children with disabilities become older, in-home care provided by a relative or baby-sitter is preferred by parents (Warfield & Hauser-Cram, 1996). These arrangements are complex and shifting—bal-ancing career goals, financial needs, and the responsibilities of family mem-bers, yet trying to ensure that the child with a disability receives proper care, developmental stimulation, and supports.

The third frequent accommodation by families—seeking information re-lated to their child's disability—is an ongoing process. Gathering informa-tion to enable more optimal family patterns of interaction and help families explain the situation to others continues to be a high priority (Mahoney & Filer, 1996). Inevitably, the information leads families to seek out a range of services for their child.

INVESTMENTS IN EARLY INTERVENTION PROGRAMS

Some families make these accommodations independently, including ser-vice-related accommodations, recognizing needs, and then identifying ser-vice agencies, family members, friends, employers, or professionals to assist them. These families have the resources and problem-solving ability to do so, particularly when the accommodations required are relatively modest. Most families, however, take advantage of state-administered early inter-vention programs authorized as part of the federal Individuals with Disabil-ities Education Act (IDEA). Part C of that act provides families of eligible infants and toddlers with a comprehensive array of services and supports at no or modest cost, including assessments, information on developmentally oriented and disability topics, therapies, and related interventions. In many respects, these programs can point to beneficial accommodations that the family may not have considered, was not certain could be done, or felt were beyond their resources.

A number of important principles guide the design of these early inter-vention programs, including maximizing child and family participation in natural environments or inclusive activities, and ensuring that intervention is family-centered such that partnerships with families are formed to strengthen a family's ability to provide a more optimal developmental environment for their child. That is, both family and child needs are considered in developing an intervention plan. In fact, the intent is consistent with providing families with an array of social supports, resource supports, and information and services. As such, the comprehensiveness of the services and supports and their coherent coordination is emphasized. Home and center-based programs are available, and many specialists can be involved.

The plan is realized through a jointly agreed on Individualized Family Service Plan (IFSP). Continued interventions are available when children reach preschool age, although the focus shifts primarily to child-oriented services through an Individualized Educational Program (IEP).

Particularly for the infant/toddler program of IDEA, family participation in early intervention is a major and sometimes extraordinary investment. Administrative, planning, and progress review meetings regarding IFSPs (or IEPs) can be time-consuming and demanding, but proper planning and monitoring are critical for their success (Shonkoff & Hauser-Cram, 1987). Being available for home visits, transporting their child to center-based activities, actively participating in therapeutic activities, involving themselves in parent groups, sifting through often contradictory information to select the most reasonable intervention program, and even advocating for more intensive or different services are common for parents participating in IDEA.

Taken together, families generally seek out resource supports, social supports, and information and services. Although their approaches may differ, families are usually responsive to stressors that can alter optimal family patterns of interaction, and are therefore working to prevent or minimize adverse effects on their child's development. To be sure, the interests of family members or broader family goals and values often compete with accommodations that would minimize stressors (Gallimore et al., 1989). Nevertheless, families are generally creative in making accommodations and organizing family routines in a manner that supports their child's development (Fiese, 2002; Gallimore et al., 1993; Kellegrew, 2000). Many families address these stressors entirely within the framework of IDEA. Even addressing sensitive and complex family issues of social isolation, depression, or marital discord are within the boundaries of IDEA, at least for infants and toddlers. Families also supplement services and supports within IDEA through other professional and personal relationships (Kochanek, McGinn, & Cummins, 1998; Shonkoff, Hauser-Cram, Krauss, & Upshur, 1992). However this is accomplished, these family investments can substantially influence their child's development in a manner consistent with the developmental model that is the framework for this discussion. Of course, even with well-planned and comprehensive early intervention programs, effects range from minimal to dramatic depending on the type of child disability, intervention quality, and active family participation (Guralnick, 1997). Nevertheless, effect sizes for well-designed programs average .50 to .75 SD, and are capable of minimizing or preventing entirely the decline in development that usually occurs in the absence of these interventions (Guralnick, 1998).

DETERMINANTS OF PARENTAL INVESTMENT

The range of parental investment in children with disabilities is extensive (see Shonkoff et al., 1992). Some families respond to a diagnosis of a disability by devoting all their time and energy to promoting their child's health and development. These parents seek out and absorb as much information as possible and involve their child in numerous medical and behavioral therapies, sometimes choosing therapeutic approaches that are highly questionable from a scientific perspective. Other parents, even those with considerable resources, take little initiative, seeking only limited information and enrolling their child in only the most basic of services.

Even beyond these extreme and unusual responses, many forces compete within the family accommodations and routines. In fact, career aspirations, financial exigencies, or concerns about devoting sufficient time and resources to other family members can lead to decisions that may not optimize family patterns of interaction.

We do know, however, that several family characteristics are associated with parent involvement in organized early intervention programs. As noted, full participation in these programs requires considerable investment in all its forms. Gavidia-Payne and Stoneman (1997) developed a structural equation model linking family education and income, social supports, stress (hassles and depression), coping (turning to religion, absence of denial, being problem focused), marital adjustment, and family functioning to parental involvement in early intervention programs. Parental involvement was indexed in a number of ways: (a) through parental attendance at IFSP or IEP meetings and attendance at workshops and related activities designed to help parents select appropriate services for their child; (b) through knowledge of their child's disability and laws governing services and supports; and (c) through parental cooperation in various projects, particularly in learning how to support their child's developmental goals in the home. Although models for mothers and fathers differed somewhat, parents with higher levels of education, more financial resources, lower stress levels, more active and diverse coping strategies, greater support from spouse, friends, and relatives, and stronger religious affiliations were more involved in early intervention programs for their children. Relations were complex but reflected important interactions among these family characteristics. For instance, family demographics (family financial income and educational levels) contributed indirectly through better family functioning and reduced stress, but also constituted an important direct path to involvement in early intervention. Social supports appeared to play an especially important role in coping strategies. In fact, the various forms of cognitive coping were important mediators of parental involvement.

The exact interrelations among family characteristics and parental involvement in early intervention remain to be determined. Nevertheless, these patterns and related research suggest that families with fewer resources and more difficulties overall are simply less able to engage in a process that requires consistent and organized involvement. Although families with limited resources tend to enroll their children in early intervention programs (Hebbeler, Wagner, Spiker, Scarborough, Simeonsson, & Collier, 2001), program effects are likely to be limited, given that child-focused programs for infants and toddlers are usually of low intensity, averaging only a few hours per month (Shonkoff et al., 1992). Moreover, the families themselves are unlikely to compensate for this lack of involvement.

As is well known, limited financial resources, low social support, marital stress, and limited education are among the family risk factors associated with adverse child developmental outcomes (Burchinal, Roberts, Hooper, & Zeisel, 2000; Sameroff et al., 1987). Of importance, these family risk factors adversely influence the same three family patterns of interaction that influence child development outcomes, thereby further increasing the vulnerability of children with established developmental disabilities (Guralnick, 1998). As a consequence, the lack of parent participation in early intervention is certain to substantially limit child developmental outcomes within the current approach to intervention services. Comprehensive services and supports and family involvement are critical elements in any successful intervention program.

Individual differences in parental investments may also reflect the extent to which both formal and informal early interventions are consistent with broad family goals, priorities, and routines (Bailey et al., 1998; Filer & Mahoney, 1996; Gallimore et al., 1993). This issue of consistency is likely to arise in many circumstances, including when families receive recommendations from an individual therapist or when participating in the IFSP or IEP early intervention program. As Bailey and colleagues (1998) pointed out, it would be especially helpful if family perceptions of the early intervention experience could be obtained with respect to their influence on both child development and well-being and family life. Without positive expectations or perceptions, the likelihood of incorporating therapeutic recommendations into family routines and taking advantage of child-focused services decreases considerably.

SUMMARY AND RECOMMENDATIONS

The challenges confronting families of young children with established developmental disabilities can be formidable. Seeking out and evaluating frequently complex and even inconsistent information, interpersonal and family distress, difficulty accessing resources, and doubting one's ability to confidently and competently parent a child with a disability are frequent problems. Unless these issues are addressed, family patterns of interaction become stressed to a point that the parents fail to support their child's optimal development. Nevertheless, parental investments in time, energy, and personal resources on their own initiative or as part of a formal early intervention system can successfully address these stressors and enhance their child's development.

Yet, the level of investment by families varies considerably. Some of this variation can be attributed to idiosyncratic responses by parents, often extreme in nature. Other sources of variation, however, appear to be linked to the way early intervention programs are organized and to certain family characteristics. In addition, many families fail to make the appropriate investments not because they lack motivation, but because early intervention recommendations are inconsistent with family goals, priorities, and daily routines.

Useful frameworks are now available or are emerging that can, if implemented properly, begin to address these issues. In particular, collaborative goal-setting strategies and techniques can be effective in identifying and resolving differences between parents and professionals in the design of early intervention programs (Bailey, 1987). Clearly, a process of negotiation must be present for a true partnership to exist. Similarly, a theoretical and practical structure is emerging in which an awareness and understanding of the accommodations that affect family routines are considered in the context of IFSP or IEP development (Bernheimer, Gallimore, & Weisner, 1990; Bernheimer & Keogh, 1995). In addition, as early intervention programs become more firmly developmental in their orientation (Guralnick, 2001; Harbin, McWilliam, & Gallagher, 2000; Spiker, Hebbeler, Wagner, Cameto, & McKenna, 2000), the relevance of assessing stressors as a means of helping strengthen family patterns of interaction will become more apparent.

Approaches to assessing child and family stressors that can facilitate this process are now being developed (Guralnick, in press). From an intervention perspective, the renewed legislative emphasis on providing supports and services in natural and inclusive environments and the availability of creative strategies for doing so (Dunst, 2001) are most compatible with family routines, thereby increasing the prospects of parental investments in their child's development.

During this negotiation process, professionals may well encounter family goals, values, and priorities that they consider not to be in the best interests of the child's development. Indeed, parental employment and daycare decisions, for example, may be designed to meet broader family needs, ones not entirely compatible with maximizing resource and social supports or information and services in relation to their child with a disability. Nevertheless, by recognizing these sometimes competing priorities, and especially by organizing early interventions to be responsive to these priorities, families are far more likely to make investments, to sustain the investments they do make, and to access programs needed to maximize their child's development.

The daycare dilemma for working parents provides a good example. As discussed earlier, a child's disability can limit families' options for quality childcare. For a variety of reasons, families prefer some form of in-home daycare, especially when children are infants. Training skilled providers and integrating services for the child continue to be a challenge, but they are essential for parents who, for financial or personal reasons, choose to work outside the home. Clearly, policies directed toward addressing this issue are vital. As a partial solution, quality childcare options in inclusive settings (which usually contain both early childhood educators and specialists in disability) are becoming available in which child-focused services and even parent support groups are integrated (O'Brien, 1997, 2001; Wesley, 1994).

However, if an inclusive childcare option is unavailable, parents must figure out how to use an early intervention program as a "home base" for resource and social supports as well as for information and services while meaningfully coordinating with the child's childcare environment (Guralnick, 2000).

From the broad family support perspective, unless early interventionists are able to adjust their time schedules to accommodate parents who are employed, few opportunities will exist for early intervention programs and services, such as parent training. Moreover, it has been extremely difficult for early intervention programs to influence family patterns of interaction, particularly parent–child transactions, in families with a child at high developmental risk owing to adverse family characteristics (Guralnick, 2000). Available evidence suggests, however, that intensive intervention-oriented daycare can prevent many developmental problems for children at risk owing to environmental factors (Burchinal, Campbell, Bryant, Wasik, & Ramey, 1997). For the increasing number of families that face high levels of stressors associated with family characteristics, ensuring the availability of and encouraging families to strongly consider this option may be in the best interests of all concerned. Although this assumption remains to be tested, the availability of intensive early intervention programs may enable parents to make a minimal investment of time, energy, and resources to achieve what may well be the best outcome for their child. Ideally, paralleling these child-oriented programs would be efforts to address the complex array of stressors generated by family characteristics (e.g., poverty, mental health problems, lack of social support).

Finally, for families to invest in early intervention programs most effectively and efficiently, the programs must be visible, accessible, and well organized, emphasize inclusive options, be consistent with generally accepted best-practice approaches, and have a well-articulated developmental framework. Such a "developmental systems" framework is now available (Guralnick, 2001), and efforts are underway to provide a blueprint for communities to adopt these principles and practices (Guralnick, in press).

REFERENCES

Affleck, G., & Tennen, H. (1993). Cognitive adaptation to adversity: Insights from parents of medically fragile infants. In A. P. Turnbull, J. M. Patterson, S. K. Behr, D. L. Murphy, J. G. Marquis, & M. J. Blue-Banning (Eds.), Cognitive coping, families, and disability (pp. 135–150). Baltimore, MD: Brookes.

Bailey, D. B. (1987). Collaborative goal-setting with families: Resolving differences in values and priorities for services. Topics in Early Childhood Special Education, 7(2), 59–71.

Bailey, D. B. Jr., McWilliam, R. A., Darkes, L. A., Hebbeler, K., Simeonsson, R. J., Spiker, D., & Wagner, M. (1998). Family outcomes in early intervention: A framework for program evaluation and efficacy research. Exceptional Children, 64, 313–328.

Baker, B. L., Blacher, J., Crnic, K. A., & Edelbrock, C. (2002). Behavior problems and parenting stress in families of three-year old children with and without developmental delays. American Journal on Mental Retardation, 107, 433–444.

Belsky, J. (1984). The determinants of parenting: A process model. Child Development, 55, 83–96.

Bernheimer, L. P., Gallimore, R., & Weisner, T. S. (1990). Ecocultural theory as a context for the Individual Family Service Plan. Journal of Early Intervention, 14, 219–233.

Bernheimer, L. P., & Keogh, B. K. (1995). Weaving interventions into the fabric of everyday life: An approach to family assessment. Topic in Early Childhood Special Education, 15, 415–433.

Booth, C. L., & Kelly, J. F. (1998). Child-care characteristics of infants with and without special needs: Comparisons and concerns. Early Childhood Research Quarterly, 13, 603–622.

Bornstein, M. H. (2003). Positive parenting and positive development in children. In R. M. Lerner, F. Jacobs, & D. Wertlieb (Eds.), Handbook of applied developmental science: Vol. 1. Applying developmental science for youth and families (pp. 187–209). Thousand Oaks, CA: Sage Publications.

Bornstein, M. H., & Tamis-Lemonda, C. S. (1989). Maternal responsiveness and cognitive development in children. New Directions for Child Development, 48, 49–61.

Bronfenbrenner, U. (1979). The ecology of human development. Cambridge, MA: Harvard University Press.

Burchinal, M.R., Campbell, F.A., Bryant, D.M., Wasik, B. H., & Ramey, C.T. (1997). Early intervention and mediating processes in cognitive performance of children of low-income African American families. *Child Development*, 68, 935–954.

Burchinal, M. R., Roberts, J. E., Hooper, S., & Zeisel, S. A. (2000). Cumulative risk and early cognitive development: A comparison of statistical risk models. *Developmental Psychology*, 36, 793–807.

Carmichael, B., Pembry, M., Turner, G., & Barnicoat, A. (1999). Diagnosis of fragile-X syndrome: The experiences of parents. *Journal of Intellectual Disability Research*, 43, 47–53.

Crnic, K., & Stormshak, E. (1997). The effectiveness of providing social support for families of children at risk. In M. J. Guralnick (Ed.), *The effectiveness of early intervention* (pp. 209–225). Baltimore, MD: Paul H. Brookes.

Dunst, C. J. (1985). Rethinking early intervention. *Analysis and Intervention in Developmental Disabilities*, 5, 165–201.

Dunst, C. J. (2001). Participation of young children with disabilities in community learning activities. In M. J. Guralnick (Ed.), *Early childhood inclusion: Focus on change* (pp. 307–333). Baltimore, MD: Paul H. Brookes.

Dunst, C. J., Trivette, C. M., & Jodry, W. (1997). Influences of social support on children with disabilities and their families. In M. J. Guralnick (Ed.), *The effectiveness of early intervention* (pp. 499–522). Baltimore, MD: Paul H. Brookes.

Fiese, B. H. (2002). Routines of daily living and rituals in family life: A glimpse at stability and change during the early child-raising years. *Zero to Three*, 22 (4), 10-13.

Filer, J. D., & Mahoney, G. J. (1996). Collaboration between families and early intervention service providers. *Infants and Young Children*, 9 (2), 22–30.

Gallimore, R., Keogh, B. K., & Bernheimer, L. P. (1999). The nature and long-term implications of early developmental delays: A summary of evidence from two longitudinal studies. In L. M. Glidden (Vol. Ed.), *International review of research in mental retardation* (Vol. 22, pp. 105–135). San Diego: Academic Press.

Gallimore, R., Weisner, T. S., Bernheimer, L. P., Guthrie, D., & Nihira, K. (1993). Family responses to young children with developmental delays: Accommodation activity in ecological and cultural context. *American Journal on Mental Retardation*, 98, 185–206.

Gallimore, R., Weisner, T. S., Kaufman, S. Z., & Bernheimer, L. P. (1989). The social construction of ecocultural niches: Family accommodation of developmentally delayed children. *American Journal on Mental Retardation*, 94, 216–230.

Gavidia-Payne, S., & Stoneman, Z. (1997). Family predictors of maternal and paternal involvement in programs for young children with disabilities. *Child Development*, 68, 701–717.

Georgieff, M. K., & Rao, R. (1999). The role of nutrition in cognitive development. In C. A. Nelson & M. Luciana (Eds.), *Handbook of developmental cognitive neuroscience*. Cambridge, MA: MIT Press.

Goffman, E. (1963). *Stigma*. Englewood Cliffs, NJ: Prentice-Hall.

Gorman, K. S. (1995). Malnutrition and cognitive development: Evidence from experimental/quasi-experimental studies among the mild-to-moderately malnourished. *Journal of Nutrition*, 125, 2239S–2244S.

Guralnick, M. J. (Ed.). (1997). *The effectiveness of early intervention*. Baltimore: Brookes.

Guralnick, M. J. (1998). The effectiveness of early intervention for vulnerable children: A developmental perspective. *American Journal on Mental Retardation*, 102, 319–345.

Guralnick, M. J. (2000). The early intervention system and out-of-home child care. In D. Cryer & T. Harms (Eds.), Infants and toddlers in out-of-home care (pp. 207–234). Baltimore: Brookes.

Guralnick, M. J. (2001). A developmental systems model for early intervention. Infants and Young Children, 14(2), 1–18.

Guralnick, M. J. (2002). Les jeunes enfants trisomiques 21 dans leurs relations avec des pairs: Caractéristiques de développement et interventions envisageables [The peer relations of young children with Down syndrome: Developmental characteristics and intervention approaches]. Journal de la Trisomie, 21(4), 18–27.

Guralnick, M. J. (Ed.). (in press). A developmental systems approach to early intervention: National and international perspectives. Baltimore, MD: Paul H. Brookes.

Harbin, G. L., McWilliam, R. A., & Gallagher, J. J. (2000). Services for young children with disabilities and their families. In J. P. Shonkoff & S. J. Meisels (Eds.), Handbook of early childhood intervention (2nd ed., pp. 387–415). New York: Cambridge University Press.

Hebbeler. K., Wagner, M., Spiker, D., Scarborough, A., Simeonsson, R., & Collier, M. (2001). National Early Intervention Longitudinal Study (NEILS): A first look at the characteristics of children and families entering early intervention services. Menlo Park, CA: SRI International.

Kellegrew, D. H. (2000). Constructing daily routines: A qualitative examination of mothers with young children with disabilities. American Journal of Occupational Therapy, 54, 252–259.

Kelly, J. F., & Booth, C. L. (2002). The early child care study of children with special needs. In L. M. Glidden (Ed.), International review of research in mental retardation (Vol. 25, pp. 71–106). San Diego: Academic Press.

Kochanek, T. T., McGinn, J., & Cummins, C. (1998). Beyond early intervention: Utilization of community resources and supports by families with young children with disabilities. Providence, RI: Early Childhood Research Institute, Rhode Island College.

Krauss, M. W., Upshur, C. C., Shonkoff, J. P., & Hauser-Cram, P. (1993). The impact of parent groups on mothers of infants with disabilities. Journal of Early Intervention, 16, 8–20.

Ladd, G. W., Profilet, S. M., & Hart, C. H. (1992). Parents' management of children's peer relations: Facilitating and supervising children's activities in the peer culture. In R. D. Parke & G. W. Ladd (Eds.), Family–peer relationships: Modes of linkage (pp. 215–253). Hillsdale, NJ: Lawrence Erlbaum Associates.

Landry, S. H., Smith, K. E., Swank, P. R., Assel, M. A., & Vellet, S. (2001). Does early responsive parenting have a special importance for children's development or is consistency across early childhood necessary? Developmental Psychology, 37, 387–403.

Landry, S. H., Smith, K. E., Swank, & Miller-Loncar, C. L. (2000). Early maternal and child influences on children's later independent cognitive and social functioning. Child Development, 71, 358–375.

Mahoney, G., & Filer, J. (1996). How responsive is early intervention to the priorities and needs of families? Topics in Early Childhood Special Education, 16, 437–457.

National Research Council and Institute of Medicine. (2000). From neurons to neighborhoods: The science of early child development. Committee on Integrating the Science of Early Childhood Development. J. P. Shonkoff & D. A. Phillips (Eds.), Board on Children, Youth, and Families, Commission on Behavioral and Social Sciences and Education. Washington, DC: National Academy Press.

NICHD Early Child Care Research Network (2001). Nonmaternal care and family factors in early development: An overview of the National Institute of Child Health and Human Development (NICHD) Study of Early Child Care. *Applied Developmental Psychology, 22*, 457–492.

O'Brien, M. (1997). *Inclusive child care for infants and toddlers: Meeting individual and special needs.* Baltimore, MD: Brookes.

O'Brien, M. (2001). Inclusive child care for infants and toddlers: A natural environment for all children. In M. J. Guralnick (Ed.), *Early childhood inclusion: Focus on change* (pp. 229–251). Baltimore, MD: Paul H. Brookes.

Osofsky, J. D. (1995). The effects of violence exposure on young children. *American Psychologist, 50*, 782–788.

Pianta, R. C., Marvin, R. S., Britner, P. A., & Borowitz, K. C. (1996). Mothers' resolution of their children's diagnosis: Organized patterns of caregiving representations. *Journal of Infant Mental Health, 17*, 239–256.

Roach, M. A., Orsmond, G. I., & Barratt, M. S. (1999). Mothers and fathers of children with Down syndrome: Parental stress and involvement in childcare. *American Journal on Mental Retardation, 104*, 422–436.

Sameroff, A. J. (1993). Models of development and developmental risk. In C. H. Zeanah, Jr. (Ed.), *Handbook of infant mental health* (pp. 3–13). New York: Guilford.

Sameroff, A. J., Seifer, R., Barocas, R., Zax, M., & Greenspan, S. (1987). Intelligence quotient scores of 4-year-old children: social–environmental risk factors. *Pediatrics, 79*, 343–350.

Santelli, B., Turnbull, A., Sergeant, J., Lerner, E. P., & Marquis, J. G. (1996). Parent to parent programs: Parent preferences for supports. *Infants and Young Children, 9*(1), 53–62.

Shonkoff, J. P., & Hauser-Cram, P. (1987). Early intervention for disabled infants and their families: A quantitative analysis. *Pediatrics, 80*, 650–658.

Shonkoff, J. P., Hauser-Cram, P., Krauss, M. W., & Upshur, C. C. (1992). Development of infants with disabilities and their families. *Monographs of the Society for Research in Child Development, 57*(6), Serial no. 230.

Shonkoff, J.P., & Meisels, S. M. (Eds.). (2000). *Handbook of early childhood intervention* (2nd ed.). Cambridge: Cambridge University Press.

Spiker, D., Boyce, G. C., & Boyce, L. K. (2002). Parent–child interactions when young children have disabilities. In L. M. Glidden (Ed.), *International review of research in mental retardation* (Vol. 25, pp. 35–70). San Diego: Academic Press.

Spiker, D., Hebbeler, K., Wagner, M., Cameto, R., & McKenna, P. (2000). A framework for describing variations in state early intervention systems. *Topics in Early Childhood Special Education, 20*, 195–207.

Wachs, T. D. (1992). *The nature of nurture.* Newbury Park, CA: Sage.

Warfield, M. E., & Hauser-Cram, P. (1996). Child care needs, arrangements, and satisfaction of mothers of children with developmental disabilities. *Mental Retardation, 34*, 294–302.

Weisner, T. S. (1984). Ecocultural niches of middle childhood: A cross-cultural perspective. In W. A. Collins (Ed.), *Development during middle childhood: The years from six to twelve* (pp. 335–369). Washington, DC: National Academy of Sciences Press.

Wesley, P. W. (1994). Innovative practices: Providing on-site consultation to promote quality in integrated child care programs. *Journal of Early Intervention, 18*, 391–402.

6

Investments in Children Among Immigrant Families

Andrew J. Fuligni
University of California, Los Angeles

Hirokazu Yoshikawa
New York University

As a result of the dramatic increase in immigration since the 1965 Immigration Act, approximately one in five American children has at least one foreign-born parent, and this proportion is expected to rise in the coming decades (Hernandez & Charney, 1998). Given the increasing prominence of immigrant families and the many challenges that they and their children face in adapting to American society, it is important to study the pattern of family investments in children among this group of families. Understanding the pattern in this rapidly growing segment of the population is critical not only to our understanding of the immigrant population itself, but also to our understanding of parental investment within particular ethnic groups that are predominantly immigrants, such as Latin Americans and Asians. It has been estimated that as many as 60% of Latin American children and more than 90% of Asian American children in the United States hail from immigrant families (Rumbaut, in press). Ethnic variations in parental investments across these groups, therefore, may be due to their status as immigrants in addition to other factors traditionally associated with ethnicity, such as socioeconomic background or cultural beliefs and values.

Immigrant families represent an interesting case study through which we can examine the intersection of cultural, socioeconomic, and structural factors that shape the portfolios of families' investments in their children. We consider a range of investments, including education, time use, parenting, and participation in programs and policies that may increase family income and benefit children directly, including childcare subsidy use, cash, and in-kind assistance. Immigrant families often hail from societies whose cultures differ radically from American society in social norms and economic systems. The families are diverse in their educational levels, wealth, and occupational skills. Immigrants are even more socioeconomically diverse than the American-born population, with the population of foreign-born adults equally likely to have received 4-year and postgraduate degrees and less likely to have graduated from high school than American-born adults (Schmidley & Gibson, 1999). Finally, immigrant families must contend with a sometimes bewildering and constantly changing set of rules and regulations regarding their access to social institutions and public assistance (Zimmerman & Tumlin, 1999).

This chapter considers three questions regarding the investment behaviors of immigrant parents: What economic, cultural, and developmental theories of investment behaviors may be relevant to immigrant families? What are investment behaviors of immigrant parents that may be most important in influencing their children's adjustment and well-being? What factors predict investment behaviors among immigrant parents?

The discussion is organized around the unique characteristics of immigrant families that may help to explain patterns of parental investments. Throughout the chapter, we consider how investment behaviors, their determinants, and their consequences for child well-being may differ for immigrant and nonimmigrant families in the United States, and between immigrant groups. The chapter closes with a discussion of future research directions and how the evidence on investment behaviors among immigrant families may challenge prevailing theories of investment behaviors.

Although research on immigrant families has increased dramatically in the past decade, the field is still developing, and there is currently less knowledge about parental investments in these families than in American-born families. Most of the research within the field of immigration studies has focused on the economic incorporation of adult immigrants, with less attention paid to the adjustment of their children. This has changed in recent years, and a better picture of the adaptation and development of these children is gradually emerging. However, even this literature has tended to focus on the outcomes of children and not the processes that may lead to those outcomes. Therefore, there are significantly fewer systematic assessments of investment behaviors among immigrant parents than American-born parents. This chapter reports findings on the actual investment behaviors of parents when they are available. In the absence of such data, the chapter describes these behaviors based on inferences from the available evidence. In these cases, descriptions await confirmation from analyses of future data sets that will directly examine such behaviors.

ECONOMIC, CULTURAL, AND DEVELOPMENTAL THEORIES OF INVESTMENT BEHAVIORS

Economic Theories

Among economic theories of household investments in children, the most prominent is Becker's (1991) human capital theory, which applied neoclassical economic theory to families. The general model states that parents' utility (satisfaction) over the course of their children's development is determined by the parents' consumption, the adult earnings of each child, and the sum of their gifts and bequests to each child. The adult earnings of each child, in turn, are determined by human capital investments in the child and endowments, which are defined as all child characteristics that are determined prior to the process of human capital investment. The model proceeds under several assumptions, including that parents engage in consensus investment behavior, that they are altruistic, that the utility of individuals (e.g., parents) cannot be compared, and that children's independent economic behavior (defined by income generation and consumption), even if purely selfish, can be directed toward the overall well-being of the family by parents.

Although the assumptions of consensus between parents and of altruism as their motive for investing in children may be questioned, the key insight into the model is that parents invest in the human capital of their children to increase the parents' happiness. The parents will invest more when the return to these human capital investments (in terms of the parents' happiness) is higher. What determines the level of parental investments in children in this model? One obvious determinant is the level of parental wealth. Parents with insufficient wealth (or even less than very high levels of resources) often do not invest in their children's human capital as much as parents with more wealth. There is no evidence to date to suggest that this pattern is different among immigrant families in the United States; however, few studies have been conducted examining differences between immigrant and U.S.-born families in economic investments in children. Immigrant parents, on average, are poorer and less educated according to U.S. standards than U.S.-born parents; although this may suggest overall lower levels of parental investments in children among immigrant parents, many other factors (reviewed later in this chapter) may affect investments among different immigrant groups.

Parents may also invest differently across their children, a finding that could not be explained by differences in family wealth. Differences within household may be explained by differences in children's expected returns to investments. For example, cultures appear to vary in the extent to which parents with limited resources favor sons over daughters in their investments in health and human capital (Lundberg and Rose, chapter 7 in this volume). Behrman (1988) found that in rural India, parents divided nutrition equally among children who differed in sex and birth order during the surplus season, whereas during the lean season, they favored older children and sons based on cultural expectations regarding adult sons' greater economic contributions to their families compared with daughters. Because this difference in investments across children occurs only in the lean season, it suggests that both the overall level of family resources and differences across children in expected returns to investment are important determinants of parental investments.

Critiques of this theory have pointed out that assumptions of human capital theory are questionable (Behrman, 1997; England & Budig, 1998; Folbre, 1994, 2001). Parents, for example, may not engage in consensus behavior or altruism. The prevalence of domestic violence across cultures, for example, may challenge both (England & Budig, 1998). Parents may not derive the same levels of utility from a marriage owing to factors such as unequal power and unequal resources; this suggests that comparisons of utility across household members are important to investigate. However, alternative human capital models of investment in children based on bargaining or game theory address some of the shortcomings of Becker's model without changing its key insight. These models proceed from the assumption that household members may have conflicting as well as consensus interests. Each individual may pursue his or her own utility, including investments, in the absence of agreement (Lundberg & Pollak, 1993; McElroy & Horney, 1981). Resources under a particular household member's control can be either shared or withheld from other members. There is evidence from both the United States and developing countries, for example, that assets and unearned income under the control of mothers is more likely to be spent on children's health and well-being (e.g., nutrition, children's clothing) than similar resources under the control of fathers (Case, Lubotsky, & Paxson, 2002; see also Lundberg & Rose, chapter 7 in this volume).

Patterns appear to be stronger in developing countries, where households have very low levels of resources. This suggests that parents do not invest equally in children, and that this imbalance may differ by nativity (Quisumbing & Maluccio, 2000; Thomas, 1990, 1994). Given that immigrants as a whole have lower levels of wealth than U.S.-born parents, this pattern may hold for immigrant parents in the United States; however, there have been no studies investigating such patterns of intrahousehold allocation among particular immigrant groups. Research on these bargaining models focuses almost exclusively on levels of consensus between parents; much of the psychological and developmental literature on children of immigrant parents, in contrast, focuses on conflicts between children and parents. Some of these conflicts may be about behaviors that contribute to household income (this is discussed more fully later in the chapter).

Cultural and Developmental Theories

Cultural and developmental models of parenting and parental investments have focused mainly on the socialization goals and parenting behaviors of parents. Parental goals are generally believed to be determined by the social and economic structure of a society, and parental behaviors and investments toward their children are expected to support these goals. Levine (1974), a cultural anthropologist, suggested a popular model that consists of a hierarchy of universal parental goals:

> (1) the physical survival and health of the child ..., (2) the development of the child's behavioral capacity for economic self-maintenance in maturity, and (3) the development of the child's behavioral capacities for maximizing other cultural values—e.g., morality, prestige, wealth, religious piety, intellectual achievement, personal satisfaction, self-realization—as formulated and symbolically elaborated in culturally distinctive beliefs, norms, and ideologies. (p. 230)

In addition to being developmentally ordered, with the earlier goals being pursued at younger stages in children's lives, these parental goals are assumed to be sensitive to the health risk and subsistence level of a family and society. Parental goals will remain at earlier levels if such goals are perceived by parents to be threatened, and later goals will only be emphasized to the extent that the earlier ones can be achieved. The hazards, demands, and opportunities of a society's social environment act as constraints on the parents' goals, and the strategies for survival that have existed within that society will be encoded as customs and traditions of childrearing.

Other well-known models of parental goals have been offered (e.g., Hoffman & Hoffman, 1973; Kohn, 1963), but Levine's model shares many of the same features of the others and is well-suited to discussions of the parental investments of immigrant families. In particular, three features of the model suggest ways to organize and understand the parenting behaviors of immigrant families. First, the goal of "developing the child's capacity for economic self-maintenance in maturity" is believed to be the primary goal of parents in a society with relatively scarce resources for subsistence, or in a position within a society that is not perceived to promise a secure economic future. Given their status as newcomers in American society, it is reasonable to assume that immigrant parents will focus on establishing economic security for their families in the present and for their children in the future. The investment behaviors of immigrant parents, therefore, should be focused on activities that they believe will help their children attain that goal and on avoiding behaviors that might threaten that goal.

Second, childrearing customs develop within societies to address chronic demands and opportunities over the generations. These customs come to be imbued with ethical and moral dimensions, which further perpetuate those customs even when the initial, precipitating conditions no longer exist. Many immigrant families originate from societies that still depend on the economic contribution of children to the household, and the socialization strategies of parents emphasize the child's membership in an interdependent network of family members. Given the moral elements of this emphasis on familial interdependence, such an orientation is likely to be evident among immigrant families in the United States and is one that could shape the nature of their investments in their children. Third, the ability of parents to meet their childrearing goals within a particular society depends on the parents' level of cultural knowledge. Native members of society have greater access to such knowledge. Therefore, it is possible that the investment behaviors of immigrant parents are constrained by their relative lack of cultural knowledge, and that they may engage in unique behaviors to meet their childrearing goals.

Developmental theories have also focused on the parenting styles within families. A dominant theory has been that authoritative parenting—a combination of parental guidance, emotional support, and the participation of children in family decisionmaking—is the most conducive to educational success and advantageous social behavior among children (Steinberg, Mounts, Lamborn, & Dornbusch, 1991). Recent studies, however, have suggested that the educational payoff from authoritative parenting may be greatest for American-born families with European backgrounds; the link is less evident among cultural groups that traditionally place a greater emphasis on parental control and obedience among children. The link, for example, is virtually nonexistent among some Asian immigrant groups (Chao, 2001; Steinberg et al., 1991). These results suggest that some traditional developmental theories of effective parenting may not apply to some immigrant groups.

UNIQUE CHARACTERISTICS AND INVESTMENT BEHAVIORS OF IMMIGRANT FAMILIES

At a general level, it can be assumed that immigrant parents share many of the same basic goals for their children as American-born parents. Foreign-born parents want to raise healthy, well-adjusted, intelligent children who can become productive adults. Nevertheless, there are some unique characteristics of immigrant families that can affect their investments. Immigrant families are unique in many ways; a small set of characteristics that may influence their investment behaviors is the focus here.

Immigration as a Family Investment

Perhaps the most distinguishing characteristic of immigrant families is that they have already made a major investment in their children, either directly or indirectly, through the act of immigration. Immigration is a major investment itself; immigrant parents often come to this country to provide their families with a better life (Caplan, Choy, & Whitmore, 1991; Gibson & Bhachu, 1991; Suárez-Orozco & Suárez-Orozco, 1995; Zhou & Bankston, 1998). Parents often view immigration as an investment that can directly affect children through better schools, better opportunity for economic advancement, and the avoidance of poverty, war, conscription, and other aspects of their native society perceived to be harmful to their children. One Nicaraguan mother said to Suárez-Orozco (1991), "We came here for them, so that they may become somebody tomorrow," suggesting that many immigrant parents see the possibility for a higher return on their children's abilities and skills in the United States than in their home countries.

Immigration can also be an indirect investment in children through the perception that better occupational and economic prospects await the parents in the United States (Portes & Rumbaut, 1996). It is difficult to think of a more substantial investment than one that involves leaving extended family and community ties and entering what can be a radically different and unfamiliar society. Parents within the United States may migrate to other areas of the country for similar reasons, but as challenging as those moves may be, they are not likely to be as dramatic as a move to another country.

Given the magnitude of the act of immigration, paying attention only to the actions of immigrant parents while here in the United States and comparing them with American-born parents may underestimate the amount of investment these families have already made in their children's potential. Neither economic nor cultural/developmental theories of family investment have examined international migration as an investment in children's education, per se. Economic theories, whether neoclassical or more recent variants, tend to emphasize individuals' or households' efforts to maximize absolute or relative income across labor markets, rather than opportunities for children's human capital development (Massey, 1999). The role of opportunities for children in the decision to emigrate is potentially an important area for research, one that would extend to studies of American-born parents' decisions to migrate to different neighborhoods or regions of the country for the sake of their children.

In addition to being an investment in itself, the act of immigration can affect the nature of the goals and behaviors of immigrant parents toward their children in a number of ways. For example, immigrant families generally feel less secure about the stability of their position in their new country because of their status as newcomers (Caplan et al., 1991; Gibson & Bhachu, 1991). Immigrant families, therefore, emphasize the development of instrumental skills and credentials that will ensure economic stability for their families and children.

Educational opportunities are often cited by immigrant families in both qualitative and quantitative research as a reason for their emigration to the United States. Education is seen by many as the key route to future economic success for their children, and their optimism toward American society leads them to believe that there will be higher returns from educational attainment than do American-born parents, particularly American-born parents in ethnic minority families (Portes & Rumbaut, 1996). Most studies that have compared immigrant and U.S.-born attitudes toward education find greater emphasis on educational success and higher aspirations for educational attainment among immigrant parents (Fuligni, 1997; Kao & Tienda, 1995; Suárez-Orozco & Suárez-Orozco, 1995).

This emphasis on education in immigrant families may be based on the perceived usefulness of schooling and educational credentials for occupational mobility and economic success, rather than a more abstract, humanistic value of education for self-exploration and improvement. As a Vietnamese refugee mother explained to Caplan et al. (1991, p. 116), "According to our culture, a well-educated person always gets respect, even when not rich. But this country is different; education goes along with the wealth. I would like my children to be well educated, both to be respected in our community and also to get a high position in this society." The emphasis on the economic usefulness of education can also be seen in the type of postsecondary majors and degrees toward which immigrant parents direct their children. On average, children from immigrant families are more likely to pursue technical and business degrees that have a clearer link to future jobs than degrees in the social sciences and humanities (Tseng, 2001). These students often cite parental emphasis on obtaining stable, well-paying occupations as one of their primary reasons for pursuing such courses of study. As another Vietnamese refugee noted to Caplan et al. (1991):

> I think that education is very important to everyone. It is the most important thing to us, the refugees .... I talk to my children about the hard life without a good career and a high education ... only a good education can help us to get out and get up higher and higher. (p. 120)

There is, however, variability between immigrant groups in the value of schooling. Parents from Asian countries generally place more value on studying and doing well in school than their counterparts from Latin American countries (although even within groups there is substantial variability; for example, Chinese immigrant parents tend to place a more consistently strong value on education than parents from the Philippines; Fuligni, 1997; Kao & Tienda, 1995). In contrast to the differences between immigrant and American-born parents, the variation between immigrant groups tends to be largely due to the socioeconomic background of the parents. For example, parents from Asian countries tend to have higher levels of education and income than those from Latin American countries. The socioeconomic differences between the immigrant populations are very large, even larger than the differences among the American-born population, and this variability is a significant reason for differences in parental educational values and investments by national origin (Fuligni, 1997, 1998).

The act of immigration also may influence parental goals and behaviors toward their children by creating the need to realize that initial investment and by avoiding activities that may threaten that investment. In terms of education, the importance of that initial investment appears to lead to considerable fear of what could happen if school success were not achieved. Most parents, regardless of immigration status, believe that schooling can enhance their children's occupational and economic potential. Yet immigrant parents are more likely to believe that not doing well in school can severely damage their children's economic potential, and by extension, lessen one of the primary returns to immigration. Simply put, immigrant parents tend to believe a lot more is riding on their children's educational success than do American parents because academic failure can also mean that the initial investment of immigration would be less of a success. This, in turn, results in an especially powerful desire among children from immigrant families to persist educationally despite the many challenges that they may face, such as having lower family resources and attending poorer schools (Hernandez & Charney, 1998). In fact, the tendency for immigrant parents and their children to have higher educational aspirations than their American-born counterparts often becomes more pronounced after controlling for factors such as parental education and family income, suggesting that immigrant families place a greater value on educational success than would be predicted from their levels of human and financial capital (e.g., Kao & Tienda, 1995).

The importance of the initial investment of immigration also may shape parental response to children's problem behaviors. The concern with avoiding activities that could threaten the ability of the family to stay in the country is one reason for the remarkably low levels of problem behavior among children from immigrant families. Adolescents from immigrant families are less likely to use drugs and alcohol, to have had sex, and to engage in violent and delinquent behavior than those from U.S.-born families (Harris, 1999). The role of immigrant parents in helping their children avoid such problem behaviors is not well understood. One recent study of 317 Mexican immigrant families suggested that third-generation parents focused less on responsibility to the family in their parenting than their first- or second-generation peers (Buriel, 1993). Parents also seek to minimize their children's involvement in troublesome behavior by directing them to peers in their own community. In explaining such a strategy, a Sikh mother said to Gibson and Bhachu (1991, p. 77), "When our children get together with the White children, they start doing things that affect our family honor." In a Vietnamese community in New Orleans, youth who do not participate in the immigrant ethnic community and are not interested in their culture are considered to be the "bad kids" (Zhou & Bankston, 1998). Parental control over children's friendship choices, which have been related to lower levels of problem behavior in nonimmigrant populations, is an example of the kind of noneconomic investments that immigrant parents may make and that are generally overlooked in economic research on the family. In cultural and developmental research on the family, the particular forms that this control may take within immigrant families (e.g., directing children to co-ethnic peers) have been understudied.

Family Interdependence

Another unique feature of immigrant families that may influence investments in their children is the interdependence of goals for children and goals for the larger family. Most of the families that compose the current foreign-born population in the United States originated in societies with strong family traditions. For example, Latin American and Asian immigrants, who make up three quarters of the immigrant population (U.S. Bureau of Census, 2001), have often been characterized by their strong emphasis on the role of family members in assisting and supporting one another, and in respecting the authority of the larger family (Chilman, 1993; Ho, 1981; Shon & Ja, 1982). In addition, their status as newcomers and minorities makes family assistance immediately salient. Immigrant parents often know little about the workings of American society and frequently must accept occupations below their prior job levels because of a lack of education or an unwillingness of American employers to accept their foreign occupational credentials (Portes & Rumbaut, 1996). The cultural emphasis on family interdependence, along with the very real need for members to assist one another in a new society, could result in investments in their children that reflect the mutual dependence of the goals for their children and the larger family.

For example, a child's education is often seen as an investment for the entire family, not just the individual child (Fuligni & Tseng, 1999). This is due, in part, to the noted anticipated returns of the initial act of immigration, but also to the hope that educational success will enhance the ability of the child to provide financial support to the family during adulthood. Many immigrants come from societies in which children traditionally support their parents when the parents get older, and the perceived connection between education and economic success leads immigrant parents to see an investment in their children's educations as having potential returns for their well-being during old age.

Numerous ethnographies have highlighted how many children from immigrant families share this belief (Caplan et al., 1991; Gibson & Bhachu, 1991; Suárez-Orozco & Suárez-Orozco, 1995), and a recent study indicated that foreign-born children are more likely to financially support their families as young adults than are American-born children (Fuligni & Pedersen, 2002). Latin American and Filipino young adults are typically more likely than East Asian youth to support their parents, possibly because of the greater likelihood of East Asians to pursue postsecondary education on a full-time basis. It may be the case that the East Asian youth will also support their families financially on completion of their bachelor degrees.

The greater degree of interdependence among the members of immigrant families may also result in additional benefits from educational success. Family honor and respect are strong values in both the cultural background and the current enclaves and communities of immigrant families, and the success of a family's children is an important source of such honor (Caplan et al., 1991; Gibson & Bhachu, 1991; Suárez-Orozco & Suárez-Orozco, 1995).

Paradoxically, the emphasis on family interdependence among immigrants, especially for those with low incomes, can potentially compromise the educational investments if the family faces financial distress and needs the children to provide economic support. Suárez-Orozco and Suárez-Orozco (1995), in their ethnography of Latin American immigrant families, discussed how the immediate economic needs of the poorer families often required that children assist their families by working and in other ways that interfered with their schoolwork. This pattern is similar to that observed in developing countries, where children have been found to "pay back" their parents' investments in their health and well-being sooner in the life span through contributions to the household economy, rather than by staying in school to support parents later in life (Caldwell, 1982). In this case, pressing survival needs lead some immigrant parents to forgo some of their investments in the children's education. Such a negative effect of family interdependence on education likely occurs mainly for immigrant parents with low status and unstable occupations, and could be one reason for the tendency of immigrant Latin American students to have higher school drop-out rates than American-born Latin American students (McMillen, 1997).

Yet extremely high demands placed on students from immigrant families can interfere with academic achievement and educational attainment, regardless of the family's economic needs. In our own research, we have observed that adolescents with the strongest sense of obligation to support and assist the family tended to receive lower grades in school than their peers with a more moderate sense of obligation, who tended to attain the highest levels of achievement (Fuligni, Tseng, & Lam, 1999). This may be because of the actual demands associated with a tradition of family assistance and support. A recent study of college freshmen suggests that the everyday demands placed on immigrant students to help their families can erode some of the advantages from motivation and aspirations that family obligation accords these students; this highlights how family interdependence can act as a double-edged sword in its impact on educational attainment (Tseng, 2001). These findings challenge the expectation in human capital theory that economic consequences of altruistic (as well as selfish) behaviors of family members are distributed to family members such that all benefit. In the case of these immigrant families, the household income benefits contributed by children may be counterbalanced by negative effects on children's own human capital development (school achievement). The findings also fall outside the predictions of nonconsensus models, in that these negative effects on children could occur with parent consensus. The interesting question of whether children agree to or feel coerced to contribute to household income in contexts in which native-born peers are not often expected to contribute has rarely been explored systematically, although there is some suggestion that it can be a source of familial conflict in some segments of the immigrant population (Zhou, 1997).

Immigrant families often need to provide economic assistance to extended family in their native countries. The extent of remittances can be large and of economic significance to source countries. In a recent telephone survey of 1,000 Latino immigrants, 69% of respondents had sent remittances to their source country, averaging seven remittances per year. The average amount sent per remittance was $200 (Inter-American Development Bank, 2002). The researchers estimate that remittances from Latin American immigrants totals $15 billion a year.

There is little research on how such remittances affect parental investment in children's development. Most of the research on remittances focuses on the impact on the source country (Barham & Boucher, 1998; Jones, 1998). In many cases, remittances are sent by parents who have come to the United States alone or without all of their children, and some studies indicate that remittances are spent on children in the source country. For example, Conway and Cohen (1998) found that members of two groups of rural Mexican migrants—short term or cyclical, on the one hand, and long term, on the other—commonly sent home remittances to cover school expenses and other supports for their children. In some cases, the researchers found that the decision to migrate to the United States was driven by the need to pay for children's school and other expenses.

Research on remittances challenges economic and cultural theories of family investments in that it highlights the issue of investing in children who are not present in the household, or conversely, from parents who are not present in the household or country of residence of the children. For the most part, the scant data on remittances do not challenge assumptions of altruism inherent in some theories of family investments. However, the ways in which money is spent to support children's development may vary considerably in the U.S. community compared with the source country, even within the same kinship network. In addition, it may be important to investigate how remittances affect children's developmental outcomes in sending households as well as receiving households. It is reasonable to expect that remittances reduce financial investments in children who live in the United States.

Parental Knowledge About U.S. Society

Immigrant parents generally possess less knowledge about American society than American-born parents. Immigrant parents tend to have fewer English skills and to be less informed about American institutions such as schools and social services. For example, almost one half of those from Mexico, China, and El Salvador have poor knowledge of the English language (Stevens, 1994). Many ethnographies highlight how little immigrant parents know about the workings of American schools, including which courses their children should be taking in secondary school and how to assist their children with their schoolwork. They also know little about their eligibility for public assistance (Caplan et al., 1991; Gibson & Bhachu, 1991; Suárez-Orozco & Suárez-Orozco, 1995). The relative lack of cultural knowledge of immigrant parents could influence the nature of their investment in their children by making them less likely to participate in activities that require such knowledge, and more likely participate in activities that do not require such knowledge. They may also depend more on others who do have the knowledge. The activities and actions considered here are those that directly facilitate children's education, parents' employment and earnings, particularly as they differ across gender of the parent, and use of public assistance.

In their analyses of eighth-grade students in the National Educational Longitudinal Study (NELS:88), Kao and Tienda (1995) found that across different ethnic groups, immigrant parents were generally less likely to talk to their children about current school experiences and of their plans for high school and beyond. They were also more hesitant about joining parent–teacher organizations, volunteering at school, and attending school events. Immigrant parents were more likely, however, to attend parent–teacher meetings, to provide a place to study at home, to talk to their children's teachers, and to have visited their child's classes. Similar patterns of parental involvment were observed by Nord and Griffin (1999) in their analyses of 3- to 8-year-old children in the National Household Education Survey (NHES). Children of immigrant families were just as likely as those in American-born families to have parents who taught them letters, words, or numbers in the past week. They were also just as likely to have been told or been read a story in the past week. Children in immigrant families, however, were less likely to have visited a library or to have gone to a play, concert, or live show with a family member in the past month. Immigrant parents were also less likely to be highly involved in their children's school by volunteering and attending class events, but they were equally as likely to have attended regularly scheduled parent–teacher conferences.

Together, the results from the two national surveys suggest that immigrant parents attempt to support their children's education by engaging in activities in which they feel qualified and comfortable. As one Laotian mother said to Caplan et al. (1991, p. 112), "When I get home, I always ask my children about their homework and ask them to finish doing it. We don't know how to help them with their homework because we don't have enough education, but we always ask them to do their homework." In addition, the general emphasis on education is consistently stressed: "We talk to them very often, about once a week. We want to remind them about the importance of education" (p. 113).

Comparison of different groups of immigrants suggests that Asian immigrant parents are more likely to teach their children letters and numbers, read to their children, and take their children on educational outings compared with Latin American immigrant parents (Nord & Griffin, 1999). These variations likely stem from the large differences in parental education and family income between Asian and Latin American immigrant parents. Variations in parental education, income, and English language skills also produce important variations in the educational behaviors of immigrant parents within the same group (Louie, 2001).

The likelihood of participating in the labor force is also influenced by awareness of American society and its cultural norms. Gender distinctions in employment, for example, are more prevalent in some immigrant groups, although these gender norms may change as knowledge about American society and exposure to U.S. labor markets increase. Ethnographic studies of immigrant groups from multiple countries, such as the

Dominican Republic or Vietnam, find that households become less patriarchal and more egalitarian as women gain access to social and economic resources previously beyond their reach (Espiritu, 1997; Foner, 1999; Hondagneu-Sotelo, 1994; Pessar, 1987). The question of whether the earnings of immigrant women may benefit children more than those of immigrant men has not been explored.

The relative lack of information about American institutions could also be a cause of relatively lower use, after controlling for socioeconomic background, of educational programs and social assistance among immigrant families for their children. Results from the NHES analyses (Nord & Griffin, 1999) indicate that children of immigrant parents who are not yet enrolled in kindergarten or elementary school are less likely to be enrolled in some type of early childhood program than children of American-born parents. In addition, poor children of immigrants are less likely than poor children of American-born parents to attend Head Start. It is possible that the lower use of preschool programs by immigrant parents stems from a lack of knowledge about the existence and eligibility requirements of these services, as well as fear of being noticed by authorities. School enrollment decisions during early elementary school are similar among immigrant and American-born parents, with the same proportion of children in each group attending the public schools assigned to them, public schools of their parents' choice, and private religious and secular schools. Comparing immigrant groups, Asian and Latin American parents are equally likely to enroll their children in early childhood and Head Start programs (Nord & Griffin, 1999). Asian immigrant parents, who have higher incomes, are more likely than Latin American immigrant parents to send their children to private elementary schools, suggesting that children from Asian immigrant families may benefit over the long term from their parents' ability to choose against a lower quality public school if that is the only public school choice available to the parents.

Turning to means-tested government programs, immigrant families have lower rates of use than native families, once indicators of human capital are controlled. Hofferth (1999), analyzing the Panel Study of Income Dynamics for 1990–1992, examined the use of Aid to Families with Dependent Children (AFDC), Supplemental Security Income (SSI), other welfare (General Assistance and miscellaneous state assistance), Medicaid, Food Stamps, heating assistance, and housing assistance (rent subsidies or public housing) among Mexican and Cuban immigrants. Immigrant Mexican families were less likely to receive AFDC and SSI than American-born families with Mexican backgrounds, after controlling for poverty status, region of residence, and other demographic factors. Immigrant Mexican families were even less likely to receive AFDC and SSI than American-born Whites. They were also generally less likely to use other forms of assistance, after controlling for socioeconomic and demographic factors, except for housing assistance. American-born Mexican families, in contrast, were more likely than American-born Whites to receive AFDC and SSI.

Cuban immigrant families were generally more likely than American-born Cuban families and White families to receive most forms of assistance. Hofferth (1999) attributed the findings among immigrant Mexican families to "less legal eligibility, fear of discovery among undocumented immigrants, or to a greater work ethic" and the findings among Cubans to their official status as refugees, which grants them more accessible eligibility for assistance programs.

In a study using the Survey of Income and Program Participation, Brandon and Tausky (2000), like Hofferth (1999), found that immigrant families were less likely to use AFDC and Food Stamps than American-born Whites with American-born parents, controlling for family income and other demographic factors. However, this varied by time in the United States. The authors found that first-generation Asians and Mexicans were more likely than native-born Whites with native-born parents to use public assistance. By the third generation, as in Hofferth's (1999) data, Mexicans were more likely to use AFDC, Food Stamps, and Medicaid than native-born Whites with native-born parents, whereas Western European, Eastern European, and Asian immigrants were generally less likely to use these programs. Puerto Ricans and African Americans were more likely than native-born Whites to use the full range of assistance programs, whereas Cubans overall were no more (or less) likely to use them. Finally, Brandon and Tausky (2000) found that the foreign born who emigrated before 1970 were less likely to use public assistance than those who emigrated in the 1970s or 1980s. This evidence corroborates work by Borjas and Hilton (1996) that levels of human capital have declined among successive cohorts of immigrants during those decades.

Large declines in immigrants' use of means-tested programs have occurred since passage of the Personal Responsibility and Work Opportunity Reconciliation Act in 1996. Using the 1995 and 2000 Current Population Survey, Fix and Passel (2002) found large declines between 1994 and 1999 in legal immigrants' use of programs for low-income families (declines of 60% for Temporary Assistance for Need Families (TANF), 48% for Food Stamps, 32% for SSI, and 15% for Medicaid). By 1999, low-income legal immigrant families had lower rates of TANF and Food Stamps use (although not for Medicaid) than their low-income citizen counterparts. These declines were not accounted for by increased naturalization or rising incomes among immigrant families. However, it is impossible to disentangle the influence of welfare reform legislation from improvements in the economy or other factors on these declines. Little strong causal evidence exists linking the law to these patterns of use.

These data on public assistance do not reveal the decision-making process that immigrant parents use in determining whether to apply for public assistance. We therefore know little about the perceptions of immigrant parents regarding the extent to which public assistance programs might help their children, whether they view decisions about public assistance as part of their investments in their children's development, or how such decisions are made within families.

IMPLICATIONS OF THE FINDINGS

The research to date suggests that the unique investment behaviors in children among immigrant families have their roots in the families' cultural backgrounds, socioeconomic standing, and the structure and politics of public assistance in American society. Immigrant parents, regardless of their country of origin, appear to view their entrance into American society as an investment in and of itself, and they place a particularly strong emphasis on education in developing their children's potential in order to realize that initial investment. The specific educational and public assistance behaviors of immigrant families result from complex interactions among culture, socioeconomics, and the rules regarding social assistance. For example, the cultural emphasis on family interdependence appears to interact with the socioeconomic standing of immigrant families in determining whether they invest in education as a route to the family's future economic success, or whether they need their children's more immediate assistance to support the family. Socioeconomic background appears to be a better explanation of variations among immigrants themselves than of differences between immigrant and American-born families. Finally, the structure and political climate of public assistance in American society appears to explain both variations in the use of such assistance among immigrant groups (e.g., refugees versus others) and lower use, compared with nonimmigrants, of AFDC and SSI, the latter because of confusion over eligibility and fear of official harassment and prosecution.

This section discusses the implications of these findings for intervention with immigrant families, for existing theories of parental investment, and for future research on this unique and rapidly growing group of American families.

Implications for Theories of Investment Behaviors

What Are the Investments, and What Child Outcomes Do They Support?

Some of the data reviewed suggest that immigrant parents attempt to prevent their children from engaging in problem behaviors by controlling friendships (e.g., directing children toward co-ethnic peers and away from peers of other groups). Such parenting behaviors are rarely investigated in economic studies of family investments in children, or in the developmental literature. In addition, these findings suggest that some immigrant parents may view problem behaviors as an impediment to economic and educational success. Although this aligns with much of the developmental literature linking socioemotional outcomes with cognitive and school outcomes, the prevailing economic theories of investment behaviors do not consider how human capital development is influenced by behaviors such as antisocial behavior, delinquency, early sexual activity, and substance use.

Who Makes Investments, and What Is the Decision Process Involved? As reviewed previously, human capital theories assume parental consensus in decisions about family investments in children. In contrast, bargaining models directly explore parental disagreements. Studies of immigrant families suggest, however, that parent–child conflict can often erupt concerning matters relevant to investment behaviors, such as obligations to contribute to the household income, to help parents navigate government agencies, and other family demands. The role of intergenerational conflict in influencing investment behaviors is neglected by both human capital and bargaining models. In addition, gender norms regarding who invests in children in families may change with immigration. The evidence reviewed suggests that for some immigrant families, gender norms regarding women's work may change after emigrating. This may explain patterns of increased earnings among women in these families. If, as some economic studies suggest, women's assets and earnings are more likely to be spent on child expenses than are men's, child investments may rise as a result of immigration. Other studies reviewed found that children in immigrant families, especially low-income families, contribute directly to household income. These behaviors may influence family investment behaviors and child development in complex ways that neither economic nor developmental theories have elucidated.

What Are the Effects of Family Investment Behaviors in Countries of Origin Versus the United States? An important influence of the research on immigration has been to shift the level of analysis from the individual to the household, and from the household to the kinship network, in both countries of origins and host countries. Neoclassical economic theories, for example, tend to emphasize individual decision making concerning human capital investment. Developmental and cultural theories, although better at examining family-level influences, do not often assess them across international borders.

Implications for Future Research

This review suggests a number of areas for continued research into the investments in children of immigrants. First, there should be more direct assessments of actual parental behaviors across the years of childhood and adolescence. The value placed on the utility of education is clearly evident among immigrant parents and their children, but exactly how that value gets transmitted to children remains unclear. Future studies could focus on precisely what messages parents give their children and other strategies parents may employ to ensure that their children internalize the messages. Ethnographies suggest that immigrant parents sometimes refer to the sacrifices they have made to provide their children with American educational opportunities, as well as refer to their own low status occupations compared with what their children's futures can hold if they study hard and do well in school (Caplan et al., 1991; Gibson & Bhachu, 1991). Research should systematically assess these types of messages and examine their relative power in instilling a value of education.

Other behaviors that should be assessed include the amount of money immigrant parents spend on education-related activities, the use of private secondary schools and "choice" public schools, and their economic support of postsecondary education. As in much of the literature on family investments in children, there are surprisingly few studies that model the effects of expenditures on children on their well-being. For immigrant families, education expenditures should be routinely measured in developmental studies. Also not explored are the expenditures that immigrant families view as improving their children's future success. These perceptions may vary by ethnicity and immigrant status.

Second, the understanding of parental investments among immigrant families would also benefit from better analyses of the returns of such investments. Educational investments of immigrant parents appear to pay off during primary and secondary school, with students from immigrant families often doing just as well in school, if not better than, their peers from American-born families, and better than would be predicted from the immigrant families' socioeconomic background (Fuligni, 1997; Kao & Tienda, 1995). Less is currently known about the returns to postsecondary education because the children from the first large surge in immigration since 1965 are only just now entering young adulthood. Early results suggest that these students continue to do well in postsecondary school, attending 2- and 4- year colleges at rates similar to American-born students (Fuligni & Witkow, in press; Kaufman, Chavez, Lauen, & Carroll, 1998; Vernez & Abrahamse, 1996). It remains to be seen if the rates of attendance translate into similar patterns of attainment, and more will be known when results from ongoing longitudinal studies become available soon.

Similarly, it is important to examine the economic returns to education in relation to parents' original investments. Current research suggests that immigrants receive lower wages for the same levels of training than American-born workers, but it is difficult to apply those findings to the children of immigrants because the findings are largely based on adult immigrants who received their educational and occupational training elsewhere (Portes & Rumbaut, 1996). American employers are often reluctant to recognize foreign credentials, and immigrants who receive their postsecondary training in the United States earn more than those who receive their training in their home countries (Schoeni, McCarthy, & Vernez, 1996). Similarly, future work should focus on the extent to which children who receive a degree and subsequent employment support their parents financially. Recent studies have suggested that immigrants are more likely to financially support and live with their families of origin, and it remains to be seen if this finding holds with continued research (Fuligni & Pedersen, 2002; Goldscheider & Goldscheider, 1993).

Third, virtually nothing is known about intrafamily variations in parental investments, despite the significant interest within the study of family economics (e.g., Behrman, Pollack, & Taubman, 1995). Immigrant families present an interesting case to study some classic issues, such as the impact of gender on parental investments. In addition, many immigrant families come from societies in which boys are often more highly valued than girls (e.g., Behrman, 1988; Ho, 1981; Rosenzweig & Schultz, 1982). It would be interesting to see whether such a pattern entirely dissipates after immigration. Research suggests that the emphasis on education extends equally to boys and girls during primary and secondary school, and that, as in American-born families, girls tend to do better in school than boys (Fuligni, 1997). Traditional views toward girls' future options can create tension when these successful girls are deciding whether to attend college (e.g., Gibson & Bhachu, 1991), but it appears that immigrant girls follow the recent national trends of receiving postsecondary education at higher rates than boys (Fuligni & Witkow, in press; Kaufman et al., 1998). Nevertheless, these findings are largely based on individually based studies, and a better understanding of the dynamics of intrafamily allocations would benefit from a greater use of family-based studies among immigrant families.

Finally, it remains to be seen whether time spent in the United Status results in a change in the investment behaviors of parents toward their children such that immigrant parents begin to look more like American-born parents. The generational comparisons suggest that this may be the case, but generational differences are very weak tests of cultural change because they often compare different cohorts who enter the country under very different historical, political, and economic circumstances. Analyses of differences among the current population of immigrants by the year of arrival tend to yield conflicting results, but even this approach is limited because it does not assess true change. Complex longitudinal designs that study entire families and that control for birth order and children's age are required to examine the true effect that time spent in the United States may have on parental investments.

ACKNOWLEDGMENTS

The authors appreciate the support of the National Institute of Child Health and Human Development, the National Science Foundation, and the William T. Grant Foundation during the preparation of this chapter.

REFERENCES

Barham, B., & Boucher, S. (1998). Migration, remittances, and inequality: Estimating the net effects of migration on income distribution. *Journal of Development Economics*, *55*, 307–331.

Becker, G. S. (1991). *A treatise on the family*, (2nd ed.). Cambridge, MA: Harvard University Press.

Behrman, J. R. (1988). Nutrition, health, birth order, and seasonality: Intrahousehold allocation in rural India. *Journal of Development Economics*, *28*, 43–63.

Behrman, J. R. (1997). Intrahousehold distribution and the family. In M. R. Rosenzweig & O. Stark (Eds.), *Handbook of population and family economics* (Vol. 1A, pp. 125–187) New York: Elsevier.

Behrman, J. R., Pollak, R. A., & Taubman, P. (1995). The wealth model: Efficiency in education and equity in the family. In J. R. Behrman, R. A. Pollak, & P. Taubman (Eds.), *From parent to child: Intrahousehold allocations and intergenerational relations in the United States* (pp. 138–182) Chicago: University of Chicago Press.

Borjas, G. J., & Hilton, L. (1996). Immigration and the welfare state: Immigrant participation and means-tested entitlement programs. *Quarterly Journal of Economics*, *111*, 575–604.

Brandon, P., & Tausky, C. (2000). Public assistance receipt across immigrant generations. *Social Science Research*, *29*, 208–222.

Buriel, R. (1993). Childrearing orientations in Mexican American families. *Journal of Marriage and the Family*, *55*, 987–1000.

Caldwell, J. (1982). *The theory of fertility decline*. New York: Academic Press.

Caplan, N., Choy, M. H., & Whitmore, J. K. (1991). *Children of the boat people: A study of educational success*. Ann Arbor: University of Michigan Press.

Case, A., Lubotsky, D., & Paxson, C. (2002). Economic status and health in childhood: The origins of the gradient. *American Economic Review*, *92*, 1308–1334.

Chao, R. K. (2001). Extending research on the consequences of parenting style for Chinese Americans and European Americans. *Child Development*, *72*, 1832–1843.

Chilman, C. S. (1993). Hispanic families in the United States: Research perspectives. In H. P. McAdoo (Ed.), *Family ethnicity: Strength in diversity* (pp. 141–163). Newbury Park, CA: Sage.

Conway, D., & Cohen, J. H. (1998). Consequences of migration and remittances for Mexican transnational communities. *Economic Geography, 74,* 26–44.

England, P., & Budig, M. J. (1998). Gary Becker on the family: His genius, impact, and blind spots. In D. Clauson (Ed.), *Required reading: Sociology's most influential books* (pp. 95–111). Amherst, MA: University of Massachusetts Press.

Espiritu, Y. L. (1997). *Asian American women and men: Labor, laws, and love.* Thousand Oaks, CA: Sage.

Fix, M., & Passel, J. (2002). *The scope and impact of welfare reform's immigrant provisions.* Washington, DC: The Urban Institute.

Folbre, N. (1994). *Who pays for the kids? Gender and the structures of constraint.* New York: Routledge.

Folbre, N. (2001). *The production of people by means of people and the distribution of the costs of children.* Amherst, MA: University of Massachusetts Press.

Foner, N. (1999). The immigrant family: Cultural legacies and cultural changes. In C. Hirschman, P. Kasinitiz, & J. DeWind (Eds.), *The handbook of international migration: The American experience* (pp. 257–274). New York: Russell Sage Foundation.

Fuligni, A. J. (1997). The academic achievement of adolescents from immigrant families: The roles of family background, attitudes, and behavior. *Child Development, 68,* 261–273.

Fuligni, A. J. (1998). Adolescents from immigrant families. In V. McLoyd & L. Steinberg (Eds.), *Research on minority adolescents: Conceptual, theoretical, and methodological issues* (pp. 127–143). Hillsdale, NJ: Lawrence Erlbaum Associates.

Fuligni, A. J., & Pedersen, S. (2002). Family obligation and the transition to young adulthood. *Developmental Psychology, 38,* 856–868.

Fuligni, A. J., & Tseng, V. (1999). Family obligations and the achievement motivation of children from immigrant and American-born families. In T. Urdan (Ed.), *Advances in motivation and achievement* (pp. 159–184). Stamford, CT: JAI Press.

Fuligni, A. J., Tseng, V., & Lam, M. (1999). Attitudes toward family obligations among American adolescents from Asian, Latin American, and European backgrounds. *Child Development, 70,* 1030–1044.

Fuligni, A. J., & Witkow, M. (in press). The post-secondary educational progress of youths from immigrant families. *Journal of Research on Adolescence.*

Gibson, M. A., & Bhachu, P. K. (1991). The dynamics of educational decision making: A comparative study of Sikhs in Britain and the United States. In M. A. Gibson & J. U. Ogbu (Eds.), *Minority status and schooling: A comparative study of immigrant and involuntary minorities* (pp. 63–96). New York: Garland.

Goldscheider, F. K., & Goldscheider, C. (1993). *Leaving home before marriage: Ethnicity, familism, and generational relationships.* Madison: The University of Wisconsin Press.

Harris, K. M. (1999). The health status and risk behavior of adolescents in immigrant families. In D. J. Hernandez (Ed.), *Children of immigrants: Health, adjustment, and public assistance.* Washington, DC: National Academy Press.

Hernandez, D. J., & Charney, E. (1998). *From generation to generation: The health and well-being of children in immigrant families.* Washington, DC: National Academy Press.

Ho, D. Y. F. (1981). Traditional patterns of socialization in Chinese society. *Acta Psychologica Taiwanica, 23,* 81–95.

Hofferth, S. L. (1999). Receipt of public assistance by Mexican American and Cuban American children in native and immigrant families. In D. Hernandez (Ed.), *Children of immigrants: Health, adjustment, and public assistance* (pp. 546–583). Washington, DC: National Academy Press.

Hoffman, L. W., & Hoffman, M. L. (1973). The value of children to parents. In J. T. Fawcett (Ed.), *Psychological perspectives on fertility*. New York: Basic Books.

Hondagneu-Sotelo, P. (1994). *Gendered transitions: Mexican experiences of immigration._* Berkeley, CA: University of California Press.

Inter-American Development Bank (2002). *Survey of remittance senders: U.S. to Latin America*. Washington, DC: Inter-American Development Bank.

Jones, R.C. (1998). Remittances and inequality: A question of migration stage and geographic scale. *Economic Geography, 74*, 8–25.

Kao, G., & Tienda, M. (1995). Optimism and achievement: The educational performance of immigrant youth. *Social Science Quarterly, 76*, 1–19.

Kaufman, P., Chavez, L., Lauen, D., & Carroll, C. D. (1998). *Generational status and educational outcomes among Asian and Hispanic 1988 eighth graders*. NCES 1999–020. Washington, DC: U.S. Department of Education.

Kohn, M. L. (1963). Social class and parent–child relationships: An interpretation. *American Journal of Sociology, 68*, 471–480.

Levine, R. A. (1974). Parental goals: A cross-cultural view. *Teachers College Record, 76*, 226–239.

Louie, V. (2001). Parental aspirations and investment: The role of social class in the educational experiences of 1.5- and second generation Chinese Americans. *Harvard Educational Review, 71*, 438–474.

Lundberg, S. J., & Pollak, R. A. (1993). Separate spheres bargaining and the marriage market. *Journal of Political Economy, 6*, 988–1010.

Massey, D. S. (1999). Why does immigration occur? A theoretical synthesis. In C. Hirschman, P. Kasinitz, & J. DeWind (Eds.), *The handbook of international migration: The American experience* (pp. 34–52). New York: Russell Sage Foundation.

McElroy, M., & Horney, M. (1981). Nash-bargained household decisions: Toward a generalization of the theory of demand. *International Economic Review, 22*, 333–349.

McMillen, M. (1997). *Dropout rates in the United States: 1995*. Washington, DC: U.S. Government Printing Office.

Nord, C. W., & Griffin, J. A. (1999). Educational profile of 3- to 8-year-old children of immigrants. In D. Hernandez (Ed.), *Children of immigrants: Health, adjustment, and public assistance* (pp. 348–409). Washington, DC: National Academy Press.

Pessar, P. (1987). The Dominicans: Women in the household and the garment industry. In N. Foner (Ed.), *New immigrants in New York* (pp. 103–129). New York: Columbia University Press.

Portes, A., & Rumbaut, R. G. (1996). *Immigrant America: A portrait* (2nd ed.). Berkeley, CA: University of California Press.

Quisumbing, A. R., & Maluccio, J. A. (2000). *Intrahousehold allocation and gender relations: New empirical evidence from four developing countries*. FCND working paper no. 94. Washington, DC.: International Food Policy Research Institute.

Rosenzweig, M. R., & Schultz, T. P. (1982). Market opportunities, genetic endowments, and intrafamily resource distribution: Child survival in rural India. *American Economic Review, 72*, 803–815.

Rumbaut, R. G. (in press). Severed or sustained attachments? Language, identity, and imagined communities in the post-immigrant generation. In N. P. Levitt & M. C. Waters (Eds.), *Transnationalism and the second generation*. New York: Russell Sage Foundation.

Schmidley, A. D., & Gibson, C. (1999). *Profile of the foreign-born population in the United States: 1997*. U.S. Census Bureau Current Population Reports, Series P23–195. Washington, DC: U.S. Government Printing Office.

Schoeni, R. F., McCarthy, K. F., & Vernez, G. (1996). *The mixed economic progress of immigrants*. Santa Monica, CA: Rand Corporation.

Shon, S. P., & Ja, D. Y. (1982). Asian families. In M. McGoldrick, J. K. Pearce, & J. Giordano (Eds.), *Ethnicity and family therapy* (pp. 208–228). New York: Guilford.

Steinberg, L., Mounts, N. S., Lamborn, S. D., & Dornbusch, S. M. (1991). Authoritative parenting and adolescent adjustment across varied ecological niches. *Journal of Research on Adolescence, 1*, 19–36.

Stevens, G. (1994). Immigration, emigration, language acquisition, and the English proficiency of immigrants in the United States. In B. Edmonston & J. S. Passel (Eds.), *Immigration and ethnicity: The integration of America's newest immigrants* (pp. 163–187). Washington, DC: The Urban Institute Press.

Suárez-Orozco, C., & Suárez-Orozco, M. M. (1995). *Transformations: Immigration, family life, and achievement motivation among Latino adolescents*. Stanford, CA: Stanford University Press.

Suárez-Orozco, M. M. (1991). Immigrant adaptation to schooling: A Hispanic case. In M. A. Gibson & J. U. Ogbu (Eds.), *Minority status and schooling: A comparative study of immigrant and involuntary minorities* (pp. 37–62). New York: Garland.

Thomas, D. (1990). Intra-household resource allocation: An inferential approach. *Journal of Human Resources, 25*, 635-664.

Thomas, D. (1994). Like father, like son; like mother like daughter: Parental resources and child height. *Journal of Human Resources, 29*, 950–989.

Tseng, V. (2001). *Family as a context for immigrant adaptation: Family interdependence, academic adjustment, and course of study among youths from immigrant and U.S.-born families*. Unpublished dissertation, New York University.

U.S. Bureau of Census. (2001). *Current population reports: profile of the foreign-born population in the U.S.: 2000*. Washington, DC: U.S. Government Printing Office.

Vernez, G., & Abrahamse, A. (1996). *How immigrants fare in U.S. education*. Santa Monica, CA: Rand Corporation.

Zhou, M. (1997). Growing up American: The challenge confronting immigrant children and children of immigrants. *Annual Review of Sociology, 23*, 63–95.

Zhou, M., & Bankston, C. L. (1998). *Growing up American: How Vietnamese children adapt to life in the United States*. New York: Russell Sage Foundation.

Zimmerman, W., & Tumlin, K.C. (1999). *Patchwork policies: State assistance for immigrants under welfare reform*. Washington, DC: The Urban Institute.

7

Investments in Sons and Daughters
Evidence from the Consumer Expenditure Survey

Shelly Lundberg
Elaina Rose
University of Washington

Child gender has important and wide-ranging effects on parental behavior and family outcomes in the United States. Recent research finds that both marital and nonmarital relationships with sons are more stable than those with daughters (Katzev, Warner, & Acock, 1994; Lundberg & Rose, 2003), fathers are more involved with the family if they have sons (Morgan, Lye, & Condran, 1988; Harris & Morgan, 1991), and parents in families with sons tend to play more traditional roles than those with only daughters (Lundberg & Rose, 2002). These findings are consistent with the fact that sons, relative to daughters, increase the net benefits, or "marital surplus," that parents gain from marriage (relative to being single). In other words, the birth of a son reduces the probability of divorce and also increases the incentive of partners to invest further in the marriage or the family as a whole.

Differing investments in sons and daughters may be reflected in a gender bias in allocated resources, such as medical care or education. However, direct spending on investments in human capital is not the only way that parents influence their children's attainments. As Haveman and Wolfe (1995, p. 1832) noted, "[P]arents make a variety of ... choices such as fertility, location, and family stability that both influence the returns to productive efforts and directly affect the well-being of members of the family." Parental investments in family life, including time spent with their partner and children and expenditures on household public goods such as recreation, shelter, and community, will both benefit children directly and contribute to the stability of the family itself.

There has been little research on what is perhaps the most obvious indicator of differential investment in American families—expenditures on children and on household public goods by families with sons and daughters. Taubman (1991) found little evidence of differential treatment of children by gender in bequests, transfers, and educational attainment. Behrman, Pollak, and Taubman (1986) found that the slightly lower education levels of daughters in one sample are consistent with equal parental concern for sons and daughters if one considers future gender wage differentials in the investment response. However, little is known about other dimensions of household spending and their relation to child gender.

This chapter tests for differences in the expenditures of U.S. households with sons and daughters. Parental gender bias could result in differences in direct spending on boys and girls, or in greater spending on child goods (as opposed to adult goods) in families with sons rather than daughters. With most expenditure data, it is impossible to assign purchases to individuals, or even to adults and children, so this type of bias is difficult to test. Recent research suggests a different behavioral response to child gender: Sons increase marital surplus and therefore shift parental spending from consumption to investment. To test this hypothesis, we focus on family public goods, such as housing and durables, using samples from the Consumer Expenditure Survey (CEX) of married-couple families with a single child or with two same-sex children.

We find that housing expenditures are substantially and significantly higher for families with a son. Housing is the primary public good purchased by American families, and this finding is consistent with our hypothesis that sons increase marital surplus, and, thus, investments in family. There are no significant effects of child gender on purchases of other durables, such as automobiles and furniture, and the housing differential is not statistically significant for two-child families. We also find little evidence that child gender affects the allocation of spending between adults and children. The only other spending categories exhibiting child-gender differences are clothing and personal services. Higher expenditures on clothing by families with a daughter can be attributed to the preferences of boys and girls (or their parents), but it is puzzling that families with a boy spend nearly 10% more on barbers, beauty salons, and health clubs than do families with a girl. We speculate that this may reflect a greater transfer of marital surplus to mothers of boys, but more disaggregated expenditure data are required to provide a convincing test of this hypothesis.

CHILD GENDER AND FAMILY INVESTMENTS

A marked preference for sons in many parts of the developing world has been documented in an extensive literature on child gender and intra-household allocation. In large parts of Asia, and particularly South Asia, parental bias results in daughters receiving poorer nutrition and health care than sons (Behrman, 1988; Chen, Huq, & D'Souza, 1981). In several countries, biased sex ratios reflect gender-selective abortion, direct female infanticide, or extreme disadvantage in allocation of resources (Rose, 1999). This marked discrimination against daughters does not appear in wealthier societies, but child gender appears to influence a variety of family outcomes, including time use, the quality of relationships, and the stability of the household.

Several authors have reported that, in the United States, having a son relative to a daughter increases the likelihood that a marriage will remain intact (Katzev et al., 1994; Morgan et al., 1988; Mott, 1994; Spanier & Glick, 1981). Other researchers, using data from countries other than the United States, have failed to find significant child gender effects on divorce rates (Bracher, Santow, Morgan, & Trussell, 1993; Diekmann & Schmidheiny, 2002). Morgan and Pollard (2002) found that sons reduced the probability of divorce during the 1960–1979 period, but they also found that the child gender effect was "attenuated sharply" in later periods. Lundberg and Rose (2003) found that the birth of a son speeds the transition into marriage when the child is born before the mother's first marriage. On net, there appears to be substantial evidence from U.S. data that sons increase the stability of their parents' relationship, but the child gender effect may have declined in recent years. A decrease in the divorce rate gap between parents of boys and girls may have been caused by a change in gender preferences among more recent parents, or to changes in the selection of couples into marriage as nonmarital childbearing has increased. If parents of a boy are more likely to marry than parents of a girl (Lundberg & Rose, 2003), then married couples with girls may become more positively selected (relative to married couples with boys) as marriage rates fall.

The most striking documented difference between families with sons and those with only daughters is the extent and type of involvement of fathers. Fathers of boys tend to have stronger ties to the family than fathers of girls. Men spend more time with their sons (Yeung, Sandberg, Davis-Kean, & Hofferth, 2001), and also with their children overall (Barnett & Baruch, 1987; Harris & Morgan, 1991), if they have sons. Fathers of sons are more involved with their children's discipline, schoolwork, and other activities than are fathers of daughters (Lamb, Pleck, & Levine, 1987; Morgan et al., 1988), and unmarried fathers engage in more caregiving and playful interactions with toddler sons than with toddler daughters (Lundberg, McLanahan, & Rose, 2003). Moreover, mothers report greater emotional attachment of their husbands to sons than to daughters (Morgan et al., 1988).

Increased father involvement is believed to have positive effects on the parents' relationship. Several authors (Barnett & Baruch, 1987; Cox, Paley, Burchinal, & Payne, 1999; Katzev et al., 1994; Mizell & Steelman, 2000) reported greater satisfaction of partners in marriages with sons than with only daughters. Teachman and Schollaert (1989) found that couples whose first child is male tend to have a subsequent child sooner, and they attribute this finding to the greater stability of the relationship associated with the birth of a son.

Child gender affects not only parental time with children, but also time devoted to market work; marriages with sons are characterized by more traditional gender roles than marriages with daughters. Lundberg and Rose (2002) found that men work about 40 hours per year more after the birth of a son relative to a daughter, and that the hourly earnings of fathers of sons increase more after childbirth than do the earnings of fathers of daughters. The increase in labor supply appears to be at the expense of men's leisure, rather than time with the child.

Clearly, family dynamics differ for couples with sons and daughters. Marriages with sons tend to be more stable and more traditional and are characterized by greater father involvement on a variety of dimensions. These patterns suggest that either the mothers or fathers, or both parents, place a higher value on father interaction with sons than with daughters, and that this increases the perceived value of marriage relative to divorce. This has important implications, not just for marital stability, but for incentives to make additional investments in the family.

These implications can be derived from an economic model of the family that has been extended to incorporate child gender effects on the gains to marriage. Standard models of the family emphasize the gains to coresidence and shared consumption that accompany marriage (or cohabitation). In addition to love (interdependent preferences) and enjoyment of shared time (leisure complementarities), there are two distinct sources of gains to marriage: returns to specialization and exchange, and joint consumption of household public goods (including children). These gains can be enhanced by the tangible and intangible investments made by a husband and wife: investments in children, in household skills, in family activities or infrastructure. These investments increase the gap between potential well-being as a married couple and as single individuals (i.e., marital surplus) but also increase the prospective losses should the marriage end.

Why might sons increase marital surplus? Our explanations focus on the paternal role and how it differs for sons and daughters. Because a mother is more likely than a father to retain a close attachment to her child both outside and within marriage, a child gender bias in her behavior need not result in son–daughter difference in the value of marriage. Also, our own work has found that the observable behavior of fathers is more sensitive to child gender than is the behavior of mothers (Lundberg & Rose, 2002; Lundberg et al., 2003). Increased father involvement in parenting can generate surplus in two distinct ways. First, if fathers are more productive at parenting sons than daughters, perhaps because they play a special role in the emotional and social development of boys, then having a son increases the value of marriage (or coresidence) relative to single parenthood. Second, fathers may simply place a higher value on marriage and family if they have a son. This preference may be owing to gender bias on the part of fathers, or to the bonding that occurs when fathers spend more time with the child and are more involved with family activities.

These two stories, although they postulate very different roles for child gender in family decision making, have a number of common predictions. Both are consistent with empirical evidence that fathers spend more time with sons than with daughters, although the motivation for parent–child activities is different. Both models also imply that sons reduce the probability of divorce. With lower probabilities of marital dissolution, couples with sons should make more marriage-specific investments. These investments may take the form of a more traditional division of labor, which is consistent with the results in Lundberg and Rose (1999), but other types of investment, such as housing expenditures or avoidance of dysfunctional behaviors, may be characteristic of families with boys as well.

One important difference in the empirical implications of these two models concerns the relative well-being of mothers and fathers. If sons directly increase the utility of fathers, then a standard bargaining model of the household predicts a shift of household resources from fathers to mothers. Thus, the increase in marital surplus will be distributed between the two parents, and mothers of sons will be better off than mothers of daughters. This redistribution is distinct from the shift from consumption to investment described earlier, and it could potentially be observed as increased leisure among mothers of sons, or increased consumption of private commodities typically consumed by women. Conversely, if increased marital surplus is generated by greater productivity of fathers of sons, then the mothers of sons need not benefit: They may pay to provide their son with a father by accepting a reduced share of family resources. This distinction is difficult to test because it is difficult to construct a measure of true leisure (as opposed to nonmarket hours) or to find a purely private consumption good.

The focus in this chapter is on differences in expenditures in "family investment" categories, such as housing and consumer durables, between families with only boys and families with only girls. Omitting families with both boys and girls provides the simplest comparison of parental response to child gender, and frees us from the need to consider how this response might depend on birth order or parity. The discussion also presents a broader comparison of expenditure patterns by one-son and one-daughter families. Because most household wealth consists of equity in housing, expenditures on housing represent the principal tangible investment made by American families. This study's comparison of housing expenditures in all-girl and all-boy families is analogous to studies of consumption patterns in developing countries, such as Deaton (1989). His approach, which has been applied to a number of countries, estimates the effect of the demographic composition of the household on the shares of expenditures on various goods. A difference in the joint effects of gender-by-age category implies gender bias in household behavior. In a variation on this approach, Deolalikar and Rose (1998) estimated the effect of the sex of a child at birth on household expenditure levels, rather than shares, by category. We are unaware of any study that has examined child gender effects on the expenditure patterns of U.S. households.

There are several possible sources of family consumption response to child gender in addition to our hypothesized investment effect, some of them reflecting son preference and others simply differences in the biology, tastes, or activities of boys and girls. For example, expenditures on food and clothing for sons and daughters may differ owing to differences in appetite or fashion consciousness.

THE CONSUMER EXPENDITURE SURVEY

The Consumer Expenditure Survey (CEX) has gathered information on the expenditures, income, and assets of a large sample of American households since 1980. The survey is conducted quarterly by the U.S. Census Bureau for the Bureau of Labor Statistics, and is used to construct consumption baskets for the Consumer Price Index. The survey consists of two parts: an interview survey that includes monthly out-of-pocket expenditures such as housing, apparel, transportation, health care, insurance, and entertainment, and a diary survey that includes weekly expenditures of frequently purchased items such as food and beverages, tobacco, personal care products, and nonprescription drugs and supplies. A household or "consumer unit" in this survey consist of all residents of a housing unit who are related by blood, marriage, adoption, or some other legal arrangement. Approximately 1,500 households are added to the survey each quarter; they are then interviewed for up to four consecutive quarters about expenditures during the past 3 months.

The study reported here uses family extracts from the CEX made available by the National Bureau of Economic Research. In these extracts, the four possible quarterly records for each household are matched to form one annual record, and the more than 600 detailed spending, income, and wealth categories in the raw data are aggregated into 109 categories that are consistent over time and that allow the data to be calibrated to National Income Account aggregates.

The first sample consists of married couple families with one resident child aged 18 or younger who was included in the CEX sample beginning in the first quarter of 1990 through the second quarter of 1998. (The third and fourth quarters of 1998 were not yet available, and the third and fourth quarters of 1995 were unavailable owing to a change in the sampling frame that made these subsamples noncomparable.) Only families that were in the CEX sample for a full year were included so that reported expenditures represent a four-quarter total. Some characteristics of this sample, and the subsamples of families with sons and with daughters, are reported in Table 7.1. The full-year restriction reduces the sample size by about 40%, and young families and renters are more likely to fail to complete the survey. However, the proportions of boys and girls in the full and restricted samples are identical, and other characteristics, such as parental education, vary only slightly. The full fertility histories are unavailable for these families: Some couples with one child will go on to have additional

TABLE 7.1

Sample Characteristics, Married Couples with One Coresident Child under Age 19, Consumer Expenditure Survey, 1990–1998

Variable	Total Sample N = 2,404		One-Son Families N = 1,214		One-Daughter Families N = 1,190	
	Mean	SD	Mean	SD	Mean	SD
Child age	7.9	6.3	7.9	6.3	7.9	6.3
Age of wife	36.5	8.6	36.6	8.7	36.4	8.4
Age of husband	39.0	9.5	39.2	9.6	38.9	9.5
Total income (in 1996 dollars, PCE deflator)	49,133	40,307	49,149	42,080	49,117	38,432

children, and some couples with more than one child will be in the sample because older children are no longer in residence, or because children from a previous marriage may be living in a different household. There are no significant differences between the parental ages, child age, or total income of one-son and one-daughter families.

Child sex at birth is a random variable, but there are some possible sources of selection into the one-boy and one-girl subsamples that must be considered in interpreting the results. First, the son effects on marriage and divorce previously discussed imply that sons are more likely to live in married-couple families, although an increase in perceived marital stability may encourage couples to have a second child sooner, removing them from the one-child sample. On the other hand, if son preference leads couples whose first child is a son to be less likely to have a second child, the one-child sample will also overrepresent sons. Finally, different coresidence decisions by teenage sons and daughters may influence the composition of the sample with older children. In general, sample selection via child gender effects on divorce, marriage, or fertility-stopping behavior is expected to lead to a smaller sample of families with girls with stronger parental preferences for girls, and this will bias the results against finding a son preference in expenditures.

One indicator of sample selection would be a difference between the sex ratio (the number of boys divided by the number of girls times 100) in the sample and in the population. However, the sex ratio of 102 is not significantly different from the sex ratio of 5- to 14-year-olds in the United States, which is 105 (U.S. Census Bureau, 2001).

The focus here is on differences in expenditures in family investment categories such as housing and consumer durables. The study also presents a broader comparison of expenditure patterns by one-son and one-daughter families. Means and standard deviations of expenditures for a wide, but not exhaustive, set of categories are presented in Table 7.2. Expenditures are deflated using the Personal Consumption Expenditure deflator, and expressed in 1996 dollars. For housing, both owner-occupied housing (the probability of home ownership, and a comprehensive cost of housing that includes mortgage payments, taxes, utilities, and maintenance) and total housing are examined. Expenditures on medical care and education reflect investments in human capital, but medical expenses may also reflect differences in health status or injury rates among boys and girls. Two other aggregate categories—transportation and entertainment/recreation—include both durable goods and services. Food, clothing, and a set of miscellaneous consumption categories suggested in the earlier discussion are also included.

TABLE 7.2
Mean Annual Expenditures in Major Expenditure Categories, Married Couples with One Child (in 1996 dollars), Consumer Expenditure Survey, 1990-1998

	Mean	SD
Total expenditure	38,390.48	24,222.95
Food	5,792.98	2,732.82
Food at home	4,197.09	1,696.34
Food away from home	1,569.45	1,634.44
Clothing and clothing services	1,809.16	1,606.45
Medical care	1,877.32	1,848.98
Drugs	160.80	360.93
Medical supplies and equipment	86.65	170.08
Physicians and dentists	617.21	1,000.49
Hospitals	108.41	535.01
Health insurance	900.79	1,105.50
Transportation	8,241.59	8,809.96
Cars, parts, and gasoline	6,831.15	8,421.59
Auto insurance	957.43	826.59
Airline fares	317.25	731.10
Entertainment and recreation	2,775.39	2,709.37
Books, publications, toys	585.44	554.35
Recreation and sports equipment	901.81	1,656.50
Recreation services	1,288.13	1,399.60
Education	1,056.17	2,279.06
Higher education	336.63	1,733.10
Nursery, elementary	626.42	1,416.17
Other education	93.12	404.51
Housing		
Homeownership	0.77	0.42
Cost of owned housing (mortgage, property tax, maintenance, utilities)	8,269.60	10,239.43
Total housing costs (rental + owned)	11,907.12	10,121.27
Utilities	1,851.52	895.24
Home maintenance	765.80	2,154.74

(continued on next page)

TABLE 7.2 (continued)

	Mean	SD
Other		
Tobacco	311.93	514.92
Alcohol	185.23	291.51
Jewelry and watches	203.33	631.90
Personal care services (barbers, beauty parlors, health clubs)	328.29	283.93
Furniture and durable household equipment	1,197.31	1,938.24
Telephone	868.63	568.59
Domestic service (insurance, babysitting, cleaning, gardening)	848.01	1,618.37
Contributions to religious, welfare, and political organizations	588.45	1451.11

CHILD GENDER AND SPENDING PATTERNS
OF ONE-CHILD FAMILIES

Table 7.3 reports the coefficient on a dummy for male child in ordinary least squares (OLS) regressions in which the dependent variable is household expenditures in 1996 dollars for selected expenditure categories. These effects control for the age of husband and wife, the education level of each, whether the child was older than age 10, total expenditure and expenditure squared. (However, a specification without these controls leads to an almost identical pattern of child gender results.) Also included in the regression are dummy variables for the quarter (from 1990:1 to 1998:2) in which the family entered the CEX sample to control for change in economic activity and seasonal effects on sample attrition.

For most expenditure categories, there are no significant differences between the spending of one-son and one-daughter families, and this is true for more detailed subcategories as well as the aggregates reported. The investment hypothesis receives some support from the differential housing expenditure of families with sons and daughters: Total housing costs are significantly higher for families with sons. The "boy effect" on housing is nearly 4% of average housing costs, and other indicators of investment in

TABLE 7.3
Effect of Male Child on Annual Expenditures, Married Couples with One Child (in 1996 dollars), Consumer Expenditure Survey, 1990-1998[a]

Number of observations	2401–2404[b]
Total consumption	253.89
Consumption aggregates	
Food	14.92
Clothing	−142.445**
Medical Care	37.00
Transportation	-248.15
Entertainment and recreation	−37.36
Education	−5.643
Housing	
Homeownership (probit)	−.012
Cost of owned housing (homeowners only)	346.60
Total housing costs	431.20*
Food, personal care, and household	
Food at home	44.31
Food away from home	−23.71
Tobacco	3.84
Alcohol	−10.13
Jewelry and watches	−6.62
Personal care services	29.13**
Furniture and durables	18.85
Domestic service	−60.10

Notes: * $p < 0.01$; ** $p < 0.1$.
[a]Controls for parent's age and education, total expenditure and expenditure squared, child age, and quarter family entered survey included.
[b]Extreme outliers more than 10 standard deviations above 99th percentile deleted.

housing, such as maintenance and renovations, show a consistently positive relation with sons, although these effects are not statistically significant.

We find evidence of neither greater investments in the education and health of either sons or daughters in one-child families, nor any indication of gender discrimination in the two purely "adult" goods (tobacco and alcohol) that are identified in the data set. Inasmuch as high levels of tobacco and alcohol consumption might also be considered indicators of low investment in the family, this result also fails to support our principal hypothesis. However, because these expenditures in particular are thought to be substantially underreported in the CEX (Gieseman, 1987), we do not have a great deal of confidence in these estimates.

Clothing expenditures by families with a daughter are significantly higher than in families with a son, but spending on "personal care services" is higher in families with sons. The latter result is somewhat surprising, and is robust to changes in specification and the sample period. It is difficult to see how this difference in a category that includes barbers, beauty salons, and health clubs could reflect direct spending on children rather than a reallocation of parental spending.

Table 7.4 takes a closer look at total housing expenditures, allowing interaction effects between child gender and the child's age, and between child gender and family income. Column 1 reports the raw difference between the housing spending of one-son and one-daughter families—more than $600 per year. Column 2 introduces the standard set of controls, as well as more detailed dummy variables for child age. Column 2 shows that, controlling for total expenditure, housing expenses decline as the child ages. The other specifications show that the positive effect of a son on housing expenses is limited to families with children age 5 or older in the sample as a whole—and for these families, the boy premium is nearly 7% of total housing expenditure. Column 4 shows that the increase in housing expenditures is roughly constant for child age categories 5 and above.

Families with above-median income exhibit a stronger son effect than low-income families even when their children are under age 5. The intensification of son–daughter differences as the children become school age is also characteristic of patterns of parental interactions with children, and with some estimates of son effects on relationship stability (Morgan et al., 1988; Morgan & Pollard, 2002; Lundberg & Rose, 2003). Other possible explanations for the observed differences in housing spending might include a need for space to accommodate the size and activity of sons (although the spending differential appears at an age when boys and girls are the same size), or a desire for a higher quality neighborhood to reduce the probability of risky behavior by boys. The latter explanation seems applicable to low-income families only and is not consistent with our finding of stronger son effects in high-income families.

Table 7.4

Effect of Male Child on Total Annual Housing Expenditures, Married Couples with One Child,*[a] Consumer Expenditure Survey, 1990–1998 (1996 dollars, standard errors in parentheses) (N = 2401)

	(1)[b]	(2)	(3)	(4)	(5)	(6)
Boy	619.95	447.34	−13.44	−13.31	−260.89	−397.44
	(345)	(218)	(339)	(339)	(371)	(407)
Boy–age interactions						
5+			789.34		761.54	1003.88
			(445)		(444)	(537)
5–9				977.54		
				(622)		
10–14				618.36		
				(618)		
15–18				777.64		
				(570)		
Boy–income interactions						
Above median income					539.19	
					(329)	
Above median income,* under age 5						844.15
						(501)
Above median income,* age 5 and older						332.25
						(417)
Child age						
5–9		−226.93	−619.79	−716.52	−622.53	−614.55
		(333)	(400)	(458)	(400)	(400)
10–14		−970.69	−1355.8	−1275.8	−1358.5	−1347.2
		(389)	(446)	(491)	(445)	(446)
15–18		−2210.2	−2609.0	−2606.7	−2605.4	−2597.2
		(410)	(467)	(501)	(467)	(467)
R-squared	0.612	0.617	0.618	0.618	0.618	0.619

Notes: * = 1 if total income is greater than sample median income, 0 otherwise.

[a]Controls for husband's age and education, wife's age and education, total expenditure and expenditure squared, and quarter family entered the sample also included.

[b]Without controls.

Housing expenditure of married couple families with two same-sex children are also compared. The sample, more than 30% smaller than the one-child sample, is described in Table 7.5. Again, there are no significant differences between the characteristics of families with only sons and those with only daughters. Table 7.6 shows that the general pattern of spending is similar to that in one-child families, but the effect of sons is smaller and no longer significant. Other specifications that control for the age of the older child, as well as the younger child, yield the same result. One possible explanation for the absence of a significant difference in housing expenditure in this sample (in addition to the smaller sample) would be a correlation between the parents' gender preferences and the probability of having a second child. Parents with a strong son preference whose first child is male may be more likely to stop with one child, rather than take the chance of having a daughter. However, if their first child is a daughter, such parents may be more likely to have a second child than a couple without a strong preference for sons. This reasoning implies that differences in gender preference between the parents of sons and daughters in the one-child sample will be greater than this difference in the two-child sample.

DISCUSSION

The objective of this chapter was to test whether child gender has a significant effect on household expenditure and, in particular, to test the hypothe-

TABLE 7.5

**Sample Characteristics, Married Couples with Two Coresident Children
Under Age 19, Same Sex**

	Total sample N = 1,617		Two-son families N = 833		Two-daughter families N = 784	
Variable	Mean	SD	Mean	SD	Mean	SD
Younger child's age	6.5	4.8	6.6	4.8	6.5	4.9
Older child's age	10.2	4.9	10.3	4.9	10.0	5.0
Age of wife	36.1	6.4	36.2	6.4	36.0	6.4
Age of husband	38.5	7.0	38.5	6.9	38.6	7.2
Total income (in 1996 dollars, PCE deflator)	49,033	38,031	49,582	37,952	48,450	38,130

TABLE 7.6

Effect of Male Children on Total Annual Housing Expenditures, Married Couples with Two Children of Same Sex,[a] Consumer Expenditure Survey, 1990–1998 (in 1996 dollars, standard errors in parentheses) ($N = 1,617$)

	(1)	(2)	(3)	(4)
Boys	218.76	224.28	83.37	−10.79
	(313)	(312)	(482)	(384)
Boy–age of younger child interactions				
5–9			495.37	
			(758)	
10–14			8.71	
			(804)	
15–18			−7.73	
			(1331)	
Boy–income interactions				
Above median income				487.76
				(463)
Younger child's age				
5–9		−1211.3	−1469.1	−1222.5
		(414)	(571)	(414)
10–14		−1026.5	−1030.2	−1027.1
		(490)	(646)	(490)
15–18		−2123.4	−2128.6	−2152.5
		(745)	(976)	(745)
R-squared	0.570	0.574	0.574	0.574

Notes: * = 1 if total income is greater than sample median income, 0 otherwise.
[a]Controls for husband's age and education, wife's age and education, total expenditure and expenditure squared, and quarter family entered the sample also included.

sis that families with sons invest more in household public goods than families with daughters. The findings support this hypothesis: Housing costs, which constitute 44% of the total expenditures reported by our sample, are 4% to 7% greater in families with one son relative to families with one daughter. The effect is more pronounced when the child is age 5 or older, and is smaller and not significant in two-child families.

Child gender differences in spending on other household public goods, such as furniture and durables and many housing subcategories, have the expected sign but are not significant in this sample of households. There are few other child gender differences in expenditure patterns beyond a positive effect of daughters on clothing expenditure and a positive effect of sons on personal service spending.

This finding might be interpreted in terms of a model of the family in which parents who enjoy a higher marital surplus—that is, who expect to be better off together than apart—expect a longer lasting relationship and are willing to make more marriage-specific investments. The shift of spending from clothing to housing by parents of boys can be regarded as a shift from consumption to investment. These findings are consistent with the picture that emerges from the research on child gender and the family overall: The presence of a boy results in greater stability, more intense father involvement, and a more traditional division of labor than the presence of a girl.

Given that the category "personal care services" is dominated by "women's goods," the fact that there are greater expenditures on this category for families with sons suggests that other factors are involved as well. In particular, this result suggests some redistribution from fathers to mothers and are consistent with the hypothesis that boys directly increase their father's utility, relative to girls.

The results of this study add to the growing research base indicating that, even in developed countries, households with sons behave differently from households with daughters. Although the differences are certainly more subtle than would be found in, say, rural India, parents in the United States clearly respond to the child's gender. Previous research has shown that marriages with boys are more stable and more traditional. Here, expenditures of families with boys exhibit a greater investment component, reflecting greater optimism in, and contributions to, the long-run prospects for the family.

ACKNOWLEDGMENT

We are grateful to Ekaterina Stepanova and Anoshua Chaudhuri for excellent research assistance, to Tom DeLeire and Sara McLanahan for valuable comments, and to NIH/NICHD for research support (R01 HD42785-01).

REFERENCES

Barnett, R. C., & Baruch, G. K. (1987). Determinants of fathers' participation in family work. *Journal of Marriage and the Family, 49,* 29–40.

Behrman, J. (1988). Intrahousehold allocation of nutrients in rural India: Are boys favored? Do parents exhibit inequality aversion? *Oxford Economic Papers, 40,* 32–54.

Behrman, J. R., Pollak, R. A., & Taubman, P. (1986). Do parents favor boys? *International Economic Review, 27*(1), 33–54.

Bracher, M., Santow, G., Morgan, S. P., & Trussell, J. (1993). Marriage dissolution in Australia: Models and explanations. *Population Studies, 47,* 403–425.

Chen, L. C., Huq, E., & D'Souza, S. (1981). Sex bias in the family allocation of food and health care in rural Bangladesh. *Population and Development Review. 7*(1), 55–70.

Cox, M., Paley, B., Burchinal, M., & Payne, D. C. (1999). Marital perceptions and interactions across the transition to parenthood. *Journal of Marriage and the Family, 61,* 611–625.

Deaton, A. (1989). Looking for boy–girl discrimination in household expenditure data. *World Bank Economic Review, 3*(1), 1–15.

Deolalikar, A., & Rose, E. (1998). Gender and savings in rural India. *Journal of Population Economics, 11*(4), 453–470.

Diekmann, A., & Schmidheiny, K. (2002). *Do parents of girls really have a higher risk of divorce? Results from an eighteen-country study with the fertility and family survey.* Unpublished manuscript, University of Bern.

Gieseman, R. (1987, March). The Consumer Expenditure Survey: quality control by comparative analysis. *Monthly Labor Review,* 8–14.

Harris, K. M., & Morgan, S. P. (1991). Fathers, sons, and daughters: Differential paternal involvement in parenting. *Journal of Marriage and the Family, 53,* 531–544.

Haveman, R., & Wolfe, B. (1995). The determinants of children's attainments: A review of methods and findings. *Journal of Economic Literature, 33*(4), 1829–1878.

Katzev, A. R., Warner, R. L., & Acock, A. C. (1994). Girls or boys: Relationship of child gender to marital instability. *Journal of Marriage and the Family, 56,* 89–100.

Lamb, M. E., Pleck, J. H., & Levine, J. A. (1987). Effects of increased paternal involvement on fathers and mothers. In C. Lewis & M. O'Brien (Eds.), *Reassessing fatherhood: New observations on fathers and the modern family* (pp.109–125). Newbury Park, CA: Sage.

Lundberg, S. J., McLanahan, S., & Rose, E. (2003, January 3–5). *Child gender and father involvement in fragile families.* Paper presented at the Allied Social Sciences Association, Washington, DC.

Lundberg, S. J., & Rose, E. (1999). *The determinants of specialization within marriage.* Unpublished manuscript, University of Washington.

Lundberg, S. J., & Rose, E. (2002). The effects of sons and daughters on men's labor supply and wages. *Review of Economics and Statistics, 84,* 251–268.

Lundberg, S. J., & Rose, E. (2003). Child gender and the transition to marriage. *Demography 40,* 333–349.

Mizell, C. A., & Steelman, L. C. (2000). All my children: The consequences of sibling group characteristics on the marital happiness of young mothers. *Journal of Family Issues, 21,* 858–887.

Morgan, S. P., Lye, D., & Condron, G. (1988). Sons, daughters and the risk of marital disruption. *American Journal of Sociology, 94,* 110–129.

Morgan, S. P., & Pollard, M. S. (2002). *Do parents of girls really have a higher risk of divorce?* Unpublished manuscript, Duke University.

Mott, F. L. (1994). Sons, daughters and father's absence: Differentials in father-leaving probabilities and in-home environments. *Journal of Family Issues, 15,* 97–128.

Rose, E. (1999). Consumption smoothing and excess female mortality in rural India. *Review of Economics and Statistics, 81*(1), 41–49.

Spanier, G. B., & Glick, P. C. (1981). Marital instability in the United States: Some correlates and recent changes. *Family Relations, 31,* 329–338.

Taubman, P. J. (1991). Discrimination within the family: The treatment of daughters and sons. In E. P. Hoffman (Ed.), *Essays on the economics of discrimination* (pp. 25–42). Kalamazoo, MI: W. E. Upjohn Institute.

Teachman, J. D., & Schollaert, P. T. (1989). Gender of children and birth timing. *Demography, 26,* 411–423.

U.S. Census Bureau. (2001). *Gender: 2000.* Washington, DC: Author.

Yeung, W. J., Sandberg, J. F., Davis-Kean, P. E., & Hofferth, S. L. (2001). Children's time with fathers in intact families. *Journal of Marriage and the Family, 63,* 136–154.

8

Expenditure Decisions in Single-Parent Households

Kathleen M. Ziol-Guest
Ariel Kalil
Thomas DeLeire
University of Chicago

In contemporary American society, 27% of children under 18 are living with a single parent (U.S. Bureau of the Census, 2001), predominantly (84%) their mother. Never-married parents head the majority (42%) and divorced parents head about one third (37%) of single-parent families (U.S. Bureau of the Census, 2001).

Single-parent family structure is recognized as a significant risk factor for children's well-being. Children from single-parent homes are more likely to display lower educational aspirations and school achievement (McLanahan & Sandefur, 1994), increased psychological distress (Aseltine, 1996; Chase-Lansdale & Hetherington, 1990; Hetherington & Clingempeel, 1992; Peterson & Zill, 1986), greater susceptibility to negative peer pressure (Steinberg, 1987), increased vulnerability to health problems (Dawson, 1991), and greater likelihood of engaging in problem behaviors or deviant activities (Cherlin et al., 1991; Dornbusch et al., 1985; McLanahan & Sandefur, 1994; Steinberg, 1987). During adolescence, these children are more likely to have a teen birth (McLanahan & Bumpass, 1988; McLanahan & Sandefur, 1994; Wu & Martinson, 1993) and are more likely to be "idle" (neither working nor in school) than children in married households (McLanahan & Sandefur, 1994). In addition, children who grow up apart from a parent are more likely to become welfare dependent (Garfinkel & McLanahan, 1986). Finally, children who are exposed to the effects of parental divorce early in life have a heightened risk of problems such as poor mental health, poverty, and nonmarital childbearing in later life (Chase-Lansdale, Cherlin, & Kiernan, 1995).

Clearly, given the potential risks to child well-being in single-parent households, understanding why these risks exist has important practical and policy implications. Previous research examining why children from single-parent homes fare less well, on average, than children from two-parent homes has often focused on two explanations: economic deprivation and socialization (McLanahan & Sandefur, 1994). The economic deprivation perspective hypothesizes that substantial economic differences between single-parent and two-parent families produce differences in child well-being. Family economic resources were shown in one study to account for approximately one half of the differences in child developmental outcomes between single-mother families and their dual-parent counterparts (McLanahan & Sandefur, 1994). Hill (1992) found that such income differences are due to single parenthood and not to characteristics that predate single parenthood (i.e., selection factors), although this issue is not resolved in the literature.

The socialization perspective hypothesizes that two parents are crucial for carrying out important parenting functions such as supervision and monitoring and, further, that children benefit from the presence of a male role model in a two-parent home. Single parents, because they typically fill the roles of economic provider as well as primary agent of children's socialization, may simply have less time to parent their children. Some research suggests that single parents are also at risk for psychological distress and social isolation and this may also affect the parenting investments they make in their children (McLoyd, 1990).

A third perspective, called the *stress hypothesis*, emphasizes the effects of family structure changes. Changes in family structure are hypothesized to increase disequilibrium in family relationships and to disrupt relationships with others outside the family as well. Disruptions in family arrangements are also associated with changes in the children's place of residence and school. These changes are posited to have a cumulative negative effect on children's developmental outcomes (Aquilino, 1996; Wu, 1996). These mechanisms are neither exclusive nor exhaustive; several mechanisms could be operating simultaneously, and different mechanisms could be operating interactively.

These different perspectives can be integrated in an economic perspective on child development. A basic economic model of child development is one of resource allocation: Families "invest" purchased inputs and their own time in their children's well-being. This well-being is sometimes referred to as *human capital* (Becker, 1993), but it can be defined more broadly to include a child's emotional health. Parents can augment children's well-being by allocating more time and resources to a child.

According to the economic model, family investment behavior is shaped by a budget constraint that is determined by family resources, time available to parents, and the "prices" of child investments. Prices of investments in children include not only market prices—for example, the cost of high-quality child care—but also the value of parents' time. Resources can include not only income, but also nonmonetary resources such as education and information. A single-parent family may have a deficit in both material resources (such as housing, food, and cognitively stimulating toys and books) and nonmaterial resources (such as education, information, and mental health). Single-parent families may have a lower capacity to invest in their children's human capital; they also lack the synergies that stem from the investments of two parents in a married-couple household. Children from single-parent families are thus likely to do less well in life.

Our goal in this chapter is to extend existing knowledge about differences in parental investments across different family structures. In particular, we compare how single and married parents spend their money. More specifically, we ask: Holding income constant, how do parents choose to allocate their resources, and does this differ in single- and married-parent families? We take the expenditure patterns of household heads as potentially important indicators of parental preferences for, or constraints on, investments in their children's well-being. In this way, our analysis extends previous research that documented differences in parental investments in children's human capital across family structure that are largely due to differences in parents' economic circumstances (e.g., the extent to which parents provide their children with books or CDs and stimulate their development with trips to museums or libraries; see also Bradley & Corwyn, chapter 1 this volume). Although economic resources matter for children (Duncan & Brooks-Gunn, 1997), the way parents use the resources they have can make a difference, too.

Given variations in material and nonmaterial resources between single- and married-parent households, we anticipate identifying differences in the way these parents spend their money. We also expect to find differences between never-married and divorced single parents: Although divorced parents often have more economic resources than never-married single parents, they have also experienced a marital disruption.

RESEARCH QUESTIONS

This chapter seeks to answer several new important and related questions. First, do families' expenditure patterns differ by family structure? Second, are any observed differences in expenditure patterns between single and married parents relevant for child well-being? Our wide array of expenditure categories allows us to make some insights into this question.

These questions are explored first by examining the dollar expenditures on several disaggregate consumption categories and, second, by examining the share of total expenditures spent on each category. Using both measures is helpful because parents may respond to changes in family structure by either reducing overall expenditures uniformly across categories, such that single parents spend the same proportion of their income on various goods as do married families, or by reducing or raising the proportion of expenditures on only some goods. The benefit of using levels of expenditures as a dependent variable is that differences between families are translated into specific dollar amounts that are more easily converted into actual purchasing decisions. The benefit of using shares as a dependent variable is that shares add up to unity by construction, and therefore can be observed as the allocation of the family's total budget.

METHOD

Data

The data used in this chapter come from the National Bureau of Economic Research (NBER) family-level extracts of the Consumer Expenditure Survey (CEX) from 1980 to 1998. Each household in the CEX reports up to 12 months of consumption data, which include expenditures on food and other nondurable household necessities; the survey also collects demographic, income, and wealth data. Information is collected from each household four times, and a new sample of households is introduced every month. The CEX Interview Survey provides the best available consumption data on a large, nationally representative set of U.S. households. Other data sets, such as the Panel Study of Income Dynamics, for example, only provide information on food expenditures.

The NBER extracts aggregate the quarterly interview surveys to the family level. The purpose of the family-level data files is to condense the original data into an organization that is consistent over time. The detailed spending, income, and wealth items from the original raw CEX quarterly interview data are aggregated into 109 income, expenditure, and wealth categories available in the family-level extracts. Although losing some of the detailed description of income and expenditure, these 109 categories are consistent over the entire time frame, making it possible to examine consumption and income changes over time.

The family-level extracts provide the opportunity to examine the spending patterns of different types of families. The entire pooled sample from 1980 through 1998 consists of over 116,000 families, both those with and without children, from a vast array of family compositions. We have defined a "family" as a household headed by an adult, where an adult is an individual who is at least 18 years old. The head of household in these analyses is the household member identified by the survey respondent as the person who owns or rents the dwelling.

The analysis is limited to families with children (more than 39,000 families) who had participated in the CEX in all four quarterly interviews, which guaranteed complete income and consumption information for all of the families over the course of one year. Including only those with full-year data also ensures that the observed expenditure patterns are not affected by seasonal factors.

A limitation, however, is that by removing families that do not participate in all four quarters, we lose a large number of less stable and more transient families. This can be seen in Table 8.1 which presents the prevalence of different family types within the CEX. By concentrating on those families in the full-year sample, we are left with a little more than 23,000 families. The largest decline from eliminating inconsistent participants was in the category of never-married families, where 58% did not participate in all four quarters. The two other family types used in this analysis were married with children and divorced with children, which saw a 37% and 48% decrease, respectively. Families who participated in all four quarters are more advantaged than families who participate in three or fewer quarters. Specifically, those who drop out are younger, more likely to be non-White, have lower educational attainment, and higher rates of government program participation than those who remain (results not shown).

As expected, most married households are male-headed, and most divorced and never-married households are female-headed. The other potential family structures in the data set are also reported in Table 8.1. We exclude separated, widowed, and married families with a female head because biological relationships with fathers cannot be determined. Although the latter might be stepfamilies, we exclude them because of reported differences in parental investments in stepfamilies versus intact families (Case, Lin, & McLanahan, 2000). Analyses (not shown here) show that married families with female heads differ from married families with male heads, in terms of both descriptive characteristics (where married female heads were much more disadvantaged), and in spending patterns. The final sample consists of 16,121 married families (headed by fathers) with children, 1,142 never-married families with children, and 2,111 divorced families with children.

Independent Variables

Demographics.   The age, gender, and race of the head of household were obtained directly from the respondent. Age is a continuous measure, whereas gender and race are dichotomous. Gender is measured using male

TABLE 8.1
Prevalence of Family Types

	Total	%**	Complete Data	%**	Full Year	%**	Drop***
Total Families*	116,087		114,393		64,458		44%
Families with Children[1]	39,364		38,798		23,128		40%
Never Married	2,732	7%	2,698	7%	1,142	5%	58%
Female-Headed	2,383		2,355		1,006		57%
Male-Headed	349		343		136		60%
Married	29,999	76%	29,554	76%	18,687	81%	37%
Female-Headed	4,413		4,365		2,566		41%
Male-Headed	25,586		25,189		16,121		36%
Divorced	4,140	11%	4,089	11%	2,111	9%	48%
Female-Headed	3,451		3,408		1,747		49%
Male-Headed	689		681		364		47%
Separated	1,903	5%	1,878	5%	839	4%	55%
Female-Headed	1,673		1,652		726		56%
Male-Headed	230		226		113		50%
Widowed	590	1%	579	1%	349	2%	40%
Female-Headed	503		494		292		41%
Male-Headed	87		85		57		33%

* total adult, hoh cu families
** percent of families with children
*** percent drop from complete data
[1] Children are biological children of head of household

as the base category, and race using non-White as the base category. An individual is coded as non-White when he or she indicates Black, American
Indian or Aleut Eskimo, Asian or Pacific Islander, or Other on the survey.
The head of household's highest level of education is measured with four
mutually exclusive, dichotomous variables. These variables correspond to
whether the reference person had not graduated high school, graduated
from high school but went no further, completed some college but did not
obtain a college degree, or graduated from college and has gone farther.

Economic Resources. Family resources are measured with four variables:
family after-tax income, head of household employment status, whether the
household receives any of its income from public cash assistance, and
whether the household receives assistance in the form of food stamps.

Family after-tax income is measured with seven dummy variables. Income was dichotomized to allow flexibility in the models. The range of family income was quite large, with incomes ranging from losses (negative
income) to a few outliers with incomes over one-half-million dollars, and
highly skewed to the right. We inflated income to 1999 dollars using the
Consumer Price Index, all urban consumers (CPI-U). Income categories
were created to account for those who reported negative income, those
whose income ranged from $0 to $20,000; $20,000–$40,000; $40,000–
$60,000; $60,000–$80,000; $80,000–$100,000; and those who reported in-
comes greater than $100,000.

Head of household employment is measured with a dichotomous variable
coded for whether he or she was employed for some part or all of the interview year in full- or part-time work (base category is unemployed). Receipt
of public cash assistance and food stamps are coded with two dichotomous
variables (base category is no public assistance).

Year Variables. Because of the panel nature of the data set, dummy variables for the first year that the family was included in the survey are included
in all of the regression analyses. These variables can highlight any time
trends and ascertain true family structure effects. Furthermore, they allow
patterns of expenditures to vary over time, without assuming a functional
form associated with the time trends.

Household Composition. Another important variable in family expenditure decisions in addition to the structure of the family is the number and
type of other individuals in the household. A continuous measure of the
number of other adults in the household was created that measures the
number of adults (not including the reference person) who report living in
the household. These individuals are age 18 or older and are related to the

head of household as a spouse, child or adopted child, grandchild, in-law, sibling, parent, other relative, or an unrelated individual.

A continuous measure of the number of other children living in the household was also created to account for living arrangements that include other related children. Individuals counted as other children include those younger than age 18 and related to the head of household as a grandchild, in-law, sibling, other relative, or unrelated to the head of household.

Finally, a continuous measure of number of children living in the household was created. This variable measures the number of the head's biological or adopted children (younger than age 18) living in the household. This measure was dichotomized to account for gender and age given the different patterns of consumption by age and gender (e.g., boys might consume more food). Eight dichotomous variables were created to account for these potential consumption differences: number of boys and girls ages 5 and younger; number of boys and girls between ages 6 and 10; boys and girls between ages 11 and 15; and boys and girls between ages 16 and 18. The age ranges used in dichotomizing this variable represent broad developmental stages.

Dependent Variables

Expenditures. All nonmedical expenditures in the data set were included as dependent variables. The focus was on nonmedical expenditures because medical expenditures for services in the data were often negative. Nonmedical expenditures were measured as the total dollars spent on various categories, including food at home, food eaten out, food eaten at work, tobacco, alcohol, nightclubs and bars, clothes, tailors, jewelry, toiletries, health and beauty, tenant-occupied rent, other rented lodging, principal and interest (as well as other transactions costs) paid on mortgages for own dwelling, furniture and durable household equipment, nondurable household supplies, electricity, gas, water, home fuels, telephone, domestic service, business services, life insurance, new and used vehicles, car payment principal and interest, auto parts, car services, gasoline, tolls, auto insurance, mass transit, other transit, airfare, books and maps, magazines/newspapers and nondurable toys, recreation and sports equipment, other recreation services, higher education, nursery and elementary and secondary school, other education services, and religious and welfare activities.

Aggregated Categories. More comprehensive expenditure categories were created from the original aggregated categories in the NBER data set. Several measures of consumption were calculated by combining several of the aforementioned categories (which are aggregates). Tobacco, alcohol at home, alcohol away from home, clothing, and jewelry are measured as the individual variables in the data set. Spending on alcohol is combined with spending on alcohol away from home for a measure of total spending on alcohol. Furthermore, the share spent on all tobacco and alcohol products is included for a collective view of expenditures not consumed by children. Food is measured by combining food consumed at home and away from home (such as in restaurants). Food at home and food away from home are measured individually as well.

Toiletries and health and beauty is a combination of these supplies as well as spending on health clubs. Transportation is measured as a combination of expenditures on vehicles, parts, car services, gasoline, tolls, auto insurance, mass transit, other transit expenses, and airfare. Utilities is a combined measure of electricity, gas, water, home fuels, and telephone. Domestic services include such services as insurance coverage and repairs, as well as expenditures on babysitting and home care services. Housing and furnishings includes purchases for the home dwelling, including furniture and durable household equipment expenditures.

Other categories include business and insurance, which encompasses occupational expenses, membership fees, and other nonhealth insurance expenses. Charitable contributions and other education expenses include education expenses not spent on K–12 education.

Child-Specific Expenditures. These expenditures focus more closely on goods that might benefit child well-being, and include shares of nonmedical expenditures on books and maps; magazines, newspapers, and toys; recreation and sports equipment; and nursery, elementary, and secondary school expenses.

Aggregated Levels of Expenditure: Regression Analysis. The aggregated categories are examined in terms of the raw level of expenditure in 1999 dollars. These measures are computed by taking the raw dollar level that the household spent on each of the categories named.

$$l_j = X'\beta_{1j} + \lambda_{1j}Nevermarried + \theta_{1j}Divorced + \varepsilon_{1j}$$

where l_j is the level of expenditure for category j,
X is the set of demographic characteristics, and
NeverMarried and *Divorced* are indicator variables (where married is omitted).

Aggregated Shares of Expenditure: Regression Analysis. All share measures are computed by dividing the total amount spent on that good by the family's total nonmedical expenditures.

$$s_j = X'\beta_{2j} + \lambda_{2j}Nevermarried + \theta_{2j}Divorced + \varepsilon_{2j}$$

where s_j is the expenditure share for category j,
X is the set of demographic characteristics, and
NeverMarried and Divorced are indicator variables (where married is omitted).

RESULTS

Descriptive Statistics

Table 8.2 presents weighted descriptive statistics of means and standard deviations of the families in this analysis. The family head of household is, on average, 37 years old and is male. Eighty-four percent of the sample is White. The majority of the sample has graduated from high school, and many have gone farther. Consistent with prior research, never-married and divorced families earn significantly less than married families. The same pattern exists in weighted per capita income, where married families earn $12,728 per capita, never-married earn $5,449 per capita, and divorced earn $9,199 per capita (results not shown). On average, there were 1.1 other adults in the household, with married families having more (recall that this measure includes spouses and own children over age 18). Furthermore, families on average have 0.1 other children in the household and 1.9 own children.

Married families are not just earning more, but, as expected, they are spending more on nonmedical goods and services, as shown in Table 8.3. Married parents also have larger families, which might contribute to the larger expenditures. On average, married families spend approximately $43,000 annually, never-married families spend approximately $16,000, and divorced families spend $27,000. Per capita spending patterns are similar to the averages. Average weighted per capita spending on total nonmedical goods for married parents is $10,771, whereas never-married heads spend $5,356, and divorced heads spend $9,246 (results not shown).

The share values in Table 8.4 can be interpreted as share of total nonmedical expenditures spent on a particular category. For example, the average family in the analysis spends 26% of its total nonmedical expenditures on housing and home furnishings. The second largest expenditure is food, consumed both at and away from home.

Analysis of Variance

Table 8.2 also reports the results of a one-way analysis of variance in demographic differences between the groups. The analysis uses the Bonferroni

TABLE 8.2
Comparison of Means—Descriptive Statistics (Weighted)

Demographics	Overall Mean	(SD)	Married (a)	Never Married (b)	Divorced (c)	Significant Differences[1]
Age of HOH	37.17	(8.83)	37.96	29.00	37.87	b < a,c
White HOH	0.84	—	0.89	0.45	0.79	b < a,c; c<a
Female HOH	0.18	—	—	0.90	0.83	c < b
Education						
No high school diploma	0.22	—	0.20	0.38	0.22	b < a,c
High school graduate	0.32	—	0.31	0.39	0.34	b,c < a; b < c
Some college	0.23	—	0.22	0.19	0.29	a < c; b < a
College graduate	0.23	—	0.27	0.04	0.15	b,c < a; b <c
Household Resources						
Income (1999 dollars)	45338.25	(31244.95)	51149.73	16750.19	26839.32	b,c < a; b < c
<$0	0.00	—	0.00	0.00	0.00	—
$0–$20K	0.20	—	0.11	0.72	0.46	—
>$20–$40K	0.29	—	0.29	0.22	0.36	—
>$40–$60K	0.25	—	0.29	0.04	0.12	—
>$60–$80K	0.14	—	0.17	0.01	0.03	—
>$80–100K	0.06	—	0.07	0.00	0.02	—

(continued on next page)

TABLE 8.2 (continued)

Demographics	Overall Mean	(SD)	Married (a)	Never Married (b)	Divorced (c)	Significant Differences[1]
>$100K	0.05	—	0.06	0.00	0.01	—
Head is employed	0.91	—	0.96	0.58	0.83	b,c < a; b < c
Household received cash assistance	0.08	—	0.03	0.51	0.17	a < b,c; c < b
Household received food stamps	0.11	—	0.04	0.58	0.22	a < b,c; c < b
Household Composition						
No. of other adults in HH[2]	1.14	(.80)	1.31	0.45	0.46	b,c < a
No. of other children in HH	10.06	(.36)	0.05	0.14	0.11	a < b,c; c < b
No. of own children in HH	1.90	(.99)	1.94	1.83	1.73	b,c < a; c < b
N	19,374		16,121	1,142	2,111	—

HOH = head of household.
[1]Computed using the Bonferroni multiple comparison test ($p < .05$).
[2]Other adults includes own children ≥ 18 and spouse.

TABLE 8.3
Comparison of Means—Levels (Weighted)

	Overall Mean	(SD)	Married (a)	Never Married (b)	Divorced (c)
Total Nonmedical Expenditures (1999 US$)	39371.48	(27498.65)	43661.28	16322.36	27200.34
Ingestibles					
Food	6643.22	(3303.18)	7190.43	3846.14	4981.56
Food at Home	5100.09	(2376.93)	5463.04	3381.65	3893.64
Food Away	1543.14	(1601.91)	1727.39	464.49	1087.92
Tobacco	382.09	(538.88)	396.75	294.65	347.15
Alcohol	317.13	(487.82)	351.78	125.02	223.31
Alcohol at Home	195.49	(316.20)	218.06	84.78	123.38
Alcohol Away	121.64	(256.55)	133.72	40.24	99.93
Tobacco & Alcohol	699.22	(781.75)	748.53	419.66	570.46
Personal Care					
Clothing	2003.20	(1766.69)	2161.54	1133.44	1568.43
Jewelry	174.65	(508.46)	198.93	48.65	103.10
Toiletries/Health/Beauty	331.61	(318.71)	358.52	184.41	257.26
Transportation	7547.50	(8336.76)	8530.12	2365.79	4684.87

(continued on next page)

TABLE 8.3 (continued)

	Overall Mean	(SD)	Married (a)	Never Married (b)	Divorced (c)
Housing Costs					
Utilities	2883.54	(1360.53)	3057.62	1831.13	2478.86
Domestic Services	752.63	(1348.17)	836.53	289.27	524.10
Housing and Furnishings	10911.91	(15245.85)	12141.23	4227.24	7484.68
Other					
Business/Insurance	1010.13	(1862.61)	1143.70	244.69	667.50
Charitable Contributions	657.81	(1917.50)	780.37	55.72	267.10
Other Education Expenses	94.07	(481.42)	105.30	19.43	73.14
Child-Specific Expenditure					
Books	142.19	(248.42)	157.85	38.20	112.91
Publications and Toys	487.87	(481.05)	544.70	208.88	306.52
Recreation	2041.25	(3056.68)	2300.27	574.82	1363.34
Education (PreK–12)	557.99	(1535.05)	608.87	264.23	429.17

TABLE 8.4
Comparison of Means—Shares (Weighted)

	Overall Mean	(SD)	Married (a)	Never Married (b)	Divorced (c)	Significant Differences[1]
Ingestibles						
Food	0.199	(.09)	0.188	0.278	0.214	a < b,c; c < b
Food at Home	0.161	(.09)	0.149	0.252	0.176	a < b,c; c < b
Food Away	0.036	(.03)	0.039	0.026	0.038	b < a,c
Tobacco	0.013	(.02)	0.012	0.020	0.017	a < b,c; c < b
Alcohol	0.008	(.01)	0.009	0.013	0.008	b < a,c
Alcohol at Home	0.005	(.01)	0.006	0.011	0.004	a < b,c
Alcohol Away	0.003	(.01)	0.003	0.006	0.003	b < a,c; a < c
Tobacco & Alcohol	0.022	(.03)	0.021	0.027	0.025	a<b,c
Personal Care						
Clothing	0.054	(.03)	0.050	0.076	0.060	a < b,c; c < b
Jewelry	0.004	(.01)	0.004	0.002	0.003	b,c < a; b < c
Toiletries/Health/Beauty	0.009	(.01)	0.009	0.011	0.010	a < b,c; c < b
Transportation	0.174	(.12)	0.185	0.101	0.150	b,c < a; b < c

(continued on next page)

TABLE 8.4 (continued)

	Overall Mean	(SD)	Married (a)	Never Married (b)	Divorced (c)	Significant Differences[1]
Housing Costs						
Utilities	0.089	(.05)	0.082	0.126	0.108	a < b,c; c < b
Domestic Services	0.018	(.03)	0.018	0.016	0.018	
Housing and Furnishings	0.260	(.13)	0.260	0.262	0.262	
Other						
Business/Insurance	0.024	(.03)	0.026	0.014	0.021	b,c < a; b < c
Charitable Contributions	0.014	(.03)	0.016	0.003	0.009	b,c < a; b < c
Other Education Expenses	0.002	(.01)	0.002	0.001	0.002	b < a,c; a < c
Child-Specific Expenditures						
Books	0.003	(.01)	0.004	0.002	0.004	b < a,c
Publications and Toys	0.013	(.01)	0.013	0.014	0.012	c < a,b
Recreation	0.047	(.04)	0.049	0.034	0.045	b,c < a; b < c
Education (PreK–12)	0.012	(.03)	0.012	0.011	0.014	b < c

[1]Computed using the Bonferroni multiple comparison test ($p < .05$)

multiple-comparison test. Several demographic details are worth noting and are comparable to findings in the research. Never-married heads are younger than divorced and married heads, and they are more likely to be both female and non-White. Married heads have higher education than other family heads, and also have higher incomes. Never-married heads are the least likely to be employed and are more likely to be receiving cash assistance and food stamps. The economic resource variables suggest that, as a whole, married families are the best off, followed by divorced and never-married families.

The residential composition of these households also differs. Never-married families have more children other than their own living in the household. Given the differences in ages of household heads, it is not surprising that never-married heads have younger children on average than married households, whereas divorced families have older children (results not shown).

Table 8.3 presents the results of a means comparison of expenditures between married, never-married, and divorced heads of household. As might be expected, married families spend more on nonmedical goods and services than the other two family structures, whereas never-married families spend the least. Married families also spend more on each category of expenditure than never-married and divorced, whereas divorced heads spend more on each category than do never-married. The exception is tobacco spending, where there is no difference between never-married and divorced. All differences are significant at .05 level.

Table 8.4 presents the results of a one-way analysis of variance in shares of expenditures on the various categories. Never-married families spend a higher share of their total expenditures on food than the other two family types. Single-parent families spend a higher proportion on alcohol and tobacco than married families.

Married families spend smaller shares on clothing, and larger shares on jewelry and transportation. These univariate differences extend to never-married and divorced families as well, with never-married families spending less on jewelry and transportation and more on clothing.

Married families spend the smallest share on utilities, followed by divorced families and, finally, never-married families. Never-married and divorced families spend a smaller share of their total nonmedical budget on business expenses and charitable contributions. Furthermore, divorced heads of household spend a larger share on other education expenses than both married and never-married heads.

Married families spend a higher share of their expenditures on recreation activities and books than never-married families. Divorced families, although spending less on publications, toys, and recreation than married families, spend more on books than do never-married families.

Regression Analysis

Regression analysis was conducted on the entire sample of married, never-married, and divorced heads. These analyses were weighted using the attrition weight—an adjusted version of the sampling weight—provided in the data set. The attrition weight available in the family-level extracts accounts for those who report complete income information, who completed all four quarterly interviews, and who did not reside in a student household. Excluding these households leads to substantial attrition bias (young renters tend to not complete the survey); therefore, the attrition weight is based on six age groups and renter-homeowner status. Finally, the analysis uses the Huber-White-Eicker Sandwich Estimator for the OLS standard errors to correct for any heteroskedasticity in the independent variables.

Regression analyses controlled for household head's age, race (non-White is base category), gender (male is base category), educational attainment (high school graduate omitted), income category ($40,000–$60,000 omitted), employed status (not employed omitted), family cash assistant receipt (not receiving welfare omitted), family food stamp receipt (not receiving food stamps omitted), number of other adults in the household, number of other children in the household, eight continuous measures of gender and age of household head's children, and year respondent began quarterly interview (1980 omitted).

Tables 8.5 and 8.6 present the results of regression analyses for expenditure levels and shares, respectively. These tables present the unadjusted levels (shares) and regression coefficients. The unadjusted levels (shares) are the average weighted levels (shares) of each category for each family type. The regression coefficients are results of the level (share) regressions described earlier controlling for all of the previously mentioned variables.

Table 8.5 presents the findings of a regression analysis predicting the levels of expenditure on the aggregate categories of total nonmedical expenditures. There are several large differences in expenditure decisions based on family structure. Single-parent families spend significantly less than married families on nonmedical expenditures. Divorced families also spend significantly less on food overall (led mostly by food consumed at home), and never-married families spend significantly more on food away from home than married families. There are also significant differences in the total spent on tobacco and alcohol products; never-married and divorced parents each spend about $200 more per year than do married heads.

Single heads also differ from married heads in several personal care items. Divorced heads spend $286 less on annual clothing expenditures than married families, whereas both never-married and divorced heads spend less on toiletries, health and beauty supplies, and transportation expenses.

TABLE 8.5
Differences in Category Levels, by Family Structure

| | Unadjusted Levels | | | Regression Coefficients | | | |
| | Married | Never Married | Divorced | Never Married | | Divorced | |
				B	SE	B	SE
Total Nonmedical Expenditures	43661.28	16322.36	27200.34	-4225.22 **	881.38	-4241.78 **	842.29
Levels							
Ingestibles							
Food	7190.43	3846.14	4981.56	9.25	137.75	-548.82 **	121.74
Food at Home	5463.04	3381.65	3893.64	-152.89	111.89	-601.30 **	101.00
Food Away	1727.39	464.49	1087.92	162.14 *	69.54	52.48	66.76
Tobacco	396.75	294.65	347.15	33.12	37.44	45.55	32.82
Alcohol	351.78	125.02	223.31	184.56 **	37.95	178.78 **	38.69
Alcohol at Home	218.06	84.78	123.38	69.00 **	21.34	58.72 **	19.93
Alcohol Away	133.72	40.24	99.93	115.56 **	22.49	120.05 **	24.05
Tobacco & Alcohol	748.53	419.66	570.46	217.67 **	58.84	224.33 **	54.61
Personal Care							
Clothing	2161.54	1133.44	1568.43	-130.66 **	67.78	-285.89 **	62.16
Jewelry	198.93	48.65	103.10	7.62	25.46	-8.85	25.22
Toiletries/Health/Beauty	358.52	184.41	257.26	-52.46 **	17.52	-56.10 **	16.15
Transportation	8530.12	2365.79	4684.87	-2188.72 **	507.36	-1936.62 **	449.81

(continued on next page)

TABLE 8.5 (continued)

	Unadjusted Levels			Regression Coefficients			
				Never Married		Divorced	
	Married	Never Married	Divorced	B	SE	B	SE
Housing Costs							
Utilities	3057.62	1831.13	2478.86	-214.55 **	72.02	-175.82 **	65.65
Domestic Services	836.53	289.27	524.10	-101.13	59.68	-70.58	54.51
Housing and Furnishings	12141.23	4227.24	7484.68	-1592.56 **	445.95	-906.13 *	449.29
Other							
Business/Insurance	1143.70	244.69	667.50	74.87	101.58	64.82	111.48
Charitable Contributions	780.37	55.72	267.10	*-78.61*	56.38	**-286.63 **	65.69
Other Education Expenses	105.30	19.43	73.14	16.36	17.86	1.06	19.55
Child-Specific Expenditures							
Books	157.85	38.20	112.91	-5.89	17.20	-0.03	17.24
Publications and Toys	544.70	208.88	306.52	*-43.67 **	21.30	***-73.37*** **	19.03
Recreation	2300.27	574.82	1363.34	-35.27	113.28	-76.80	122.33
Education (PreK–12)	608.87	264.23	429.17	-171.78 **	62.40	-124.04 *	54.05

Note: Regression controls for age, education, race, and gender of head; categorical income; categorical child age and gender; number of other adults in household; number of other children in household; employment status of head; cash assistance receipt; and food stamp receipt. **Bold** coefficients are different from each other (*p* < .05). *Italic* coefficients are jointly significant (*p* < .05). Regressions are weighted using attrition adjusted weights. Standard errors are adjusted using Sandwich Estimator.

*p < .05. **p < .01.

TABLE 8.6
Differences in Category Shares, by Family Structure

	Unadjusted Shares			Regression Coefficients				Adjusted Percent Difference	
				Never Married		Divorced		Never Married	Divorced
	Married	Never Married	Divorced	B	SE	B	SE		
Shares									
Ingestibles									
Food	0.188	0.278	0.214	0.026 **	.006	-0.005	.004	13.83%	-2.66%
Food at Home	0.149	0.252	0.176	0.019 **	.005	-0.012 **	.004	12.75% **	-8.05% **
Food Away	0.039	0.026	0.038	0.007 **	.002	0.007 **	.002	17.95% **	17.95% **
Tobacco	0.012	0.020	0.017	0.003	.002	0.005 **	.002	25.00%	41.67% **
Alcohol	0.009	0.013	0.008	0.007 **	.001	0.008 **	.001	77.78% **	88.89% **
Alcohol at Home	0.006	0.011	0.004	0.003 **	.001	0.003 **	.001	50.00% **	50.00% **
Alcohol Away	0.003	0.006	0.003	0.004 **	.001	0.005 **	.001	133.33% **	166.67% **
Tobacco & Alcohol	0.021	0.027	0.025	0.010 **	.003	0.013 **	.002	47.62% **	61.90% **
Personal Care									
Clothing	0.050	0.076	0.060	0.005 *	.002	-0.006 **	.002	10.00% *	-12.00% **
Jewelry	0.004	0.002	0.003	0.000	.001	0.000	.001	0.00%	0.00%
Toiletries/Health/Beauty	0.009	0.011	0.010	0.000	.001	-0.001 *	.001	0.00%	-11.11% *
Transportation	0.185	0.101	0.150	-0.052 **	.011	-0.020 *	.009	-28.11% **	-10.81% *

(continued on next page)

TABLE 8.6 (continued)

	Unadjusted Shares			Regression Coefficients				Adjusted Percent Difference	
				Never Married		Divorced			
	Married	Never Married	Divorced	B	SE	B	SE	Never Married	Divorced
Housing Costs									
Utilities	0.082	0.126	0.108	0.008	.004	0.004	.003	9.76%	4.88%
Domestic Services	0.018	0.016	0.018	0.001	.002	0.001	.002	5.56%	5.56%
Housing and Furnishings	0.260	0.262	0.262	**0.000**	.001	**0.015** *	.007	0.00%	5.77% *
Other									
Business/Insurance	0.026	0.014	0.021	0.005	.003	0.004	.002	19.23%	15.38%
Charitable Contributions	0.016	0.003	0.009	**-0.004** **	.002	**-0.005** **	.002	-25.00% **	-31.25% **
Other Education Expenses	0.002	0.001	0.002	0.001	.001	0.001	.001	50.00%	50.00%
Child-Specific Expenditures									
Books	0.004	0.002	0.004	**-0.001**	.000	**0.000**	.000	-25.00%	0.00%
Publications and Toys	0.013	0.014	0.012	**0.001**	.001	**-0.001**	.001	7.69%	-7.69%
Recreation	0.049	0.034	0.045	0.002	.003	0.003	.003	4.08%	6.12%
Education (PreK-12)	0.012	0.011	0.014	-0.003	.002	**-0.003** *	.001	-25.00%	-25.00% *

Note: Regression controls for age, education, race, and gender of head; categorical income; categorical child age and gender; number of other adults in household; number of other children in household; employment status of head; cash assistance receipt; and food stamp receipt. Bold coefficients are different from each other ($p < .05$). *Italic* coefficients are jointly significant ($p < .05$). Regressions are weighted using attrition adjusted weights. Standard errors are adjusted using Sandwich Estimator.

*$p < .05$. **$p < .01$.

Differences in housing costs also exist between the married and single heads. Single heads spend less on utilities than married heads. Never-married and divorced heads differ little from married heads in their spending on domestic services; however, they spend significantly less on total housing and furnishing costs. Never-married and divorced families also spend less on publications and toys, as well as children's education expenses.

Table 8.6 presents the findings from the share regression analysis, specifically the unadjusted shares, the regression coefficients, and the adjusted percentage difference. The adjusted percentage differences are computed as the percentage difference from the married unadjusted shares. The adjusted percent differences are computed using the following formulations:

$$\left(\frac{s_m + \beta}{s_m} \right) - 1$$

where s_m is the unadjusted share for married families, and β is the regression coefficient.

Never-married and divorced families each spend 18% more than married families on food outside the home, whereas divorced families spend 8% less on food for consumption at home, and never-married spend 13% more. Furthermore, never-married families spend 48% more and divorced families spend 62% more than married families on combined tobacco and alcohol purchases. Divorced heads spend a smaller share and never-married heads a larger share of their total nonmedical expenditures on clothing. Divorced heads spend a smaller share on toiletries, health and beauty, whereas both never-married and divorced heads spend less on transportation. Furthermore, divorced heads spend a significantly larger share on housing and furnishings than married heads. As might be anticipated, single heads spend a smaller share on charitable contributions. Finally, divorced heads spend 25% less than married parents on children's education.

DISCUSSION

The results suggest that expenditure patterns differ between single and married families with children, and that some of these differences may be relevant for child well-being. Differences exist not only in the total level of expenditure on various consumption categories, but also in the share of total expenditures. That is, single parents allocate their total expenditures in ways that are different from married families.

The most striking findings with respect to the expenditure categories that might be relevant for child well-being are differences in food, alcohol and tobacco, and education-related goods. Results suggest that divorced heads of household, controlling for all other factors, spend less money on food at home than do married households, and never-married heads spend significantly more money than do married heads on food consumed away from home. The difference spent on food consumed away from home by never-married heads is equivalent to just over one tenth of a standard deviation in food away from home expenditures for the entire sample.

The proportion of family budget spent also mirrors the differences in the levels. Divorced heads of household spend a smaller share of total nonmedical expenditures on food consumed at home, whereas never-married heads spend a larger portion on food at home. The finding for never-married families is not surprising given that they are much poorer than married parents, and we would expect them to spend a larger proportion of their budget on food, although these results are not true for divorced families as they are also poorer than married families. Furthermore, both never-married and divorced heads spend a larger share (10% and 12% more, respectively) of their total expenditures on food consumed away from home than do married heads.

Single parents may spend more on outside food because of the time constraints associated with being a single parent. However, this choice may compromise children's nutrition and health. Food consumed away from home often exceeds appropriate portion sizes recommended by the Food and Drug Administration (Nielsen & Popkin, 2003), potentially leading to greater obesity (Young & Nestle, 2002). Furthermore, food consumed away from home often fails to adhere to recommended nutritional requirements, containing a higher fat density and a lower fiber and calcium density than foods prepared at home (Lin, Guthrie, & Blaylock, 1996).

Both divorced and never-married heads also spend significantly more on tobacco and alcohol products relative to their married counterparts. Single parents spend over $200 more annually on these products than do married heads, which is equivalent to just over one fourth of a standard deviation in the entire sample. Much of this difference is attributed to alcohol purchases and not tobacco, especially alcohol consumed away from home. Hanson, McLanahan, and Thomson (1998) found that the period following divorce for mothers was associated with an increase in frequenting bars and taverns. The consistency in the expenditure data, both in terms of levels and shares, suggests that the single parents in the sample might be visiting more bars and clubs than married parents, perhaps because they are looking for potential partners. This is potentially problematic because the single parents in the sample have fewer economic resources than do married parents, yet they are spending more on alcohol and tobacco. Time spent consuming alcohol away from home may also reduce parental monitoring of children's activities.

Finally, never-married and divorced heads of household spend less than do married heads on publications, toys, and education. Single parents also spend a smaller share of total expenditures on children's education expenses than do married families. Prior research found strong connections between the quality of a child's learning environment and subsequent test scores and educational experiences (see Bradley & Corwyn, chapter 1, this volume). Although much research to date suggests that the quality of the home environment is highly correlated with poverty status (Brooks-Gunn, Klebanov, & Liaw, 1995; Duncan, Brooks-Gunn, & Klebanov, 1994; Garrett, Ng'andu, & Ferron, 1994), other research has illustrated a strong relation between the quality of the home environment and mother's marital status (Menaghan & Parcel, 1995; Miller & Davis, 1997; Thomson, Hanson, & McLanahan, 1994). The quality of cognitive, social, and emotional stimulation that a child receives in the home is highly associated with a variety of child outcomes, including cognitive abilities and school-readiness, even controlling for maternal education. The findings reported here show that single parents spend less on educational items that may benefit children's intellectual development, even controlling for their lower economic resources and educational attainment.

Given these differences in both the level and share of total nonmedical expenditures across different family structures, some of the spending patterns associated with family structure may be contributing to differences in child outcomes in single-versus married-parent families. Investments in child health and intellectual development appear to differ between single- and married-parent families. Because the study controlled for economic resources available to a family, the effects are likely attributable to differences in parenting resources, which could include both time and information available to the parent, as well as parental psychological resources.

Limitations

It is important to note the limitations of this study. First, because of missing data and incomplete reports, there is significant attrition, particularly by the family structures of particular interest. Attrition not only reduces the efficiency of the estimates, but it may also be systematic in some way that precludes our capturing true effects.

Second, given the nature of the marital status and relationship variables, the analysis was unable to distinguish between married families that are stepfamilies and those that are biologically related. This suggests that the estimates are lower bounds. Because stepfamilies are pooled with other married families, the positive effects on consumption from marriage may be understated. The potential effect of stepfamilies was minimized by limiting our analysis to married families headed by fathers.

Third, for many categories it was impossible to determine which individual in the household was consuming the goods and services purchased. For example, the aggregated lower education category is by its nature an expenditure on children. However, expenditures on food consumed at home and away are less clear.

Fourth, the aggregation already present in the raw data available from the NBER was not always the preferred aggregation. Specifically, publication and toy purchases are aggregated in the raw data, and we would prefer that they be separate. This is particularly important given that the family structures differ and we are unable to tell a clear story about the nature of these expenditures.

Finally, this study cannot comment on actual child outcomes. We know of no data set or study that has linked detailed purchasing decisions made by heads of the household with comprehensive child development measures. We identified expenditure decisions in single-parent versus married-parent households that *might* account for differences in child well-being, however. Identifying the source of these differences and whether they matter for child well-being remains an important task for future research.

ACKNOWLEDGMENTS

We are grateful to Rachel Dunifon for helpful comments.

REFERENCES

Aquilino, W. S. (1996). The lifecourse of children born to unmarried mothers: Childhood living arrangements and young adult outcomes. *Journal of Marriage and the Family, 58*, 293–310.

Aseltine, R. (1996). Pathways linking parental divorce with adolescent depression. *Journal of Health and Social Behavior, 37*, 133–48.

Becker, G. S. (1993). *A Treatise on the Family* (enlarged ed.). Cambridge, MA: Harvard University Press.

Brooks-Gunn, J., Klebanov, P. K., & Liaw, F. R. (1995). The learning, physical, and emotional environment of the home in the context of poverty: The Infant Health and Development Program. *Children and Youth Services Review, 17*, 251–276.

Case, A., Lin, I-F., & McLanahan, S. (2000). How hungry is the selfish gene? *Economic Journal, 110*, 781–804.

Chase-Lansdale, P. L., Cherlin, A., & Kiernan, K. (1995). The long-term effects of parental divorce on the mental health of young adults: A developmental perspective. *Child Development, 66*, 1614–34.

Chase-Lansdale, P. L., & Hetherington, E. M. (1990). The impact of divorce on life-span development: Short and long term effects. In P. Baltes, D. Featherman, & R. Lerner (Eds.), *Life span development and behavior* (Vol. 10, pp. 107–151). Hillsdale, NJ: Lawrence Erlbaum Associates.

Cherlin, A., Furstenberg, F., Chase-Lansdale, P. L., Kiernan, K., Robins, P., Morrison, D., & Teitler, J. (1991). Longitudinal studies of the effects of divorce on children in Great Britain and the United States. *Science, 252*, 1386–89.

Dawson, D. (1991). Family structure and children's health and well-being: Data from the 1988 National Health Interview Survey On Child Health. *Journal of Marriage and the Family, 53*, 573–84.

Dornbusch, S., Carlsmith, J., Bushwall, S., Ritter, P., Leiderman, H., Hastorf, A., & Gross, R. (1985). Single parents, extended households, and the control of adolescents. *Child Development, 56*, 326–41.

Duncan, G. J., & Brooks–Gunn, J. (Eds.). (1997). *Consequences of growing up poor.* New York: Russell Sage.

Duncan, G. J., Brooks–Gunns, J., & Klebanov, P. K. (1994). Economic deprivation and early childhood development. *Child Development, 65*, 296–318.

Garfinkel, I., & McLanahan, S. (1986). *Single mothers and their children: A new American dilemma.* Washington, DC: The Urban Institute.

Garrett, P., Ng'andu, N., & Ferron, J. (1994). Poverty experiences of young children and the quality of their home environments. *Child Development, 65*, 331–345.

Hanson, T. L., McLanahan, S., & Thomson, E. (1998). Windows on divorce: Before and after. *Social Science Research, 27*, 329–349.

Hetherington, E. M., & Clingempeel, W. (1992). *Coping with marital transitions: A family systems perspective.* Monographs of the Society for Research in Child Development, 57 (2–3, Serial No. 227), Boston: Blackwell.

Hill, M. S. (1992). The role of economic resources and remarriage in financial assistance for children of divorce. *Journal of Family Issues, 13*, 156–178.

Lin, B., Guthrie, J., & Blaylock, J. R. (1996). *The diets of America's children: Influence of dining out, household characteristics, and nutrition knowledge.* Agricultural Economic Report No. 746US. Washington, DC: U. S. Department. of Agriculture, Economic Research Service.

McLanahan, S. S., & Bumpass, L. L. (1988). Intergenerational consequences of marital disruption. *American Journal of Sociology, 94*, 130–152.

McLanahan, S., & Sandefur, G. (1994). *Growing up with a single parent: What hurts, what helps.* Cambridge, MA: Harvard University Press.

McLoyd, V. C. (1990). The impact of economic hardship on black families and children: Psychological distresses, parenting and socioemotional development. *Child Development, 61*, 311–346.

Menaghan, E. G., & Parcel, T. L. (1995). Social sources of change in children's home environments: The effects of parental occupational experiences and family conditions. *Journal of Marriage and the Family, 57*, 69–84.

Miller, J. E., & Davis, D. (1997). Poverty history, marital history, and quality of children's home environments. *Journal of Marriage and the Family, 59*, 996–1007.

Nielsen, S. J., & Popkin, B. M. (2003). Patterns and trends in food portion sizes, 1977–1998. *Journal of the American Medical Association, 289*(4), 450–453.

Peterson, J. L., & Zill, N. (1986). Marital disruption, parent–child relationships, and behavior problems in children. *Journal of Marriage and the Family, 48*, 295–307.

Steinberg, L. (1987). Single parents, stepparents, and the susceptibility of adolescents to antisocial peer pressure. *Child Development, 58*, 269–75.

Thomsuch, E., Hanson, T. L., & McLanahan, S. (1994). Family structure and child well-being: Economic resources vs. parental behaviors. *Social Forces, 73*, 221–242.

U.S. Bureau of the Census. (2001). *America's families and living arrangements: June 2001.* Current Population Reports, P20–537. Washington, DC: Author.

Wu, L. L. (1996). Effects of family instability, income, and income instability on the risk of a premarital birth. *American Sociological Review, 61,* 386–406.

Wu, L. L., & Martinson, B. C. (1993). Family structure and the risk of premarital birth. *American Sociological Review, 58,* 210–232.

Young, L. R., & Nestle, M. (2002). The contribution of expanding portion sizes to the U.S. obesity epidemic. *American Journal of Public Health, 92* (2), 246–249.

9

Parent- Versus Child-Based Intervention Strategies for Promoting Children's Well-Being

Katherine A. Magnuson
Columbia University

Greg J. Duncan
Northwestern University

In the course of human development, there are abundant avenues for interventions aimed at promoting children's well-being. This chapter focuses primarily on the relative effectiveness of parent-based strategies designed to augment human capital and reduce problem behavior, particularly among children reared in economically disadvantaged families.

The goals of most parent-based strategies are to enhance either parents' parenting skills or economic resources in hopes that parents will be better able to teach, nurture, or in other ways provide for their children, and in so doing enhance their children's productive capacities and well-being. Because wise policymakers choose the best among competing alternative strategies, this chapter compares the effectiveness of various parent-based strategies. The chapter also considers the relative effectiveness of parent- versus child-focused strategies.

The chapter opens with an overview of parent- and child-focused interventions and an explanation of the logic that underlies policy–economic choices among them. It then reviews parent-based strategies, focusing on both direct parenting interventions and the broader questions of whether and how increasing parental resources such as income and education promotes children's development. The findings suggest that, although many parent-based interventions improve parenting, few of these improvements translate into improved academic outcomes among low-income children. On the other hand, parenting interventions focused on problem behavior among children with high levels of externalizing behavior problems have been shown to be modestly effective. Unfortunately, the research to date does not explain whether parenting programs are unsuccessful in improving children's achievement because they fail to produce sufficiently large improvements in parenting, or because the types of changes in parenting that are achieved are not strongly related to children's academic outcomes.

Boosting parental economic resources, as recent welfare reform experiments demonstrate, can have a positive impact on younger children's school achievement but may worsen adolescent behavior. The nonexperimental research suggests that increasing the resources of deprived families may be more beneficial for children's cognitive development than increasing the incomes of middle-class families. In addition, earlier may be better: Boosting family income appears to benefit preschoolers more than older children.

The evidence is mixed on whether promoting parents' education can improve their children's school-readiness. Some intriguing evidence suggests that this is indeed the case, but most adult schooling interventions do not result in substantial educational gains for mothers. This may be why adult-based human capital programs have failed to improve children's academic achievement or behavior.

After reviewing the evidence for parent-based interventions, the chapter examines the more promising research on interventions that target children's human capital. A number of careful studies have demonstrated that expensive early education interventions provide a handsome social profit. In addition, some programs that treat children's severe behavior problems appear successful. All in all, child-focused programs appear more promising than parent-focused programs if the goal is to promote the well-being of children. Finally, combining these approaches may be particularly useful in reducing children's problem behaviors.

PARENTING INTERVENTIONS

The review of interventions distinguishes two types of parenting programs—parenting education and parenting management training. Parenting education programs seek to boost parents' general knowledge about parenting and child development. Information is provided in conjunction with instrumental and emotional support. Home visitation programs for new mothers and parent–teacher programs are perhaps the most familiar examples. Management training programs are designed for parents of children with problem behavior, usually conduct disorders. Clinical therapists teach parents concrete behavioral strategies designed to improve their children's behavior. Typically, parents are taught how to reinforce their child's positive behavior and punish negative behavior appropriately.

Two theoretical assertions undergird most parenting interventions. First, parental behavior has a strong influence on children's healthy development. Second, positive parenting can be learned or, in the case of economic interventions, improved by increases in economic resources. Both of these assertions are controversial.

That parents influence children is beyond debate; however, the relative contribution of environmental, including parental, and genetic influences to development remains a point of contention (Bradley & Corwyn chapter 1, this volume; Neiderhiser & Reiss, chapter 2, in this volume). Developmentalists such as Scarr (1992) argued that genetic forces leave little room for developmental consequences on the part of all but the most extreme family conditions. Collins, Maccoby, Steinberg, Hetherington, and Bornstein (2000) acknowledged that past studies may have overstated parental influence on children by failing to attend to the potential effects of genetics, but they countered that parenting may still be a profoundly important influence on children. They also pointed out that parenting behaviors appear to have differing, but systematic, influences on children with different genetically determined characteristics. Therefore, although one type of parenting may not have an effect on all children, it may have substantial effects on particular types of children.

Even if pathways of parental influence are identified correctly, and children benefit from changes in parent–child interaction patterns, or in the quality of their home learning environments, the success of parent-based interventions is premised on the ability of interventions to improve parents' behavior in cost-effective ways. The research reviewed here suggests that effecting change in parents through parenting programs is indeed possible, although more difficult than previously thought.

Parenting education and training programs make demands on the time and effort of parents—demands that, for some parents, appear too high. Work conflicts, stress, and lack of motivation result in non-participation rates as high as 50% in some programs (Prinz & Miller, 1994; Webster-Stratton & Spitzer, 1996). In addition, parental engagement appears to be a function of parents' perceptions of how well their needs are met by a particular program (Brooks-Gunn, Berlin, & Fuligni, 2000). Furthermore, even when parents do participate in the program, they are not all equally engaged or capable of implementing and maintaining the strategies they are taught. Unfortunately, parents of children most at risk of academic or behavior problems—single and low-income parents—appear least able to participate in programs and maintain changes in parenting behavior (Prinz & Miller, 1994; Webster-Stratton & Hammond, 1990).

OTHER TYPES OF PARENT-FOCUSED INTERVENTIONS

Another parent-based avenue to improved child well-being targets parental socioeconomic resources such as income and education in hopes that enhancing these resources will promote children's development (Haveman & Wolfe, 1994; Brooks-Gunn, Brown, Duncan, & Moore, 1995). Causal links between these resources and child well-being are controversial questions in the social sciences. Research in psychology, sociology, and economics demonstrates strong associations between children's developmental outcomes and such resources as family income, parental education, and composite indicators of socioeconomic status. Yet, many of these studies have been criticized because they fail to adjust for genetic or other biological factors that may be driving the associations (Rowe, 1994; Rowe & Rodgers, 1997) or, as discussed later, employ unconvincing empirical techniques (Mayer, 1997).

Economic models of child development (e.g., Becker, 1981) view families with higher economic resources as better able to purchase or produce important "inputs" into their children's development—for example, nutritious meals; enriched home learning environments and child-care settings outside the home; safe and stimulating neighborhood environments; and, with older children, higher quality schools and college education. The most commonly used measure of household economic resources is household income, which is the sum of income from all sources received by all members of the household over a given time period.

Human capital constitutes a second form of family resources and includes parental skills acquired in both formal and informal ways (Becker, 1975). The most common measure of parents' human capital is their educational attainment. Parents' formal education may influence children's well-being by enhancing cognitive stimulation in the home learning environment and promoting more verbal and supportive teaching styles (Harris, Terrel, & Allen, 1999). Although most developmental researchers believe that parent–child interactions account for the bulk of parental education's effects on children (e.g., Laosa, 1983), the skills acquired through formal education may also enhance parents' abilities to organize their daily routines and resources in a way that enables them to accomplish their parenting goals effectively (Michael, 1972, 1982). Finally, improving parental education may improve child outcomes by boosting other household resources, most notably income.

POLICY EVALUATION

In thinking about the diverse array of parent- and child-focused intervention strategies, it is helpful to be reminded of the economic dimensions of such interventions. An important source of tension between the science and policy of intervention programs lies in the fact that science often addresses the question of "What works?" and "How does it work?" whereas policymakers and practitioners seek evidence on real-world programs with the "biggest bang for the buck."

Seeking to establish whether intervention programs might indeed produce long-lasting impacts, program designers often develop very expensive "efficacy" interventions, with per-participant costs exceeding $10,000, and the quality of the intervention much higher than what is possible in a "scaled up" national or regional program. Shadish, Cook, and Campbell (2002) have aptly argued that informed policy requires that "efficacy" trials be followed by "effectiveness" trials in which interventions are implemented in a variety of real-world settings and with realistic levels of quality.

Even if effectiveness trials establish program impacts, policymakers require research-based answers to additional questions. If research trials demonstrate a convincing causal link between intervention A and outcomes B and C, what are the costs of a feasible large-scale program that changes A and what is the value of benefits associated with the resulting change in outcomes B and C? How big an impact must an intervention produce to be worthwhile? Is a cheaper-by-half, scaled-back version of a proven but very expensive parenting program likely to provide at least half the benefits of the original program? If several interventions have proven benefits, but funding constraints limit the scope of implementation, how should one choose among the alternatives?

Cost–benefit frameworks (Gramlich, 1990; Levin, 1983) address all these issues. Key is a systematic assessment based on a careful (ideally random-assignment) comparison of participants offered the program services and otherwise similar participants not offered program services. When both costs and benefits can be quantified, a cost–benefit accounting can produce an estimate of a program's "social rate of return;" that is, the return on the investment of public dollars in the intervention.

However, the questions remain: which child impacts to measure and how to assign a dollar value to them. In the case of long-run impacts, labor market employment and earnings are obvious outcomes. In the short term, IQ and school achievement are commonly measured outcomes for young children. Presumably IQ gains, if maintained, translate into academic success and increased productivity. Even small gains may be profitable if, as research suggests, small increases in IQ result in substantial increases in lifetime earnings. Krueger (2003), for example, estimates that the one fifth standard deviation increase in tests scores from the Tennessee STAR class-size experiment increased future earnings by between $5,000 and $50,000, depending on assumed discount and future earnings growth rates. However, abundant developmental evidence documents the importance of other developmental domains, in particular physical and emotional health, in promoting academic success and well-being in adulthood (Shonkoff & Phillips, 2000). The value to society of reducing problem behavior can easily exceed the value of IQ-based productivity gains. For example, in a careful evaluation of the High/Scope Perry Preschool program (Schweinhart, Barnes, & Weikart, 1993), the cost savings from reductions in criminal behavior were much larger than savings stemming from increased earnings or reductions in welfare.

EVIDENCE ON PARENTING PRACTICES AND INTERVENTIONS

Parenting interventions have generally, although not exclusively, focused on low-income families, whose parenting practices are sometimes considered lower quality and whose children are at greater risk for academic problems. A long line of research (reviewed in McLoyd, 1990, 1998) has established that, compared with middle-class parents, low-income parents are more likely to use an authoritarian and punitive parenting style and less likely either to support their children or to provide them with stimulating learning experiences in the home. Low-income parents are more likely to use physical punishment and other forms of power-assertive discipline, and they are less likely to ask children about their wishes, reward children for positive behavior, or to respond to children's expressed needs. In the extreme, these behaviors may lead to child abuse or neglect, both of which are more common among poor than advantaged parents (Trickett, Aber, Carlson, & Cicchetti, 1991). However, some aspects of power-assertive discipline may be an adaptive response to dangerous neighborhoods or other perceived threats. Consequently, these parenting practices may not be harmful among some low-income populations (Deater-Decker, Dodge, Bates, & Petit, 1994).

Depending on the particular domains considered and the extent to which research designs account for omitted variable biases, the associations between parenting and children's outcomes range from weak to moderate (McLoyd, 1998). Some evidence suggests that the home learning environment is most closely linked to children's cognitive development and achievement, whereas parent–child warmth and discipline practices have the strongest associations with children's behavior (McGroder, 2000; Bradley & Corwyn, chapter1, this volume).

Parenting Education Programs

Assuming that these differences in parenting contribute to low-income children's poorer academic achievement and problem behavior, interventions have set out both to teach parents how to parent better and to connect parents with supportive services in their community. Parenting interventions may include home visits, supportive parenting group meetings, and informational sessions. Some combine both parent-focused and child-focused strategies into a single program. Parenting interventions typically provide mothers with some form of social support, emotional and instrumental, as well as instructional information about child development. The expectation is that this combination of services will improve mothers' capacities to provide their children with sensitive caregiving as well as other experiences that promote healthy development (Gomby, Culross, & Behrman, 1999; Seitz & Provence, 1990).

Disappointingly, although programs focused solely on parents have demonstrated an ability to improve some aspects of parenting, they have not consistently improved the cognitive development or social behavior of low socioeconomic status (SES) children (Brooks-Gunn Berlin, & Fuligni, 2000; Yoshikawa, 1994). See Table 9.1 for a summary of the various types of interventions reviewed in this chapter. Brooks-Gunn and colleagues (2000) reviewed evaluations of 24 parent-focused home interventions for low-SES children. Remarkably, 19 of these programs produced favorable effects on parenting outcomes, including more sensitive parenting and a higher quality home environment. However, positive program impacts on parenting usually failed to translate into significant positive impacts on children's cognitive or behavioral outcomes.

A popular example of parenting education programs is Parents as Teachers (PAT), a home-visiting program for parents of children from birth to age 3. The program began in Missouri in the early 1980s and has since expanded to 49 states. During monthly home visits, the parent educators follow a set curriculum designed to strengthen parenting skills and parents' knowledge of child development. The home visits include periodic screenings of children's health and referrals for needed community services. In addition, voluntary group meetings are offered to parents. Results of an evaluation of PAT programs that served working- and middle-class families found positive effects on children's home environments, an important aspect of parenting, but no effects on children's development or well-being (Owen & Mulvihill, 1994). A subsequent evaluation with primarily low-income families found that the program did not consistently affect either parenting practices or child outcomes for most families, although it did show some favorable impacts on Spanish-speaking mothers and children (Wagner & Clayton, 1999).

TABLE 9.1

Summary of Experimental Evaluations of Interventions

Program type	Examples of Programs	Effectiveness of Programs
		Parent-Focused
Parenting education	Parents as Teachers, Home visiting programs	With a few noteworthy exceptions, most parenting programs are ineffective at improving children's academic outcomes and behavior outcomes.
Parent Management Training	PARTNERS	Among children with identified behavior problems, these programs have proved modestly effective at reducing children's problem behavior in the short term, particularly in the home setting. There is no evidence that these programs have positive effects on children's academic outcomes. In addition, there is some evidence that these programs are less effective with disadvantaged populations and children with severe behavior problems.
Parental income	Earned Income Tax Credit, minimum wage	Boosting poor families' economic resources appears to improve children's achievement modestly; this effect may be stronger at younger ages. Little evidence of impacts on children's problem behavior.
Parental schooling	NEWWS, Even Start	Mixed evidence that promoting parental human capital improves children's academic outcomes. No evidence that it reduces problem behavior.
		Child-Focused
Early Education	Head Start, childcare quality improvements, Perry Preschool	Some evidence that intensive education programs produce large long-term gains, mostly by reducing problem behaviors; uncertain impacts for less intensive programs.
School-based reforms	Reductions in class size, upgrading teacher credentials	Class size matters for early grades; impacts of other school inputs is unclear.
Cognitive problem-solving skills training	Peer Coping Skills, PATHS	Among children with identified problem behaviors, these programs have a modest positive effect on children's behavior at home, but there is no indication of whether children's academic achievement is improved.

The Early Head Start evaluation study also provides some recent evidence on the effectiveness of home-visiting programs for low-income families with children (Love et al., 2002). Services were provided between birth and age 3. Seven sites in the larger evaluation provided programming primarily through weekly home visits and biweekly parent–child socialization activities. The programs also provided case management and health screenings. The evaluation assessed the program's effects on several aspects of children's development and family life when the children were aged 2 and 3. Response rates were low for portions of the study, but the rates were equally low for both experimental and control groups. Of the families enrolled in home-visiting programs, 90% participated for at least one visit, and although most of these had more than one visit, only 30% of families participated in weekly home visits. Rates of home-visiting in the control group were significantly lower, but not insubstantial, with close to one third reporting that they received a home visit during the first 3 years of their child's life.

The evaluation study reports the effects of home-visiting programs for those families who participated in Early Head Start Services, rather than the effect of the program on those who were offered the services (Love et al., 2002). Assuming that the programs would not benefit or harm the nonparticipating families, with 10% of families not participating, the program's impacts are likely to be 10% lower than reported. As is the case with other studies of home-visiting programs, this study found a few modest effects of the program on measures of participants' parenting. For example, observers rated mothers as more supportive while playing with their children, and mothers reported lower levels of parenting stress. However, the effect sizes were quite modest, about 0.16 and 0.14 of a standard deviation, respectively. With a few exceptions, experimental-control differences in parents' mental health, children's home learning environments, and harsh parenting favored the experimental group, but almost none of these differences was statistically significant at conventional levels.

With such modest effects on parenting, one might not expect large positive effects on children. Indeed, the reported program impacts on children's cognitive development and socioemotional development at age 3 were positive, but not statistically significant. The effect of the program on participating children's cognitive development translated into effect sizes of about 0.10. Effect sizes for program impacts on measures of children's socioemotional development ranged from 0.02 to 0.19 of a standard deviation, with most below 0.10. Taken together, these findings support the conclusion that home-visiting programs can result in modest improvements in some aspects of parenting; however, such modest changes will yield few and small changes in children's developmental outcomes. Whether children's outcomes would have improved if programs resulted in larger impacts on parenting is unclear. The failure of these programs to result in improvements in children's outcomes may be due either to their failure to produce large improvements in parenting, or to the lack links between the types of parenting behaviors targeted and the types of outcomes considered.

The successes of a few intensive parenting intervention programs are noteworthy. Most famously, the experimental evaluation of an intensive nurse home visitation program by Olds and colleagues (1999) in Elmira, New York, found that the program had lasting effects on important indicators of disadvantaged children's well-being. In particular, a 15-year follow-up study found that unmarried mothers assigned to the program group had fewer verified reports of child abuse and neglect than mothers assigned to the control group. Furthermore, their children had fewer emergency health-related visits, reported arrests, and lifetime sex partners, and they reported less tobacco and alcohol use than did children in the control group. Olds and colleagues have undertaken replication studies in two sites—Memphis and Denver. Results from a 3-year follow-up study of the Memphis program indicate positive, but more limited, impacts on parenting and child outcomes. However, these programs did appear to reduce the likelihood that mothers would have subsequent births, which may bring about more positive outcomes in the long run. Evidence from additional follow-up studies in Memphis and Denver will provide important information about the likelihood of replicating the success of the Elmira program.

Involving an average of nine visits by registered nurses during the pregnancy and 23 visits during the first 2 years of the child's life, and costing approximately $6,000, Olds' program was clearly at the intensive end of parenting programs. As with early education programs, it is crucial to ask whether the positive child impacts from intensive programs such as Olds' would carry over to more practical, less intensive programs. As suggested by Gomby and colleagues (1999), the answer appears to be no. Given the different program designs and populations served by parenting education programs, it is difficult to determine whether the lack of consistently positive impacts is owing to flaws in implementing the programs or weaknesses in the theoretical models underpinning them.

Parent Management Training Programs

In contrast to parent education programs, parent management training programs appear to be a more promising strategy, at least for improving the behavior of children with severe behavior problems. These programs were developed in response to research showing that maladaptive parenting and parent–child interaction patterns are common in families of severely conduct-disordered children (Kazdin, 1997; Kazdin & Weisz, 1998; Taylor & Biglan, 1998). Often described as coercive, this type of parenting involves harsh but inconsistent punishment for children's problem behavior, and a failure to attend to positive child behavior (Dumas, 1989; Patterson, DeBaryshe, & Ramsey, 1989). Parent management training programs teach parents to respond more appropriately to their children's behavior. Specifically, parents are taught to reward and attend to their children's positive behavior, but to ignore or punish their child's problem behavior appropriately and consistently. Parents are taught to identify and react to their children's behavior in new ways. Treatment sessions provide parents with the opportunity to observe appropriate parenting skills as well as practice and refine their own use of these skills. Families involved in these types of programs include, but are not limited to, low-income families.

A successful example of parenting management training is Webster-Stratton's group discussion videotape program, now known as the PART-NERS program (Webster-Stratton, Kolpacoff, & Hollinsworth, 1988). The evaluation of this program involved random assignment of parents to one of three variations of the treatment (individual videotape only, group discussion only, or videotape and group discussion) or to a control group that received no training. In the group discussion videotape treatment, parents of children with severe behavior problems attended clinic-based training sessions for 10 to 12 weeks. During these sessions, parents watched videotapes that contained 2-minute vignettes that modeled parenting skills. Each vignette was followed by a focused discussion in which a trained therapist highlighted the important points and solicited parents' questions and reactions to the material. All three variations of the program treatment had positive effects on observational and parent-report measures of parent–child interactions as well as parent and teacher reports of children's behavior. However, program impacts were more consistent and pronounced among families in the group discussion videotape treatment. A 1-year follow-up indicated that the positive gains among the experimental groups were maintained (Webster-Stratton et al., 1988).

More generally, reviews of evaluations of parent management training programs show that these programs can lead to meaningful reductions in children's problem behaviors. One review suggests that approximately two thirds of the children exhibit clinically significant improvements in behavior at the completion of the program (Taylor & Biglan, 1998). Another review suggests that the average effect size was 0.87 of a standard deviation, a large effect (Durlak, Fuhrman, & Lampman, 1991).

The reviews also suggest that parent management training may be less effective with adolescents than with younger children. Differential effects, however, may be owing to the severity of the problem behavior rather than the child's age (Ruma, Burke, & Thompson, 1996). Adolescents' behavior problems tend to be more severe than young children's, and for this reason, parent management training may be less successful in improving their behavior. Parents of adolescents are more likely to drop out of parenting training programs, which may also explain why adolescents benefit less from parent-focused programs (Dishion & Patterson, 1992).

Although reviews of parent management training programs conclude that these programs can reduce children's problem behavior substantially, whether such conclusions hold up depends on the quality of the research reviewed. Not all of the included studies used random assignment, sample sizes were typically quite small, and attrition rates, if reported, were high. Perhaps most worrisome is that when families dropped out of treatment, they were not included in the follow-up study, suggesting that the evaluation findings reflect the effect of completing the program. Few studies have follow-up data beyond 6 months after program treatment and, therefore, the long-term benefit of parenting programs is still questionable (Greenberg, Domitrovich, & Bumbarger, 2000). None of these studies provides an accounting of program costs and benefits.

Finally, it is important to keep in mind that most parents who participated in these studies were referred for treatment or were seeking help for their children's behavior. For example, to be admitted to Webster-Stratton's group videotape program, parents had to be referred to the clinic for children's "excessive noncompliance, aggression, and oppositional behavior for more than six months" (Webster-Stratton, 1990, p. 145). One reason that parenting interventions may be more successful in reducing severe problem behavior than in promoting academic achievement is that parents of children with severe behavior problems may feel they are "under siege" and thus be more engaged in parenting programs than parents of children with less severe problems (Webster-Stratton & Spitzer, 1996).

Family Resource Interventions

Interventions that target family economic resources show mixed results. In four income-maintenance experiments in the 1960s and 1970s, treatment families received an income supplement that varied with the family's income from work and other sources (Institute for Research on Poverty, 1976l; Kershaw & Fair, 1976; Salkind & Haskins, 1982; U.S. Department of Health and Human Services, 1983). School performance and attendance were affected positively in some sites among elementary school-aged children, but not among high school adolescents. In the two sites reporting program impacts on high school completion and advanced education, these outcomes were higher for the experimental group. Parenting and child outcomes were not measured very well.

Child and family outcomes were more of a measurement priority in a number of welfare-to-work experiments begun in the 1990s. Some of these programs augmented family economic resources, whereas others did not (Morris,

Huston, Duncan, Crosby, & Bos, 2001). In all cases, participants were randomly assigned to a treatment group that received the welfare reform package or to a control group that continued to abide by the old welfare rules.

Comparable analyses of these data by Morris et al. (2001) revealed that welfare reforms that both increased work and provided financial supports for working families generally promoted children's achievement and positive behavior, although children's achievement appeared to improve more than their behavior. In contrast, welfare reforms that mandated work but did not support it financially had few impacts, positive or negative, on children. Thus, it appeared that merely increasing maternal employment had no impact on children's achievement but increasing both work and income did.

Welfare reform effects on children depended crucially on the ages of the children studied. Elementary school children were helped by reforms that increased family resources, and, for the most part, unsupportive ones did not harm them. For adolescents, more limited evidence suggested that even generous reforms that promoted maternal employment may have increased school problems and risky behavior (Gennetian, Duncan, Knox, Vargas, Clark-Kaufman, & London, 2002), although nonexperimental evidence focused on welfare-to-work transitions (as opposed to changes in policy) has found improvements in adolescent mental health (Chase-Lansdale et al., 2003). In the experimental data, adolescents with younger siblings were more likely than their control group counterparts to be suspended or expelled from and to drop out of school. Assuming the responsibility of caring for their younger siblings when their mothers worked may explain some of the negative effects of these programs on adolescents. Program group adolescents without younger siblings, for example, were more likely than their control group counterparts to participate in out-of-school activities and experienced few effects on school outcomes.

Stepping back from the successful impacts on children's achievement, it is interesting to ask whether programs included in the Morris et al. (2001) synthesis affected parents. In fact, almost all of them increased parental employment rates, but, interestingly, there were virtually no significant effects on either mothers' mental health or their parenting. Thus, the hopes of welfare reformers that market work would transform family life for the better failed to materialize. Nor did the worst fears of reform nay-sayers materialize, who argued that work would add unbearable levels of stress to already struggling families.

Despite this experimental evidence, whether family resources affect child development remains a controversial issue that has generated a large nonexperimental literature (Blau, 1999; Brooks-Gunn & Duncan, 1997; Haveman & Wolfe, 1995; Mayer, 1997). Duncan and Brooks-Gunn (1997) provided a recent look at links between poverty and children's development by coordinating analyses of 12 groups of researchers working with 10 different nonexperimental developmental data sets. On the whole, the results suggest that family income may have substantial, but selective, associations with children's academic attainments. The selective nature of effects include the following: (a) family income has much larger associations with measures of children's ability and achievement than with measures of behavior, mental health, and physical health; (b) family economic conditions in early childhood appear to be more important for shaping ability and achievement than are economic conditions during adolescence; and (c) the association between income and achievement appears to be nonlinear, with the biggest impacts at the lowest levels of income. These conclusions were reinforced by Duncan, Brooks-Gunn, Yeung, and Smith's (1998) analyses, which found that children's completed schooling was more closely associated with household incomes in early childhood than middle childhood.

Not all of the sophisticated studies support these conclusions. Using the Panel Study of Income Dynamics and the National Longitudinal Survey of Youth (NLSY), Mayer (1997) provided a set of tests for omitted-variable bias and found large reductions in the estimated impact of parental income on achievement and behavior problems, leading her to conclude that much of the estimated effects of parental income on children is spurious. Blau (1999) used data from the NLSY to estimate a number of models relating income and other aspects of parental family background to children's ability, achievement test scores, and behavior problems. In general, he found small and insignificant effects of current income and larger (though still modest) effects of long-run income.

The question for policymakers is just how much money does it take to produce a meaningful effect? If one assumes that redistribution policies could successfully boost poor children's family incomes by, say, $5,000 per year for 5 years, what impact could we expect on children's developmental outcomes? If estimates by Duncan and colleagues (1998) are accurate, a $5,000 increment to income averaged over the first 5 years of a low-income child's life would produce nearly a half-year increase in completed schooling, and a 70% increase in the odds of finishing high school, but it would have no significant impact on the risk of a nonmarital teen birth for females. A comparable income increment in middle childhood or adolescence would be associated with no significant increases in any of the measured schooling or fertility outcomes. Furthermore, the nonlinear nature of the family income–child outcome relation estimated in Duncan et al. (1998) suggests that the reduction in income of more affluent families needed to finance the $5,000 increments to low-income families would not significantly reduce schooling or increase teen fertility among them.

The more general message of the welfare reform experiments (and Duncan and Brooks-Gunn, 1997) is that family resource increments are more likely to improve children's achievement than other aspects of their development. To the extent that it is both profitable and important to improve children's social behavior, it appears prudent to look beyond economic redistribution and to direct intervention as a way of enhancing children's outcomes.

Second-Generation Consequences of Boosting Adult Skills

Substantively large and statistically significant positive correlations between parental education levels and children's well-being, particularly academic achievement, are among the most replicated results from developmental studies. Haveman and Wolfe's (1995) review of published studies suggests that maternal education is more closely related to children's academic performance than fathers' education. Furthermore, parents' completion of high school or a year or two of postsecondary education appears to have a larger effect than additional years of postsecondary education beyond that level.

Nevertheless, surprisingly little is known about the causal nature of these associations (Mercy & Steelman, 1982). Most work in this area does not establish that these findings are attributable to mothers' relative schooling per se, as opposed to genetic differences or other characteristics that differentiate mothers who acquire different levels of schooling. A long list of spurious factors could be driving the maternal education–child development correlation, the most obvious of which is genetically endowed maternal cognitive abilities. Few studies attempt to control statistically for maternal cognitive ability and the many other factors that might bias nonexperimental estimation strategies; those that do, however, find that these controls reduce the association between maternal education and children's outcomes (e.g., Rosenzweig & Wolpin, 1994; Yeates, MacPhee, Campbell, & Ramey, 1983).

To date, three experimental studies with measures of child outcomes have been designed to increase maternal education: the National Evaluation of Welfare-to-Work Strategies Child Outcome Study (NEWWS-COS; McGroder, Zaslow, Moore, & LeMenestrel, 2000), New Chance (Quint, Bos, & Polit, 1997), and Even Start (Gamse, Conger, Elson, & McCarthy, 1997; the Even Start program also provided children with early education.)

None of the programs had more than marginal impacts on maternal education, in some cases because mothers in the control groups also participated in educational programs. For example, New Chance study mothers assigned to the experimental condition participated in educational programs for only 3 weeks longer than mothers in the control condition (Quint et al., 1997). In the NEWWS-COS, approximately one half of the mothers assigned to the educational treatment stream did not participate in an educational program (McGroder et al., 2000). The Even Start program succeeded in increasing mothers' participation in adult education, but this did not translate into improved basic skills.

Neither the NEWWS-COS nor New Chance evaluations found significant differences in the cognitive development and academic achievement of experimental and control group children. Even Start had positive short-term benefits for children's development, but control group children caught up to the experimental group children within a year of the program's completion. Benefits to children from these programs were unlikely in the absence of substantial gains in maternal education.

Taking advantage of the experimental design of the NEWWS-COS study, Magnuson and McGroder (2002) used an instrumental variables approach to estimate the effect of maternal schooling on 5- to 7-year-old children's academic school-readiness. They estimate that an additional 9 months of schooling causes one fourth of a standard deviation increase on a test of children's school-readiness. This suggests that there may indeed be merit to programs that are able to boost mothers' formal education. With high rates of mothers returning to school without any interventions, welfare programs appear ineffective at increasing mothers educational participation beyond these levels. The key to realizing the two-generation gain for an education-based program appears to be designing and implementing programs that successfully increase mothers' education.

EVIDENCE ON CHILD-BASED INTERVENTIONS

The sensibility of funding parent-based intervention programs depends in part on the relative profitability of alternative approaches to improving child well-being. What follows is a very brief summary of intervention evidence for programs that bypass parents and focus directly on children.

Most child-focused early education intervention programs are designed to provide children in a classroom-based setting with cognitively stimulating and enriching experiences that their parents may be unlikely to provide at home. These programs provide developmentally appropriate learning curricula and a variety of enriching activities. Most of these programs also offer some activities for parents, although typically such activities are much less intensive than the child-focused activities.

Several recent comprehensive reviews of experimental evaluations of early child-focused, center-based programs have concluded that intensive child-focused programs improve children's short-term cognitive development and long-term academic achievement and reduce children's special education placement and grade retention (Barnett, 1995; Farran, 2000; Karoly et al., 1998). Furthermore, some of these programs also improve children's later social adjustment and behavior, as reflected in fewer arrests and reports of delinquent behavior (Reynolds, Temple, Robertson, & Mann,

2001; Yoshikawa, 1994). For example, the evaluation of the Perry Preschool Program found that its participants had significantly better labor market outcomes compared with the control group nearly 27 years after the program ended (Schweinhart et al., 1993).

Regrettably, looking beyond the evaluations of these intensive "efficacy" interventions, there are virtually no experimental evaluations of more policy-relevant, less intensive, child-focused programs. Nonexperimental evaluations of less intensive programs provide some suggestive evidence that these programs may be effective. For example, Barnett's (1995) review of large-scale early childhood education programs concluded that these programs demonstrate short-term impacts on children's school outcomes, such as grade retention and special education placement, both of which impose large resource costs on schools. However, very few studies have collected data on whether these program impacts persist into children's later years or affect children's social behavior. One quasi-experimental study of the Parent Child Development Centers in Chicago (Reynolds et al., 2001) found that children who were involved in the early childhood education program had higher rates of high school graduation and lower rates of juvenile delinquency than a comparison group of children.

Cost–benefit studies have been conducted for two child-focused, early childhood education programs—Perry Preschool and the Chicago Child-Parent Center (CPC). Karoly's (2002) review of these studies found that each provided benefits that were more than three times the cost of the program, suggesting that these programs are a good investment. Lacking randomized, long-term studies of less intensive child-focused interventions, it is impossible to determine whether such programs would produce benefits in excess of their more modest costs.

Evidence on the profitability of interventions beyond the preschool years is tentative. Evidence on the impacts of improving the quality of schooling is somewhat contradictory (Card & Krueger, 1996; Hanushek, 1986). Hanushek (1997) argued that there is little systematic evidence that increasing school resources increases student performance. Reanalysis of his and other data has led other authors to claim more systematic impacts for expenditures and teacher experience (Hedges, Laine, & Greenwald, 1994) and class size (Krueger, 1999a). In addition, experimental evidence from a large class-size experiment in Tennessee confirmed that reducing class size, especially in the early grades, improves student achievement, particularly among Black and disadvantaged students (Krueger, 1999b; Nye, Hedges, & Konstantopoulos, 2001). For young students who show early signs of school failure, one-on-one instruction or tutoring appears to be an effective means to improve their short-term academic outcomes (Elbaum, Vaughn, Hughes, & Moody, 2000). Perhaps a safe conclusion from this research is that spending more money on the quality of their schooling years has, at best, selective payoffs, with much to be learned about the dimensions of school quality that matter the most for improving children's academic outcomes.

Child-focused problem behavior treatments are based on research showing that children with severe problem behaviors, particularly aggressive or externalizing behaviors, demonstrate deficiencies in a large range of cognitive and social skills. Aggressive children tend to misinterpret the actions of others and attribute hostile intent to others in situations in which the cues are ambiguous (Dodge, 1993). Furthermore, such children tend to lack problem-solving skills and have difficulties managing impulses, maintaining attention, and developing positive relationships with peers and adults.

Child-based treatments for disruptive behavior disorders include three related programs: problem-solving skills training, cognitive behavioral treatments, and social skills programs. Although each type of program emphasizes slightly different dimensions of children's deficits, the overarching goal is to teach children how to approach and react to interpersonal situations and problems more appropriately. Although programs vary in the techniques employed, children are taught how to self-direct their thoughts, control anger, and to use step-by-step approaches to solve problems in real world situations. To correct maladaptive problem-solving strategies, programs seek to foster new skills, such as identifying and perceiving problems, generating alternative solutions, choosing a solution, and evaluating an outcome (Dumas, 1989).

In general, evaluations of these child-based interventions suggest that they are often successful. In a meta-analysis of cognitive behavioral treatments for children, Durlak and colleagues (1991) found that the mean effect size of the program treatment was 0.50 of a standard deviation at program completion and 0.56 approximately 4 months later.

As was the case with the parent management training studies, reviews of completed studies are encouraging, but should be qualified by taking into account study design flaws. Most studies have small sample sizes, are plagued by high rates of attrition, and do not have long-term follow-up studies. Durlak and colleagues (1991) reported that the average follow-up study was conducted just 4 months after the completion of the treatment. Given the evidence that other types of interventions produce positive short-term gains that fade over time, establishing whether child-based programs will yield long-term benefits is an important area for further research. At least one study found that program-induced improvements in children's externalizing behavior had disappeared 2 to 3 years after program completion (Lochman, 1992). Again, an accounting of program costs and benefits is almost never provided, and thus it is unclear whether the social rate of return from these programs is positive.

COMBINED PARENT AND CHILD APPROACHES

Does adding parenting education programs to child-based programs result in additional benefits for children? Unfortunately, the evidence is inconclusive. The most successful early childhood education programs have included some form of parenting program, which suggests that the parenting component may contribute to the program's effectiveness. For example, Perry Preschool included weekly home visits to mothers, and in several other programs, parental involvement in the classroom was an explicit goal of the program (e.g, Abecedarian, CPC). However, it is difficult to evaluate the relative importance of these parenting components of early childhood education programs. The evaluation studies do not provide much information about parents' participation in the program or about program effects on parenting.

To date, there are no available studies that compare a child education program to the same child education program combined with parenting education, and this type of study would provide an important contribution to our knowledge base.[1] The information that is available comes from nonexperimental studies of programs that combined child and parent programs. Two studies have examined whether early education programs improved aspects of parenting or parent well-being, and if so, whether these program effects were related to the programs' impacts on children. Burchinal, Campbell, Bryant, Wasik, and Ramey (1997) examined whether improvements in either children's home learning environments or parents' authoritarian parenting attitudes accounted for some of early education programs' positive impacts on children. Analyses revealed that these programs did not have a positive effect on children's home learning environments or parents' authoritarian attitudes. Consequently, these avenues could not have been responsible for the program's success.

Using data from the Infant Health and Development Program (IHDP), Klebanov, Brooks-Gunn, and McCormick (2001) examined whether reductions in maternal distress and improvements in mothers' coping strategies accounted, at least in part, for positive program impacts on children. The IHDP included a home-visiting program for mothers during the child's first 3 years, in addition to an intensive early education program. The home-visiting program used a problem-solving curriculum and emphasized forming an emotionally supportive relationship between mothers

---

[1]Although the Early Head Start study estimates the effects of three types of programs—home-visiting programs, center-based programs, and programs that used a combination of home-visiting and center-based programming—the authors point out that the sites did not offer more than one program, and consequently the populations that received these programs differed. Therefore, it is not appropriate to attribute differential impact to program type, rather than differences in the populations served.

and the home visitor. Results indicate some selective positive effects on mothers. The program reduced maternal distress, although it did not improve mothers' coping strategies. Improvements in maternal well-being did not contribute to the program-induced improvements in children's academic achievement or behavior. Although research has not fully discounted a contribution, the bulk of the evidence indicates that it is unlikely that these parent programs have a positive effect on children's academic achievement.

In contrast, there is reason to believe that including parent management training in child-based programs for problem behavior yields better results. Parent- and child-based interventions target distinct domains of developmental models of problem behavior, and for this reason, the treatment is complementary. Child-focused programs improve children's cognitive-behavioral repertoires, whereas parent training programs ensure that children's positive social behavior is supported. Two studies have compared the benefits of combined parent and child programs with the benefits of child- and parent-only programs (Kazdin, Siegal, & Bass, 1992; Webster-Stratton & Hammond, 1997). Results from both studies indicate that although parent- and child-only programs benefited children, the benefits of the combined approach exceeded that of the other approaches, although neither study formally tested the question of whether program impacts were significantly different. For example, Kazdin and colleagues (1992) evaluation of these approaches with children ages 7–13 found that parental reports of child behavior problems were within a normative range one year after treatment completion only among children whose family was assigned to the combined parent and child program. Ongoing evaluations of multicomponent programs, such as the Fast Track prevention program, will yield important information about the ability of these programs to effect long-term change in children's problem behavior (Conduct Problems Prevention Research Group, 2002).

CONCLUSION

The years in which children live with parents provide abundant opportunities for parent-focused interventions designed to enhance human potential. This chapter focused on the extent to which parent-based programs promote children's achievement and positive behavior, and sought to place such programs within the broader context of policy approaches to improving children's well-being. The gaps in knowledge are many and, therefore, drawing firm conclusions is unwarranted. The field is particularly hampered by a lack of the studies that document the long-term effects of interventions, replicate exemplar programs in real-world settings, and estimate the costs and benefits associated with the programs.

Although the typical parenting education program appears to have modest effects on parenting practices, it has not demonstrated significant impacts on children's academic achievement. If a program produced more substantial and systematic improvements in parenting, would we see larger improvements in children's achievement? Unfortunately, the answer is unclear. It may be that programs must produce large changes in parenting if children are to benefit. However, it is also possible that the types of parenting that programs target are not strongly associated with children's academic outcomes, and consequently even large changes in parenting behavior would not lead to substantial improvements in children's academic outcomes. The typical parent management program for parents of children with severe problem behaviors appears to be a more promising avenue of intervention. Some of these programs reduce children's problem behavior, at least in the short term. These programs are more effective for children rather than adolescents and for families with greater resources.

Turning to economic interventions, evidence from recent welfare-to-work programs indicates that increasing the economic resources of low-income families promotes positive achievement and behavior for children, although the effect sizes are modest, and we do not know how long the positive impacts will be maintained.

Interventions targeting young children directly may be the most effective of all in promoting academic achievement and reducing problem behavior. Although a handful of careful studies of very intensive early-education programs support this view, the lamentably small amount of evidence on the payoffs to more practical, less expensive programs should leave interested parties cautious about drawing definitive conclusions regarding the long-term benefits of these programs. Similarly, child-focused problem-behavior interventions, including problem-solving skills training, have resulted in short-term reductions in children's problem behavior. These programs, however, have not yet proved their long-term worth, and it may be that the combination of parent- and child-based programming is the most effective form of intervention.

There are lessons to be learned from the fact that parenting programs appear more successful in reducing problem behavior than in promoting academic achievement. In particular, screening children and directing services to those with a demonstrated need may be particularly important for producing cost-effective program benefits. However, to effectively develop programs, it is necessary to understand the developmental progression of school failure. Remarkably little research addresses the developmental processes that contribute to academic underachievement, and more generally establish academic trajectories (Alexander & Entwisle, 1988). With a greater understanding of the processes that determine a child's academic course, intervention services may be better designed and targeted to promote children's academic achievement.

Our preoccupation with the economic aspects of interventions is rooted in a desire to inform policymakers about choices among competing real-world intervention programs as well as "interventions" that alter family resources with tax and transfer policies. Although much more is to be learned, our tentative conclusion is that the bulk of intervention resources should be focused on child-based, especially preadolescent child-based programs. It may also make sense to tilt transfer programs explicitly toward families with young children, as the French have done with single-parent benefits that end with the child's third birthday, or that countries could do with age-graded child allowances or tax credits.

ACKNOWLEDGMENTS

We are grateful to the Family and Child Well-being Research Network of the National Institute of Child Health and Human Development (2 U01 HD30947-07) for supporting this research and to Robert LaLonde for helpful comments.

REFERENCES

Alexander, K. L., & Entwisle, D. R. (1988). Achievement in the first two years of school: Patterns and processes. *Monographs of the Society for the Research in Child Development, 53* (2) (Serial 218).

Barnett, W. S. (1995). Long-term effects of early childhood programs on cognitive and school outcomes. *The Future of Children, 5*(3), 25–50.

Becker, G. S. (1975). *Human capital: A theoretical analysis with special reference to education.* New York: National Bureau of Economic Research.

Becker, G. S. (1981). *A treatise on the family.* Cambridge, MA: Harvard University Press.

Blau, D. M. (1999). The effect of income on child development. *The Review of Economics and Statistics, 8,* 261–276.

Brooks-Gunn, J., Berlin, L. J., & Fuligni, A. (2000). Early childhood intervention programs: What about the family? In S. Meisels & J. Shonkoff (Eds.), *The handbook of early intervention* (2nd ed., pp. 549–588). New York: Cambridge University Press.

Brooks-Gunn, J., Brown, B., Duncan, G., & Moore, K. A. (1995). Child development in the context of family and community resources: An agenda for national data collection. In National Research Council Institute of Medicine (Eds.), *Integrating federal statistics on children: Report of a workshop* (pp. 27–97). Washington, DC: National Academy Press.

Brooks-Gunn, J., & Duncan, G. (1997). The effects of poverty on children and youth. *The Future of Children, 7,* 55–71.

Burchinal, M. R., Campbell, F. A., Bryant, D. M., Wasik, B. H., & Ramey, C. T. (1997). Early intervention and mediating processes in cognitive performance of children of low–income African American families. *Child Development, 68,* 935–954.

Card, D., & Krueger, A. (1996). School resources and student outcomes: An overview of the literature and new evidence from North and South Carolina. *Journal of Economic Perspectives, 10*, 31–50.

Chase-Lansdale, P. L, Moffit, R. A., Lohman, B. J., Cherlin, A., Coley, R. L., Pittman, L. D., et al. (2003). Mothers' transitions from welfare to work and the well-being of preschoolers and adolescents. *Science, 229*(March 7), 1548–1552.

Collins, W. A., Maccoby, E. E., Steinberg, L., Hetherington, E. M., & Bornstein, M. H. (2000). Contemporary research on parenting: The case for nurture and nature. *American Psychologist, 55*, 218–232.

Conduct Problems Prevention Research Group. (2002). Evaluation of the first three years of the Fast Track Prevention trial with children at high risk for adolescent conduct problems. *Journal of Abnormal Child Psychology, 30*, 19–35.

Deater-Decker, K., Dodge, K. A., Bates, J. E., & Petit, G. S. (1994). Physical discipline among African–American and European American Mothers: Links to children's externalizing behaviors. *Developmental Psychology, 32*, 1065–1072.

Dishion, T. J., & Patterson, G. R. (1992). Age effects in parent training outcome. *Behavior Therapy, 23*, 719–729.

Dodge, K. (1993). Social-cognitive mechanisms in the development of conduct disorder and depression. *Annual Review of Psychology, 44*, 559–84.

Dumas, J. E. (1989). Treating anti-social behavior in children: Child and family approaches. *Clinical Psychology Review, 9*, 197–222.

Duncan, G., & Brooks-Gunn, J. (Eds.). (1997). *Consequences of growing up poor*. New York: Russell Sage.

Duncan, G., Brooks-Gunn, J., Yeung, J., & Smith, J. (1998). How much does childhood poverty affect the life chances of children? *American Sociological Review, 63*, 406–423.

Durlak, J. A., Fuhrman, T., & Lampman, C. (1991). Effectiveness of cognitive–behavioral therapy for maladapting children: A meta-analysis. *Psychological Bulletin, 2*, 204–214.

Elbaum, B., Vaughn, S., Hughes, M. T., & Moody, S. W. (2000). How effective are one-on-one tutoring programs in reading for elementary students at risk for reading failure? A meta-analysis of the intervention research. *Journal of Educational Psychology, 92*, 605–619.

Farran, D. C. (2000). Another decade of intervention for children who are low-income or disabled: What do we know now? In J. Shonkoff & S. Meisels (Eds.), *Handbook of early childhood intervention* (2nd ed., pp. 510–548). New York: Cambridge University Press.

Gamse, B. C., Conger, D., Elson, D., & McCarthy, M. (1997). *Follow-up study of families in the Even Start in depth study*. Cambridge, MA: Abt Associates.

Gennetian, L., Duncan, G., Knox, V. W., Vargas, W., Clark-Kaufman, E., & London, A. S. (2002). *How welfare and work policies for parents affect adolescents*. New York: Manpower Demonstration Research Corporation.

Gomby, D. S., Culross, P. L., & Behrman, R. E. (1999). Home visiting: Recent program evaluations analysis and recommendations. *The Future of Children, 9*(1), 4–26.

Gramlich, E. (1990). *A guide to cost–benefit analysis*. Englewood Cliffs, NJ: Prentice-Hall.

Greenberg, M., Domitrovich, C., & Bumbarger, B. (2000). *Preventing mental disorders in school-age children: A review of the effectiveness of prevention programs*. Working paper, Prevention Research Center for the Promotion of Human Development College of Health and Human Development, Pennsylvania State University. Available: http://www.prevention.psu.edu/CMHS.PDF

Hanushek, E. A. (1986). The economics of schooling: Production and efficiency in pub-
    lic schools. *Journal of Economic Literature, 24*, 1141–1177.
Hanushek, E. A. (1997). Assessing the effects of school resources on student perfor-
    mance: An update. *Educational Evaluation and Policy Analysis, 19*, 141–164.
Harris, Y. R., Terrel, D., & Allen, G. (1999). The influence of education context and be-
    liefs on the teaching behavior of African American mothers. *Journal of Black Psychol-
    ogy, 25*, 490–503.
Haveman, R., & Wolfe, B. (1994). *Succeeding generations: On the effect of investments in
    children.* New York: Russell Sage Foundation.
Haveman, R., & Wolfe, B. (1995). The determinants of children's attainments: A re-
    view of methods and findings. *Journal of Economic Literature, 23*, 1829–1878.
Hedges, L. V., Laine, R. D., & Greenwald, R. (1994). Does money matter? A meta-anal-
    ysis of studies of the effects of differential school inputs on student outcomes. *Educa-
    tion Researcher, 23*, 5–14.
Institute for Research on Poverty. (1976). *The rural income maintenance experiment.* Mad-
    ison: University of Wisconsin.
Karoly, L. (2002). Investing in the future: Reducing poverty through human capital pro-
    grams. In S. Danziger & R. Haveman (Eds.), *Understanding poverty in America: Prog-
    ress and problems* (pp. 314–346). Cambridge, MA: Harvard University Press.
Karoly, L. A., Greenwood, P. W., Everingham, S. S., Houbé, J., Kilburn, M. R., Rydell, C.
    P., et al. (1998). *Investing in our children: What we know and don't know about the costs
    and benefits of early childhood interventions.* Santa Monica, CA: RAND.
Kazdin, A. E. (1997). Parent management training: Evidence, outcomes, and issues.
    Journal of the American Academy of Child and Adolescent Psychiatry, 36, 1349–1356.
Kazdin, A. E., Siegal, T. C., & Bass, D. (1992). Cognitive problem-solving skills training
    and parent management training in the treatment of anti-social behavior in chil-
    dren. *Journal of Consulting and Clinical Psychology, 60*, 733–747.
Kazdin, A., & Weisz, J. R. (1998). Identifying and developing empirically supported
    child and adolescent treatments. *Journal of Consulting and Clinical Psychology, 66*,
    19–36.
Kershaw, D., & Fair, J. (1976). *The New Jersey income maintenance experiment (Vol. 1).*
    New York: Academic Press.
Klebanov, P. K., Brooks-Gunn, J., & McCormick, M. C. (2001). Maternal coping strate-
    gies and emotional distress: Results of an early intervention program for low birth
    weight young children. *Developmental Psychology, 37*, 654–667.
Krueger, A. B. (1999a). *An economist's view of class size research.* Unpublished working
    paper, Princeton University.
Krueger, A. B. (1999b). Experimental estimates of education production functions.
    Quarterly Journal of Economics, 114, 497–532.
Krueger, A. B. (2003). Economic considerations and class size. *Economic Journal, 113*
    (485), F34–F65.
Laosa, L. (1983). School, occupation, culture and family. In E. Sigel & L. Laosa (Eds.),
    Changing families (pp.79–135). New York: Plenum Press.
Levin, H. (1983). *Cost effectiveness: A primer.* Beverly Hills, CA: Sage.
Lochman, J. E. (1992). Cognitive-behavioral intervention with aggressive boys: A
    three-year follow-up and preventive effects. *Journal of Consulting and Clinical Psychol-
    ogy, 60*, 426–432.
Love, J. M., Kisker, E. E., Ross, C. M., Schochet, P. Z., Brooks-Dunn, J., Paulsell, D. et al.
    (2002). *Making a difference in the lives of infants and toddlers and their families: The im-*

pacts of Early Head Start. Volume 1: Final technical report. Princeton, NJ: Mathematica Policy Research.

Magnuson, K. A., & McGroder, S. (2002). *The effect of increasing welfare mothers' education on their young children's academic problems and school readiness.* Joint Center for Poverty Research working paper no. 280. Evanston, IL: Northwestern University.

Mayer, S. (1997). *What money can't buy: The effect of parental income on children's outcomes.* Cambridge, MA: Harvard University Press.

McGroder, S. (2000). Parenting among low-income African American single mothers with preschool-age children: Patterns, predictors, and developmental correlates. *Child Development, 71,* 752–771.

McGroder, S. M., Zaslow, M. J., Moore, K. A., & LeMenestrel, S. M. (2000). *National evaluation of welfare-to-work strategies impacts on young children and their families two years after enrollment: Findings from the child outcomes study.* Washington, DC: U.S. Department of Health and Human Services.

McLoyd, V. (1990). The impact of economic hardship on black children and families: Psychological distress, parenting, and socio-emotional development. *Child Development, 61,* 311–346.

McLoyd, V. (1998). Socioeconomic disadvantage and child development. *American Psychologist, 53,* 185–204.

Mercy, J. A., & Steelman, L. C. (1982). Familial influence on the intellectual attainment of children. *American Sociological Review, 47,* 532–542.

Michael, R. T. (1972). *The effect of education on efficiency in consumption.* New York: Columbia University Press.

Michael, R. T. (1982). Measuring non-monetary benefits of education: A survey. In W. W. McMahon & T. G. Geske (Eds.), *Financing education: Overcoming inefficiency and inequality* (pp.119-149). Chicago: University of Illinois Press.

Morris, P. A., Huston, A. C., Duncan, G. J., Crosby, D. A., & Bos, J. M. (2001). *How welfare and work policies affect children: A synthesis of research.* New York: Manpower Demonstration Research Corporation.

Nye, B., Hedges, B., & Konstantopoulos, S. (2001). The long-term effects of small classes in early grades: Lasting benefits in mathematics achievement at grade 9. *Journal of Experimental Education, 69,* 245–257.

Olds, D., Henderson, C. R., Kitzman, H. J., Eckenrode, J. J., Cole, R. E., & Tatelbaum, R. C. (1999). Prenatal and infancy home visitation by nurses: Recent findings. *The Future of Children, 9,* 44–65.

Owen, M. T., & Mulvihill, B. A. (1994). Benefits of a parent education and support program in the first three years. *Family Relations, 43,* 206–212.

Patterson, G. R., DeBaryshe, B. D., & Ramsey, E. (1989). A developmental perspective on anti-social behavior. *American Psychologist, 44,* 329–335.

Prinz, R. J., & Miller, G. E. (1994). Family-based treatment for childhood anti-social behavior: Experimental influences on dropout and engagement. *Journal of Consulting and Clinical Psychology, 62,* 645–650.

Quint, J., Bos, H., & Polit, D. (1997). *New Chance: Final report on a comprehensive program for young mothers in poverty and their children.* New York: Manpower Research Demonstration Corporation.

Reynolds, A. J., Temple, J. A., Robertson, D. L. & Mann, E. A. (2001). Long term effects of an early childhood intervention on educational achievement and juvenile arrest: A 15-year follow-up of low income children in public schools. *Journal of the American Medical Association, 285,* 2339–46.

Rosenzweig, M. R., & Wolpin, K. I. (1994). Are there increasing returns to the intergenerational production of human capital? Maternal schooling and child intellectual development. *Journal of Human Resources, 29*, 670–693.

Rowe, D. C. (1994) *The limits of family influence: Genes, experience and behavior.* New York: Guilford.

Rowe, D. C., & Rodgers, J. L. (1997). Poverty and behavior: Are environmental measures nature and nurture? *Developmental Review, 17*, 358–375.

Ruma, P. R., Burke, R. V., & Thompson, R. W. (1996). Group parent training: Is it effective for parents of all ages? *Behavior Therapy, 27*, 159–169.

Salkind, N. J., & Haskins, R. (1982). Negative income tax: The impact on children from low-income families. *Journal of Family Issues, 3*, 165–180.

Scarr, S. (1992). Developmental theories for the 1990s: Development and individual differences. *Child Development, 63*, 1–19.

Schweinhart, L., Barnes, H., & Weikart, D. (1993). *Significant benefits: The High/Score Perry Preschool study through age 27.* Ypsilanti, MI: High Scope Press.

Seitz, V., & Provence, S. (1990). Caregiver-focused models of early intervention. In S. J. Meisels & J. P. Shonkoff (Eds.), *Handbook of early childhood intervention* (pp. 400–427). New York: Cambridge University Press.

Shadish, W. R., Cook, T., & Campbell, D. T. (2002). *Experimental and quasi-experimental designs for generalized causal inference.* New York: Houghton Mifflin.

Shonkoff, J. P., & Phillips, D. A. (Eds.). (2000). *From neurons to neighborhoods: The science of early childhood development.* Washington, DC: National Academy Press.

Taylor, T. K., & Biglan, A. (1998). Behavioral family interventions for improving child-rearing: A review of the literature for clinicians and policy makers. *Clinical Child & Family Psychology Review, 1*, 41–60.

Trickett, P. K., Aber, L. J., Carlson, V., & Cicchetti, D. (1991). Relationship of socioeconomic status to the etiology and developmental sequelae of physical child abuse. *Developmental Psychology, 37*, 148–158.

U.S. Department of Health and Human Services. (1983). *Overview of the Seattle-Denver Income Maintenance Experiment and Final Report.* Office of Income Security Policy. Washington, DC: Author.

Wagner, M. M., & Clayton, S. L. (1999). The Parents as Teachers program: Results from two demonstrations. *The Future of Children, 9*(1), 91–115.

Webster-Stratton, C. (1990). Long-term follow-up with young conduct problem children: From preschool to grade school. *Journal of Clinical Child Psychology, 19*, 144–149.

Webster-Stratton, C., & Hammond, M. (1990). Predictors of treatment outcomes in parenting training with conduct problem children. *Behavior Therapy, 21*, 319–337.

Webster-Stratton, C., & Hammond, M. (1997). Treating children with early onset conduct problems: A comparison of child and parent training interventions. *Journal of Consulting and Clinical Psychology, 65*, 93–109.

Webster-Stratton, C., Kolpacoff, M., & Hollinsworth, T. (1988). Self-administered videotape therapy for families with conduct problem children: Comparison with two cost-effective treatments and a control group. *Journal of Consulting and Clinical Psychology, 56*, 558–566.

Webster-Stratton, C., & Spitzer, A. (1996). Parenting a young child with conduct problems. New insights using qualitative methods. In T. H. Ollendick & R. J. Prinz (Eds.), *Advances in clinical child psychology* (pp. 1–62). New York: Plenum Press.

Yeates, K. O., MacPhee, D., Campbell, F. A., & Ramey, C. T. (1983). Maternal IQ and home environment as determinants of early childhood intellectual competence: A developmental analysis. *Developmental Psychology, 19*, 731–739.

Yoshikawa, H. (1994). Prevention as cumulative protection: Effects of early family support and education as chronic delinquency and its risk. *Psychological Bulletin, 115*, 28–54.

10

A Cross-National Perspective on Policies to Promote Investments in Children

Jane Waldfogel
Columbia University

Countries vary greatly in the amount that they spend on children and on promoting parental investments in children. Countries also vary in their choice of policy instruments for these investments. This chapter considers those choices of expenditures and policy instruments, the rationale that underlies them, and what is known about their effects on parental investments and, ultimately, child outcomes. Recent social policy reforms in the United Kingdom are used as a case study of the choices that governments make in how much to invest in children, and by what instruments.

There is much research in economics and related disciplines that considers why and how governments invest in children (see, e.g., Barr, 1998). Generally, in economics, public investments in children are seen as being justified if they promote efficiency or equity. That is, if there are benefits to investments in children that accrue not just to their families but also to society at large, then public investments in children may be efficient. Also, if the distribution of parental resources, and hence potential investments, in children is uneven, then government spending may promote a more equitable distribution of investments. Outside economics, public expenditures on children are also sometimes justified on the grounds that children have the right to receive certain services or resources, or that children's quality of life and experiences matter as ends in and of themselves. One concern with regard to government investments is the possibility of their crowding out parental investments; see, for example, the research on Medicaid expansions in the United States, which notes all three of these features (health care as a public good, the goal of equitable distribution, but also substantial crowd-out).

There is also a fairly large body of research that compares how much different countries spend on social welfare programs (see Organization for Economic Cooperation and Development [OECD], 2002a, 2002b; and Kamerman & Kahn, 1997a,1997b). This research points to considerable variation across countries and also indicates that although the United States spends significant amounts in absolute terms on social welfare programs, it is less generous than other countries when considering expenditures as a share of gross domestic product (GDP). The United States ranks 20th out of 21 Organization for Economic Cooperation and Development (OECD) countries in its share of GDP spent on social welfare programs (Table 10.1). The picture, of course, is complicated by the fact that U.S. state and local governments play an important role in social welfare spending. Although state and local expenditures are included in Table 10.1, to simplify the discussion, the distinction between federal, state, and local government is ignored in the text.

Of course, not all social welfare expenditures go to children. Ideally, comparisons would consider expenditures for children separately from other social welfare expenditures (which might flow to working-age adults or the aged). However, this is not a simple exercise and has not been done across countries. Alternatively, comparisons might look at some specific programs targeted to children. As an illustration, Table 10.2 shows the share of GDP that countries devoted in 1998 (the most recent year for which data are available) to three large programs targeted to children or families with children: primary and secondary education, family cash benefits, and family services. In addition, the table shows contributions to one large program that reaches children as well as other individuals—health. When the analysis is limited to these four programs, the U.S. position improves somewhat from where it stood in Table 10.1, but it remains a comparative laggard. It is in the bottom half of the pack (in the bottom 9 or 10 of the 21 countries) in terms of the share of GDP spent on education, family services, and health, and at the bottom of the pack (outspent by 19 of 21 countries) in the share of GDP spent on family cash benefits.

Social welfare expenditures play an important role in reducing child poverty and in equalizing post-tax and transfer incomes. Generally, countries that spend more on social welfare as a share of GDP do more to reduce child poverty and to equalize incomes than countries that spend less. In particular, the United States does a poor job comparatively of reducing child poverty and income inequality (Smeeding, Rainwater, & Burtless, 2001). (Of

TABLE 10.1

Government Social Welfare Expenditure as Percentage of GDP in OECD Countries, 1960 to 1998 (Countries Ranked by Percentage in 1998)

Rank	Country	1960	1975	1985	1990	1998
1	Sweden	15.6	27.4	32.0	39.6	35.5
2	Denmark	9.0	27.1	33.9	33.9	34.1
3	France	14.4	26.3	34.2	31.9	32.9
4	Switzerland	8.2	19.0	20.5	NA	32.3
5	Norway	11.0	23.2	23.5	35.5	31.4
6	Finland	14.9	21.9	22.8	33.8	30.2
7	Germany	17.1	27.8	25.8	27.5	30.1
8	Austria	17.4	26.0	28.8	29.9	30.0
9	Italy	13.7	20.6	26.7	NA	28.5
10	United Kingdom	12.4	19.6	20.9	27.6	28.1
11	Belgium	NA	28.7	35.8	30.6	28.0
12	Netherlands	12.8	29.3	30.7	34.4	26.9
13	New Zealand	12.7	19.0	19.8	NA	25.6
14	Greece	NA	10.0	19.5	NA	25.0
15	Australia	9.5	17.3	18.4	17.7	24.2
16	Spain	NA	NA	NA	23.8	23.0
17	Portugal	NA	NA	NA	20.8	22.4
18	Canada	11.2	20.1	22.6	25.5	21.7
19	Ireland	11.3	22.0	25.6	25.2	19.0
20	United States	9.9	18.7	18.2	20.1	18.0
21	Japan	7.6	13.7	16.2	15.3	17.5

Notes: OECD = Organization for Economic Cooperation and Development; GDP = gross domestic product. Data for 1960 to 1990 from Kamerman and Kahn (1997b), Table 4.1, p. 94. Data for 1998 from OECD (2002a), "Public social expenditures by main category, 1980–1998"; and OECD (2002b), Table B2.1b, "Expenditures on educational institutions as a percentage of GDP."

TABLE 10.2
Government Social Welfare Expenditures as Percentage of GDP
in OECD Countries. 1998, by Selected Programs

Country	Health	Education	Cash Benefits	Services
Australia	6.0	3.2	2.2	0.4
Austria	5.8	4.0	1.9	1.1
Belgium	6.1	3.5	2.1	0.2
Canada	6.4	3.7	0.8	NA
Denmark	6.8	4.3	1.5	2.2
Finland	5.3	3.7	1.9	1.4
France	7.3	4.1	1.5	1.2
Germany	7.8	2.8	1.9	0.8
Greece	4.7	2.3	1.2	0.7
Ireland	4.7	3.2	1.6	0.2
Italy	5.5	3.4	0.6	0.3
Japan	5.7	2.8	0.2	0.3
Netherlands	6.0	3.0	0.8	0.4
New Zealand	6.6	4.6	2.6	0.1
Norway	7.1	4.4	2.2	1.4
Portugal	5.1	4.2	0.7	0.3
Spain	5.4	3.3	0.3	0.1
Sweden	6.6	4.5	1.6	1.7
Switzerland	7.6	4.0	1.2	0.1
United Kingdom	5.6	3.4	1.7	0.5
United States	5.9	3.4	0.2	0.3

Notes: OECD = Organization for Economic Cooperation and Development; GDP = gross domestic product. Data from OECD (2002a), "Public social expenditures by main category, 1980–1998"; and OECD (2002b), Table B2.1b, "Expenditures on educational institutions as a percentage of GDP."

course, social welfare expenditures have many other aims beyond reducing child poverty and income inequality. However, there are few, if any, studies that link the share of GDP spent on specific social programs for children to child outcomes—other than poverty or inequality—across countries.)

The social welfare expenditure data shown in Tables 10.1 and 10.2 reveal only one portion of the resources invested in children—the share from government expenditures. Missing are the resources that parents contribute, thus understating the total resources invested in children.

The magnitude of parents' investments can be seen in recent work by Bainbridge and Garfinkel (2002; see also Bainbridge, 2002; Garfinkel, 1996; Haveman & Wolfe, 1995). Bainbridge and Garfinkel estimated that parents' investments of time and money make up roughly 58% to 64% of all resources invested in children (a range of estimates is provided because the results are sensitive to method and, in particular, to how one values parental time). Although government investments are particularly important for the lowest income families (i.e., those from the lowest quintile of market income), even here the parental share is not negligible (see Table 10.3). As a result, when including parental investments, the share of GDP that is invested in children rises substantially. According to Bainbridge and Garfinkel (2002), roughly $1 trillion was invested in children in the United States in 1996, an amount equal to roughly 12% to 15% of GDP that year. However, only about $415 billion of that money (about 5% of GDP) came from the government.

Similar cross-country comparisons of the share of parental and government investment in children are unavailable. This is particularly unfortunate because if the shares vary substantially, then cross-country comparisons of government expenditures on children will not accurately capture the relative position of countries' total investments in children. Smeeding and coauthors (Osberg, Smeeding, & Schwabish, 2002; Smeeding, 2002) recently estimated both government support for children and the market incomes of families with children in the United States and in some European countries using data from the Luxembourg Income Study (LIS). It is possible to use their estimates to calculate the resources available to children from government benefits and from families' private market incomes.

As Table 10.4 shows, the United States ranks much higher in total income potentially available to children when one takes families' market incomes into account. Consider, for example, a child from a family with a median income in the United States (Panel B of Table 10.4). Looking only at cash transfers, the child ranks 12th of 13 countries, receiving less income in transfers than the median child in any other country except Switzerland. However, accounting for the relatively lower U.S. tax rate, that median-income child moves into sixth position. Add spending on noncash benefits, and the child ranks fifth. After adding in family market income, the median

TABLE 10.3

U.S. Government and Parental Expenditures on Children, 1996, by Income Quintile
(in billions of dollars, and as a percentage of total expenditures on children)

	1st quintile	2nd	3rd	4th	5th	Total
Government expenditures						
in billions of dollars	100–105	75–78	70–71	74–75	87–94	414
share of total	63–73%	42–50%	33–41%	30–39%	27–33%	
Parents' money						
in billions of dollars	10	49	74	90	153	376
share of total	6–7%	26–32%	34–44%	37–48%	47–59%	
Parents' time						
in billions of dollars	27–52	26–60	26–73	25–81	21–81	123–346
share of total	20–31%	17–32%	15–33%	13–33%	8–26%	
Total expenditures on children						
in billions of dollars	142–162	154–185	171–217	239–246	260–328	976–1138
share of total	100%	100%	100%	100%	100%	100%

Note: Author's calculations based on data in Bainbridge and Garfinkel (2002), Table 4.

TABLE 10.4
Resources Available to Children by Percentile (in 1997 $US)

A. 10th percentile

	(1)	(2)	(3)	(4)
	Cash benefits	Net Cash benefits	Cash & non–Cash benefits	Total (cash, noncash, & market income)
Australia	8,551	8,352	12,449	14,178
Belgium	8,730	8,730	14,700	18,292
Canada	8,036	7,525	12,745	17,179
Denmark	7,081	1,883	8,561	18,962
Finland	9,795	7,718	12,598	17,493
France	5,866	5,811	9,982	16,493
Germany	5,650	4,264	8,216	15,154
Netherlands	8,453	4,996	8,640	15,339
Norway	8,467	6,589	15,028	23,362
Sweden	7,417	3,497	9,354	19,298
Switzerland	6,867	4,519	10,749	18,356
United Kingdom	8,087	7,977	11,514	12,162
United States	5,984	5,537	12,453	16,527

B. 50th percentile

Australia	2,175	–3,367	730	27,061
Belgium	3,597	3,597	9,567	30,895
Canada	2,678	–6,066	–846	33,584
Denmark	5,558	–7,279	–551	32,997
Finland	6,041	–2,060	2,821	26,791
France	5,716	5,147	9,318	28,509
Germany	2,191	–6,204	–2,252	26,917

TABLE 10.4 (continued)

	(1)	(2)	(3)	(4)
	Cash benefits	Net Cash benefits	Cash & non–Cash benefits	Total (cash, noncash, & market income)
Netherlands	3,350	–6,126	–2,473	25,820
Norway	3,902	– 5,715	2,723	35,801
Sweden	8,925	315	6,171	28,503
Switzerland	0	–6,812	–582	36,476
United Kingdom	9,408	5,226	8,764	22,873
United States	1,875	–2,738	4,773	31,953
C. 90th percentile				
Australia	571	–10,981	– 6,885	38,682
Belgium	2,958	2,958	8,928	40,996
Canada	2,116	–12,109	–6,889	47,560
Denmark	5,101	–12,141	–5,413	38,414
Finland	7,348	–8,978	–4,097	42,920
France	2,935	897	5,068	42,485
Germany	2,283	–11,550	–7,597	37,839
Netherlands	3,238	–13,189	–9,535	34,263
Norway	3,939	–9,986	–1,547	43,418
Sweden	5,163	–7,682	–1,825	32,846
Switzerland	600	–7,295	–1,065	52,303
United Kingdom	1,580	–12,830	–9,293	38,6
United States	1,759	–15,129	–7,468	56,514

Notes: Author's calculations using data from Smeeding (2002), Table A–1. Columns are defined as follows: (1) cash benefits include government transfers; (2) net cash benefits include both taxes and transfers; (3) cash and noncash benefits include government taxes and transfers plus government spending on health and education; (4) total includes cash and noncash benefits plus families' market income (earnings).

U.S. child remains in fifth position. Thus, the relative standing of this median child, in terms of available public and private resources, is considerably better than when only considering cash transfers.

However, because families' market incomes are unevenly distributed, their impact on children's resources is uneven as well. For a U.S. child at the 90th income percentile, the impact of private resources is very striking. Although this child receives few government transfers (ranking 10th of 13 countries), the low tax rate, relatively high levels of spending on noncash benefits, and especially high private incomes in the United States mean that a child at the top of the U.S. income distribution enjoys a level of combined public and private resources unparalleled in any country.

The situation is quite different, however, for a child at the bottom of the income distribution. A child at the 10th percentile in the United States fares worse than in most other countries in terms of cash benefits (9th of 13 countries) and remains in the bottom half of the income distribution (8th of 13 countries) even after taking family market income into account. (Note that these calculations include tax credits such as the Earned Income Tax Credit, which is a very important support for low-income families in the United States.)

These comparative data on social welfare expenditures reveal two things about the United States. The first is that the United States spends less than other countries on social welfare benefits, and particularly on cash benefits. The second is that the impact of this lower level of social welfare spending is different at different points in the income distribution, with low-income children (who would tend to receive more benefits in other countries) relative losers and high-income children (who benefit the most from the heavier reliance on private market incomes) relative winners.

Beyond these noted limitations (the inability to distinguish spending on children as distinct from other groups, and the inability to capture parents' contributions), social welfare expenditure data also do not capture the full extent and range of government activity in promoting investments in children. Governments choose from among a set of policy instruments to invest directly in children, encourage parents to make particular investments in children, or alter the quality of investments made in children (see, e.g., discussions in Haveman & Wolfe, 1995, and Kamerman & Kahn, 1997b). The following section presents seven categories of policy instruments and considers the rationale underlying each and what is known about its effects on parental investments and ultimately child outcomes.

POLICY INSTRUMENTS TO PROMOTE INVESTMENTS IN CHILDREN

There are seven main types of policy instruments that governments use to promote investments in children: (a) direct government provision; (b) vouchers and related benefits; (c) cash benefits; (d) time benefits; (e) programs to boost parents' employment and earnings; (f) parenting or family support programs; and (g) government mandates or regulations specifying certain activities on the part of programs or parents. Countries vary widely in the choices they make about which of these instruments to use, and for which children.

Direct Government Provision

Direct government provision of primary and secondary education is common across all industrialized countries. Many countries also use direct government provision in other parts of the social welfare system, such as health care and early childhood care and education, although the United States does not. Direct government provision, like other forms of government intervention, can be justified on the grounds of efficiency or equity, or on the grounds of children's right to receive certain services or experiences. In contrast to the other types of policy instruments, direct government provision tends to be used in arenas where universal and equitable access is a goal, whether on the grounds of social cohesion or inclusion (as in education) or public goods (as in some aspects of health care), and where private market provision is either not feasible or not desirable. Direct government provision, however, can also be used in targeted programs. For instance, in the United States and United Kingdom, government directly provides free or low-cost school meals to low-income children, and many countries directly provide housing to at least some low-income families.

Direct government provision, particularly when it is universal, is generally effective in reaching its target population. Estimating its effects on child outcomes, however, is not straightforward in the absence of a control group that does not receive the services. It is striking that the large body of research on cross-country differences in government expenditures on children has not linked those differences with differences in child outcomes. One recent study (Harknett, Garfinkel, Bainbridge, Smeeding, & Folbre, 2002) took advantage of the variation in expenditures on children within the United States and found that higher public expenditures on children are linked to better outcomes for children. However, because the study used data from just one point in time, it cannot clearly establish that increases in investments lead to improved outcomes.

Thus, we know that there is variation across countries in the share of GDP spent on schooling or health (see Table 10.2), but we do not know to what extent this variation is linked with variation in outcomes for children.

Vouchers and Related Programs

Vouchers and related programs are popular policy instruments when the government wants to promote a specific type of investment in children, but prefers to let parents choose the provider, mode of provision, or product because private markets are already well established or because parental choice is important in a particular sector. In the United States, vouchers are the dominant mode for delivering child care benefits (through the now consolidated Child Care Development Fund) and food and nutrition benefits (via programs such as Food Stamps and Women, Infants, and Children [WIC]), and also play an important role in the housing sector (via Section 8 and other vouchers). The U.S. government-funded health insurance programs for low-income children (i.e., Medicaid and the State Children's Health Insurance Program) also fit this category.

In principle, vouchers and related benefits could be as (or more) effective in promoting investments in children as direct government investments. However, when using vouchers, the government has less direct control over the quality of the services delivered. Another general problem with vouchers and related benefits is low use. As a result, the effect of these programs on child outcomes is necessarily diluted, given that many of the intended beneficiaries do not, in fact, participate in the program. Calculations of these programs' effects also vary depending on whether participation is taken into account or whether effects are estimated over the entire population offered the benefit. With this caveat in mind, there is nevertheless evidence of positive effects on child outcomes of childcare programs (see reviews by Currie, 2001; Karoly et al., 1998), food and nutrition programs (Currie, 1995; Devaney, Bilheimer, & Schore, 1992), and housing voucher programs (Katz, Kling, & Liebman, 2001; Ludwig, Ladd, & Duncan, 2001; Rosenbaum, 1995). There is also evidence of positive effects of health insurance coverage for children, although at a high cost (Currie & Gruber, 1996a, 1996b).

Child care is one of the most important voucher programs in the United States. Whether provided directly or funded through vouchers, child care may be valued for several reasons: as an investment in children's future success; as a means to promote parents' employment; or as an important experience for children in and of itself. Prior research has found that the level of public support for child care varies a great deal across countries, with the United States lagging in public provision and public funding, particularly for children aged 0–2 (see, e.g., Kamerman & Kahn, 1997a; Waldfogel, 2001b).

Cash Benefits

Cash benefits are an important type of policy instrument to promote parental investments in children. The rationale for these benefits is that parents
face additional expenditures with the birth of each child, and that ensuring
that parents invest adequately in children will yield returns not just to the
parent and children but also to society. As noted earlier, these benefits can
also be justified on equity grounds, if they are redistributive and help raise
incomes for families at the bottom of the income distribution. Cash benefits
are potentially more efficient than restricted voucher-type benefits because
they allow parents to purchase the right amount of food, or child care, or
housing for their particular family (whereas voucher-type programs may
give a family more than they want or need of one good and not enough of
another). Cash benefits, however, are also subject to the concern that parents may not always act in their children's best interests in making their purchasing decisions.

Most industrialized countries have a basic child benefit or child allowance that is provided to all families with children and that increases with
family size. These are typically not means-tested but may be taxed back for
higher income families. Countries may also have other child benefits targeted to specific groups or specific children. Higher benefits to families with
infants intended to offset the additional costs associated with a newborn, for
instance, are quite common. Virtually all countries have some system of additional income support for the lowest income families with children. The
rules governing child benefits and child allowances are complicated and
vary considerably by country (for details, see Kamerman & Gatenio, 2002,
and the Clearinghouse on International Developments in Child, Youth, and
Family Policies [www.childpolicyintl.org]).

When one compares countries, however, the United States stands out
by not having a universal child benefit or child allowance. Although the
United States has a system of child tax credits, until recently, these tax
credits were nonrefundable (and even now are only partially refundable).
As a result, child tax credits have mainly benefited families with incomes
high enough to pay taxes, rather than the lowest income families. The
Earned Income Tax Credit (EITC), of course, is refundable and is partially
linked to the number of children, with an especially large increase in the
size of the EITC for the first child. However, an interesting distinction between the United States and other countries is its decision to link this
child credit to earnings.

There are no known studies that directly estimate the effect of a universal
child benefit or child allowance on child outcomes. There is a small body of
research that examines the impact of such benefits on household child expenditures. This research is important because one of the concerns about

cash benefits is how much will actually be spent on investments in children and how much on other goods not benefiting children. An important study by Lundberg, Pollak, and Wales (1997) estimated the effect in the United Kingdom of giving a cash benefit to the mother rather than the father. Analyzing expenditures on clothing, this study found that shifting the benefit from the "wallet" to the "purse" resulted in more money being spent on goods for women and children and less on men. There is also, of course, a significant amount of research that finds that children from higher income families have better outcomes on a number of dimensions (see, e.g., Duncan & Brooks-Gunn, 1997). The extent to which income is causally related to child outcomes, however, and thus the extent to which increased cash benefits would improve child outcomes, is unclear (Mayer, 1997).

Time Benefits

Time benefit policies give parents time to invest in children. The rationale for these policies is similar to the rationale for cash benefits—if there are benefits to parental time with children and if those benefits flow not just to the children and parents but to society more generally, then it may be worthwhile for government to invest resources in promoting parental time investments. These policies generally focus on investments in young children, through provisions for maternity leave, paternity leave, or parental leave. Policies promoting time investments in older children, however, also exist. For instance, it is fairly common (outside the United States) for governments to support paid sick leave, which allows parents to take time off work to care for an ill child as well as their own illness. Some countries, such as Finland and Sweden, also give parents the right to reduce their working hours without losing their job while they have preschool or school-aged children.

The generosity of time benefit policies varies widely across countries. Table 10.5 shows childbirth-related leave policies in the United States and 10 peer nations. The United States stands out as providing the shortest period of leave and by being the only country in the group to not provide paid leave. (The United States also differs from the others in providing leave rights only to qualifying workers, thus excluding about half of the private-sector workforce from coverage.)

There is little direct evidence about the effect of such time benefit policies on parents' time investments in children and on children's outcomes. The evidence that does exist suggests that more generous leave entitlements encourage parents to stay home with a young child for a longer period after a birth (see Waldfogel, 2001a). The evidence also suggests that longer leave entitlements are associated with better health outcomes for children (Ruhm, 2000). These types of benefits could be particularly conse-

TABLE 10.5
Childbirth–Related Leave Policies in the United States & 10 Peer Nations, in 2002

Country	Type of Leave	Total months	Payment
Austria	16 weeks maternity leave	27.7	100% prior earnings
	2 years parental leave		18 mos @ unemployment benefit rate, 6 weeks unpaid
Canada	17 weeks maternity leave	12.0	15 wks @ 55% pay
	35 weeks parental leave		55% prior earnings
Denmark	28 weeks maternity leave	18.5	60% prior earnings
	1 year parental leave		90% unemployment benefit
Finland	18 weeks maternity leave	36.0	70% prior earnings
	26 weeks parental leave		70% prior earnings
	Childrearing leave until child is 3		Flat rate
France	16 weeks maternity leave	36.0	100% prior earnings
	Parental leave until child is 3		Unpaid for 1 child; flat rate (income–tested)
Germany	14 weeks maternity leave	39.2	100% prior earnings
	3 years parental leave		2 yrs flat rate, 3rd unpaid
Italy	5 months maternity leave	11.0	80% prior earnings
	6 months parental leave		30% prior earnings
Norway	52 weeks parental leave	36.0	80% of prior earnings
	2 years childrearing leave		Flat rate
Sweden	18 months parental leave	18.0	12 mos @ 80% pay,
			3 mos flat rate, 3 unpaid
United Kingdom	18 weeks maternity leave	7.2	90% pay for 6 weeks, flat rate for 12 weeks (if sufficient work history, otherwise flat rate for 18 weeks)
	13 weeks parental leave.		Unpaid
United States	12 weeks family leave	2.8	Unpaid

Notes: From Waldfogel, 2001b. The information for Canada reflects the extensions to parental leave that came into effect in 2002. The information for the U.K. does not include the April 2003 extensions.

quential in the U.S. context, where women return to work much earlier after a birth than in other countries, and where early returns, particularly to full-time employment, have been associated with poorer child health outcomes (Berger, Hill, & Waldfogel, 2003) and poorer child cognitive development (Brooks-Gunn, Han, & Waldfogel, 2002; Waldfogel, Han, & Brooks-Gunn, 2002). Such policies could potentially have negative effects on women's wages if they are imposed through employer mandates; this is less of a concern if they are delivered through government insurance programs (Gruber, 1994; Waldfogel, 2001a).

Programs to Boost Parents' Employment or Earnings

Although policies to increase parents' employment or earnings have not typically been viewed as part of social welfare systems or governments' systems of investments in children, they have become increasingly important as tools to promote parents' investments in children, as is evident in recent welfare reforms in the United States and the United Kingdom. One rationale for such policies is that the greater the number of parents in work, and the higher their earnings, the greater children's incomes will be, and the less of a challenge governments will face in providing benefits adequate to move the families of nonworking or low-income, working parents out of poverty. Moreover, the political will to provide these benefits will be greater if families are perceived as working as much as they possibly can.

It is unclear a priori whether parental employment is good or bad for children (see, e.g., Duncan & Chase-Lansdale, 2002). On the one hand, working parents may be better for children to the extent that they provide more positive role models, a more organized daily routine, and so forth. On the other hand, parental work may be harmful if it results in more parental stress or in less time to monitor children's activities, help with schoolwork, and so forth. Developmental theory and prior research on families not exposed to welfare-to-work reforms suggest that the effects of parental work vary by other child and family circumstances, by the type and quality of child care, and by the age of the child. In particular, maternal employment in the first year of life, especially if it is for long hours, can have adverse effects on children's cognitive outcomes (Brooks-Gunn et al., 2002; Waldfogel et al., 2002).

Evidence from recent welfare-to-work random assignment experiments in the United States found generally neutral or positive effects on outcomes for children who were preschool, elementary, or middle school age at the time of the intervention, but some negative effects on outcomes for children who were adolescents (Morris, Huston, Duncan, Crosby, & Bos, 2001). Outcomes for infants and toddlers have not been studied.

Parenting or Family Support Programs

Parenting and family support programs seek to improve the quality of time that parents spend with children and also to increase the time that parents spend in specific activities (such as reading books to children) considered to be beneficial to child development. Programs may also induce parents to purchase specific goods (such as child safety seats or educational toys) to benefit their children.

Home visiting programs for families with newborns are an example of this type of program. Long provided universally in most European countries, home visiting programs are expanding rapidly in the United States, motivated in large part by the recent attention to the early years as an opportune moment for investments in children. Although the enthusiasm for such programs has been tempered by the recognition that investments must be made throughout childhood, and not only in the early years (Bruer, 1999), and by the recognition that not all home visiting programs are equally effective (Gomby, 1999; Guterman, 2000), some early home visiting programs can nevertheless be effective in improving outcomes for children. For instance, a program designed by David Olds and collaborators that used nurse home visitors was effective in reducing child abuse and in promoting parental employment among high-risk families (Karoly et al., 1998). More recently, Early Head Start programs that combine home-based services to parents with center-based services to children were found to improve specific parenting behaviors (for example, reducing the use of spanking and increasing the use of alternative methods of discipline), but with less consistent effects for programs that provide home-based services only (Love et al., 2002; see also Magnuson and Duncan, chapter 9 in this volume.)

Government Mandates or Regulations

Beyond providing services directly or providing funding for parents to purchase services, governments also set standards for those services by specifying curricula, minimum health and safety or staffing requirements, protocols for care, and so forth. Governments also impose mandates on parents (such as requiring children to be immunized or to attend school) and create policies to prevent parents from abusing or neglecting their children or otherwise providing inadequate care. Although not usually considered child investment policies, these mandates are clearly motivated to ensure a child's adequate care. As with other policy instruments, the empirical evidence of their effects is rather thin, but trends over time in such indicators as immunization rates or school enrollments have clearly shown improvement. One recent study of child care regulations (Currie & Hotz, 2001) illustrates some of the complexities of this type of policy instrument, finding that stricter child care regulations prevent accidents, but also raise costs, thus closing out some low-income children from formal child care settings.

VARIATION ACROSS COUNTRIES IN THE USE OF THESE POLICY INSTRUMENTS: A CASE STUDY OF THE UNITED KINGDOM

This section examines the recent social policy reforms in the United Kingdom, a main goal of which has been to promote investments in children as a means to reduce child poverty and combat social exclusion. The following case study provides a brief background for the reforms, describes the reforms and the policy instruments that have been used, and summarizes the evidence on their effects to date.

Background of U.K. Reforms

Tony Blair and New Labour were elected in 1997 at a time when child poverty in Britain was at a record high level, with about 25% of children in poverty, compared with only 10% in the 1960s and 1970s (Gregg, Harkness, & Machin, 1999). A further concern was that about 20% of children were living in "workless households," compared with only 7% in 1979 (Gregg & Wadsworth, 1996). Many individuals and areas seemed to suffer from an accumulation of disadvantages, both economic and social, such that they were isolated from mainstream society, or "socially excluded."

As used in the United Kingdom, the term *social exclusion* tends to be "a short-hand label for what can happen when individuals or areas suffer from a concentration of linked problems such as unemployment, poor skills, low income, poor housing, high crime, bad health, and family breakdown" (Social Exclusion Unit, 2001, p. 4). Social exclusion is related to poverty, but differs from the usual American definition of poverty in three main ways: (a) it concerns relative rather than absolute poverty; (b) it takes into account social as well as economic dimensions of disadvantage; and (c) it considers disadvantage as a dynamic rather than static problem.

The Blair government has taken two highly visible steps to signal its commitment to tackle social exclusion and child poverty. First, shortly after taking office in 1997, the Blair government established a Social Exclusion Unit, reporting directly to the Prime Minister and charged with tackling the most difficult social problems, including homelessness; truancy; school expulsions; teen parenthood; 16- to 18-year-olds not in work, education, or training; young runaways; and bad neighborhoods.

The second signal of its commitment, made in a speech given in 1999 at Toynbee Hall, a settlement house in East London, was the declaration of the goal of ending child poverty in the next 20 years. Blair (1999) declared, "Our historic aim will be for ours to be the first generation to end child poverty. It is a 20-year mission but I believe it can be done." Blair and the Chancellor of the Exchequer, Gordon Grown, subsequently made this commitment more specific, announcing interim goals of halving child poverty in 10 years, and reducing it by a quarter in 5 years. In making these commitments, the government was influenced by research, using the United Kingdom's rich birth cohort and longitudinal data sets, on the long-term effects of childhood poverty and disadvantage, as well as research on the effectiveness of child-based interventions in breaking the cycle of disadvantage (Brewer & Gregg, in press; Hills & Waldfogel, 2003). Much of this research was presented at a conference at the Treasury in fall 1999 and subsequently published jointly by the Treasury and the Centre for Analysis of Social Exclusion (CASE) at the London School of Economics (see CASE/HM Treasury, 1999). An accompanying report by the Treasury (HM Treasury, 1999) asserted:

> The Government attaches the highest priority to supporting families with children, tackling the causes of childhood poverty and ensuring that all children have the opportunity to succeed. It is investing an additional £19 billion in education over the next three years and increasing the financial support available to families with children. By the end of this parliament the Government will be providing an additional £6 billion a year in financial support for children (p. 34).

A Three-Part Strategy

To reduce social exclusion and child poverty, the United Kingdom adopted a three-part strategy: investments in children and communities; policies to promote work and to make work pay; and improved benefits for children, including those whose parents are unable to work (for further detail, see Hills & Waldfogel, 2003; Waldfogel, 2001c). The philosophy is that all three components are necessary to improve the life chances of children—that children need both better services and better incomes, and that better incomes can best come about through increased benefits coupled with increased parental earnings (see, e.g., statements by Blair [1999] and Brown [HM Treasury, 2001]).

The first set of reforms—investments in children and communities—includes a mix of policy instruments, making use of direct government provision, vouchers and related programs, cash benefits, time benefits, parenting and family support programs, and mandates. These instruments include:

1. Public spending for direct government provision of health and education rising as a share of GDP from 2000–2001, and with spending on education set to rise by 5.4% a year from 2003–2006.

2. Sure Start, an area-based early years intervention that includes both additional funding for government services and funding for parenting and family support programs, initially covering 100,000 children and rising to 400,000 children (one third of all poor children under the age of 4) by 2006, and with a budget rising to £500 million per year in 2003–2004.

3. A new Children's Fund (flexible funds available over a 3-year period to local areas for programs for children aged 5–13, with £100 million in 2001–2002, £150 million in 2002–2003, and £200 million in 2003–2004.

4. Education Action Zones, funding targeting the worst-performing school districts for improvements.

5. Connexions, an initiative to provide services to adolescents to help young people aged 13–18 make the transition to adulthood.

6. Educational Maintenance Allowances—cash grants to encourage youth from low-income families to stay in school.

7. A heightened focus on school performance, particularly efforts to boost basic skills (e.g., national literacy and numeracy strategies that require schools to spend specific amounts of time on reading and math; funding to reduce class sizes in the primary grades).

8. National child care strategy, using a voucher-type program to guarantee a part-time child care place in a public or private nursery school for every 3- and 4-year-old whose family wants one (with universal coverage for 4-year-olds accomplished by 1998, and universal coverage for 3-year-olds planned by September 2004), and with spending on child care to double from 2002 to 2005, including funding for local children's centers to deliver integrated services and support to children, parents, and child care providers.

9. Expanded maternity leave benefits (with increases in the payment rate, and an extension of payments from 18 weeks to 26 weeks); the introduction of parental leave benefits (in line with the European Union directive); and the introduction of 2 weeks of paid paternity leave (starting in April 2003).

10. A Neighborhood Renewal Fund for the most disadvantaged communities, with a budget of £100 million in 2001–2002, £300 million in 2002–2003, and £400 million in 2003–2004 (allocation detail in HM Treasury, 2000, 2002).

The second strand— policies to promote work and to make work pay— makes use of several programs to boost parents' employment and earnings, including:

1. More generous in-work benefits, through the Working Families Tax Credit;
2. A new Child Care Tax Credit, within Working Families Tax Credit;
3. The New Deal for Lone Parents, which began by offering single parents employment services on a voluntary basis and now requires a work-focused interview for all single parents receiving benefits (although single parents are still not required to seek or take a job after the interview);
4. Other New Deal programs;
5. A national minimum wage introduced in April 1999.

The third strand of reforms consists of improved cash benefits for children, including those whose parents are unable to work. These include:

1. Higher universal Child Benefit (an increase from £10.05 to £15.50 per week for the first child, and from £9 to £10.35 per week for additional children);
2. More generous Income Support (cash welfare) for children under age 11 (an increase of £14.70 per child per week), with smaller increases for children aged 12–17;
3. More generous maternity allowances, especially for low-income parents;
4. A new Child Tax Credit (which will be in place only from April 2001 to April 2003);
5. A new Baby Tax Credit (double the value of the Child Tax Credit in the first year of life);
6. An integrated Child Credit (to replace Child Benefit and the child portions of Income Support, Child Tax Credit, and Working Families Tax Credit starting April 2003, such that there will be one unified system of child benefits, usually paid to the mother, regardless of the parents' employment or benefit status); and
7. Proposals for "Baby Bonds" (£400 to £800 per child, not to be spent until the child's 18th birthday).

The Policy Instruments That Have Been Implemented

The U.K. reforms put into place during the past 5 years are both numerous and varied. They include examples of each of the seven types of policy instruments previously discussed.

There has been a substantial increase in direct government provision, with substantial resources directed to education, and an even larger increase planned for the 2003–2006 spending cycle. The New Labour government retained the strategy put forward by the previous Conservative government on vouchers and related programs of expanding child care provision by means of vouchers and other forms of government subsidy for mixed public and private provision, rather than through direct government provision. The third type of policy—cash benefits to parents—has played an important role in the U.K. government program, with its sizable increases in child benefit and in means-tested cash benefits for families with children. Altogether, direct financial support for families rose by 58% from 1997 to 2002 (Brewer & Gregg, in press; this includes the increases in universal child benefit, the means-tested Income Support, and the cash supports to families with working parents.) Time benefits have been expanded as well, with new government initiatives in maternity leave, paternity leave, and parental leave, and new rights for parents to request part-time work schedules.

As in the United States, policies to promote parents' employment, and to raise their earnings from employment, have also been an important component of the overall reforms. Prior to the reforms, a single parent with child care costs of £50 per week would have gained only £15 per week by going to work for 16 hours per week. As a result of the reforms, by 2001, she or he would instead have gained £48 per week (Brewer & Gregg, in press). Programs delivered to parents, or programs to improve the quality of care or services parents provide to children, have also been emphasized. Sure Start is the most important example; however, the government has supported other parenting programs and has also established a National Family and Parenting Institute as a center of expertise. Government mandates have also played a role, as in the new literacy or numeracy standards and in the heightened emphasis on performance standards for all public agencies receiving increased government funding.

Thus, the first conclusion to be drawn from the U.K. reforms of the past 5 years is that they have used all of the policy instruments identified earlier. This, however, does not indicate which types of instruments have received greater emphasis. In the recent U.S. welfare reforms, initiatives to boost parents' employment and their incomes if they were employed clearly played a central role. This is not as true in the United Kingdom, where many elements of the reforms bear no obvious relation to employment or earnings, at least for the current generation of parents. Rather, one striking difference is that the U.K. reforms have emphasized several other types of investments in children, in addition to policies to boost parents' employment and earnings.

Although it is difficult to assess the relative importance of different elements of the reforms, one way to produce at least a rough estimate is to assess where the money was spent. Clearly, large amounts were spent on increased benefits for families with children and on measures to boost families' employment and earnings, and as a result, incomes rose. The Treasury estimates that the average family with children is £1,200 better off annually as a result of the reforms undertaken from 1997 to 2002, and that low-income families, from the bottom fifth of the population, gained even more, and are now £2,400 better off per year (HM Treasury, 2002, p. 13). Large amounts were also spent on education. In the initial 3-year period from 1997 to 2000, government increased educational spending by roughly £6 billion per year while increasing cash supports to families by about the same. By comparison, services to families received less funding—currently, about £500 million a year for Sure Start (serving children aged 0–4), £200 million a year for the Children's Funds (serving children aged 5–13), and an indeterminate amount on youth programs (serving young people aged 13–18). Thus, government has expressed a preference for spending on education and on cash benefits for families over other services to families, and for services to preschoolers over services to school-aged children.

The Effects of Reforms on Child Outcomes

The reforms have already had some notable successes. As the government's Children and Young People's Unit (2001) proclaimed:

> Since 1997, there have been real improvements in children and young people's lives. Every 4-year-old now has the opportunity to take up a free educational place; 28% fewer young people left school this year without a qualification compared to 1997; over one million children will be lifted out of poverty as a result of the tax and benefit reforms we have announced since the 1997 budget; over 250,000 young people have moved into sustained jobs as a result of the New Deal (pp.1–2).

However, for the most part, it is still too early to judge what effects the reforms will have on child outcomes. Many of the measures have only recently been enacted or announced, and several have not yet gone into effect. During the first 2 years of the Blair government (1997–1999), public spending faced tight constraints, and inequality and relative poverty continued to rise until at least 1999–2000. However, projections now indicate that government's strategy will significantly reduce child poverty. Whether the reforms will result in other improvements in the lives of children still remains to be seen.

Focusing on the poverty impacts, projections from the Microsimulation Unit at Cambridge University (Piachaud & Sutherland, 2001) indicated that the benefits of the Blair government policies have been well targeted to the lowest income families. They estimate that the child poverty rate is now 10 percentage points lower than it would have been in the absence of the policies (16% versus 26%), with particularly large effects for single-parent families.

Evidence on other outcomes is, for the most part, unavailable. Evaluations have found that the New Deal programs have resulted in small increases in employment among single parents (Hasluck, McKnight, & Elias, 2000) and among young people (White & Riley, 2002), and that the Educational Maintenance Allowances have increased the numbers of young people staying in school (Ashworth et al., 2001). An evaluation of Sure Start is underway. Most other programs, however, are too new to have been evaluated. Because a major aim of the government's program has been to break the intergenerational cycle of poverty and promote better life chances for children, many of the important outcomes cannot be assessed for many years to come. Thus, it will be some time before the effectiveness of the United Kingdom's multifaceted strategy can be determined.

CONCLUSION

Comparing policies to promote investments in children is more complicated than just adding up the money spent on social welfare programs. Social welfare expenditure figures include money that is spent on groups other than children, and the figures also fail to capture money that is spent on children by someone other than government (in particular, parents).

At the same time, variation in government investments in children is not just about differences in total expenditures. It is also about differences in the policy instruments that governments use to make those investments. The recent U.S. welfare reforms, for instance, focused primarily on policies to increase parents' employment and earnings and, helped by a strong economy, were successful in achieving those goals. The U.K. reforms, in contrast, set more ambitious child-directed goals and used a wider variety of policy instruments to achieve those goals. Only time will tell which overall strategy and which specific policy instruments will prove to be most effective in promoting investments in children.

There are clearly many questions for further research. One challenge is to better isolate government expenditures on children from other social welfare expenditures and, at the same time, to produce estimates that reflect private investments in children. Researchers also must do a more thorough job of documenting the full range of policy instruments that governments use to promote investments in children and, most important, to assess their relative effectiveness in promoting investments and in improving child outcomes.

ACKNOWLEDGMENTS

This chapter was written during a visit to the Centre for Analysis of Social Exclusion at the London School of Economics. I am grateful to John Hills and other colleagues there for many helpful conversations and to Paul Gregg for help documenting and understanding the recent reforms in the

United Kingdom. I am also grateful to Sheldon Danziger, Irv Garfinkel, and Sheila Kamerman for helpful comments on an earlier draft.

REFERENCES

Ashworth, K., Hardman, J., Woon-Chia, L., Maguire, S., Middleton, S., Dearden, L., et al. (2001). *Education maintenance allowance: The first year.* London, UK: Department for Education and Employment.

Bainbridge, J. (2002). *Who supports children in the U.S.?* Unpublished doctoral dissertation, Columbia University, New York, NY.

Bainbridge, J., & Garfinkel, I. (2002). *Inequality in supports for U.S. children.* New York, NY: Columbia University.

Barr, N. (1998). *The economics of the welfare state* (3rd ed.). Oxford, UK: Oxford University Press.

Berger, L., Hill, J., & Waldfogel, J. (2003, June 14). *Parental leave policies, early maternal employment, and child outcomes.* Paper presented at the 17th Annual Meeting of the European Society of Population Economics, New York City, NY.

Blair, T. (1999). Beveridge revisited: A welfare state for the 21st century. In R. Walker (Ed.), *Ending child poverty: Popular welfare for the 21st century* (pp.1–10). Bristol, UK: Policy Press.

Brewer, M., & Gregg, P. (in press). *Eradicating child poverty in Britain: Welfare reform and children since 1997.* In R. Walker and M. Wiseman (eds) *The welfare we want.* Forthcoming from Policy Press, Bristol, UK.

Brooks-Gunn, J., Han, W., & Waldfogel, J. (2002). Maternal employment and child cognitive outcomes in the first three years of life: The NICHD study of early child care. *Child Development, 73*(4), 1052–1072.

Bruer, J. (1999). *The myth of the first three years: A new understanding of early brain development and lifelong learning.* New York, NY: Free Press.

CASE/HM Treasury. (1999) *Persistent poverty and lifetime inequality: The evidence.* CASE report 5, HM Treasury occasional paper no. 10. London, UK: London School of Economics and HM Treasury.

Children and Young People's Unit (2001). *Building a strategy for children and young people.* London, UK: Author.

Currie, J. (1995). *Welfare and the well-being of children.* Chur, Switzerland: Harwood Academic Publishers.

Currie, J. (2001). Early childhood education programs. *Journal of Economic Literature, 15*(2), 213–238.

Currie, J., & Gruber, J. (1996a). Health insurance eligibility, utilization of medical care, and child health. *Quarterly Journal of Economics, 11*(May), 431–466.

Currie, J., & Gruber, J. (1996b). Saving babies: the efficacy and the cost of the recent changes in the Medicaid eligibility of pregnant women. *Journal of Political Economy, 104*(December), 1263–1296.

Currie, J., & Hotz, J. (2001). Accidents will happen? Unintentional injuries and child care policies. Mimeo, University of California at Los Angeles.

Devaney, B., Bilheimer, L., & Schore, J. (1992). Medicaid costs and birth outcomes: The effects of prenatal WIC participation and the use of prenatal care. *Journal of Policy Analysis and Management, 11*, 573–592.

Duncan, G., & Brooks-Gunn, J. (Eds.). (1997). *Consequences of growing up poor.* New York, NY: Russell Sage Foundation.

Duncan, G., & Chase-Lansdale, L. (2002). *For better and for worse: Welfare reform and the well-being of children and families.* New York, NY: Russell Sage Foundation.

Garfinkel, I. (1996). Economic security for children: from means-testing and bifurcation to universality. In I. Garfinkel, J. Hochschild, & S. McLanahan (Eds.), *Social policies for children* (pp. 33–82). Washington, DC: The Brookings Institution.

Gregg, P., Harkness, S., & Machin, S. (1999). Poor kids: Trends in child poverty in Britain, 1968–1996. *Fiscal Studies, 20*(2), 163–188.

Gregg, P., & Wadsworth, J. (1996). More work in fewer households. In J. Hills (Ed.), *New inequalities* (pp. 181–207). Cambridge, UK: Cambridge University Press.

Gomby, D. (1999). Home visiting: Recent program evaluations—executive summary. *The Future of Children, 9*(1), 2–7.

Gruber, J. (1994). The incidence of mandated maternity benefits. *American Economic Review, 84*(3), 622–641.

Guterman, N. (2000). *Stopping child maltreatment before it starts: Emerging horizons in early home visitation services.* Thousand Oaks, CA: Sage.

Harknett, K., Garfinkel, I., Bainbridge, J., Smeeding, T., & Folbre, N. (2002, May). *Returns on investments? Public expenditures on children and child outcomes across the fifty U.S. states.* Paper presented at the Annual Meeting of the Population Association of America, Atlanta, GA.

Hasluck, C., McKnight, A., & Elias, P. (2000) *Evaluation of the new deal for lone parents: Early lessons from the phase one prototype,* DSS research report 110. Leeds, UK: Corporate Document Services.

Haveman, R., & Wolfe, B. (1995). The determinants of children's attainments: a review of methods and findings. *Journal of Economic Literature, 33*(4), 1829–1878.

Hills, J., & Waldfogel, J. (2003). *Welfare reform in the UK: What are the lessons for the US?* London, UK: London School of Economics

HM Treasury. (1999). *Persistent poverty and lifetime inequality: The evidence.* HM Treasury occasional paper no. 10 and CASE report no. 5. London, UK: Author & London School of Economics.

HM Treasury. (2000). *Spending review 2000: New public spending plans 2001–2004.* London, UK: Author.

HM Treasury. (2001). *Tackling child poverty: Giving every child the best possible start in life.* London, UK: Author.

HM Treasury (2002). *Budget 2002—The Strength to Make Long–Term Decisions: Investing in an Enterprising, Fairer Britain.* London, UK: The Stationery Office.

Kamerman, S., & Gatenio, S. (2002). *Tax day: How do America's child benefits compare?* New York, NY: Clearinghouse on International Developments in Child, Youth, and Family Policies. Available online at www.childpolicyintl.org (posted: August 21, 2002).

Kamerman, S., & Kahn, A. (1997a). *Starting right: How America neglects its youngest children and what we can do about it.* New York, NY: Oxford University Press.

Kamerman, S., & Kahn, A. (1997b). Investing in children: Government expenditures for children and their families in western industrialized countries. In G. A. Cornia & S. Danziger (Eds.), *Child poverty and deprivation in the industrialized countries: 1945–1995.* Oxford, UK: Clarendon Press.

Karoly, L., Greenwood, P., Everingham, S., Hoube, J., Kilburn, R., Rydell, P. et al. (1998). *Investing in our children: What we know and don't know about the costs and benefits of early childhood interventions.* Santa Monica, CA: Rand.

Katz, L., Kling, J., & Liebman, J. (2001). Moving to opportunity in Boston: Early results of a randomized mobility experiment. *Quarterly Journal of Economics 116*(2), 607–654.

Love, J., Kisker, E., Ross, C., Schochet, P., Brooks-Gunn, J., Paulsell, D., Boller, K. et al. (2002). *Making a difference in the lives of infants and toddlers and their families: The impacts of early Head Start.* Princeton, NJ: Mathematica Policy Research.

Ludwig, J., Ladd, H., & Duncan, G. (2001). Urban poverty and educational outcomes. In W. Gale & J. R. Pack (Eds.), *Brookings-Wharton Papers on Urban Affairs 2001.* Washington, DC: Brookings Institution.

Lundberg, S. J., Pollak, R. A., & Wales, T. J. (1997). Do husbands and wives pool their resources? Evidence from the United Kingdom child benefit. *Journal of Human Resources, 32*(3), 463–480.

Mayer, S. (1997). *What money can't buy.* Cambridge, MA: Harvard University Press.

Morris, P., Huston, A., Duncan, G., Crosby, D., & Bos, J. (2001). *How welfare and work policies affect children: A synthesis of research.* New York, NY: Manpower Demonstration Research Corporation.

Organization for Economic Cooperation and Development (2002a). *Social Expenditure Database, 1980–1998* (3rd ed.). Available online at www.oecd.org/EN/links_abstract/0,,EN-links_abstract-19-nodirectorate-no-no-1152-19,00.html (posted July 26, 2002).

Organization for Economic Cooperation and Development (2002b). *Education at a Glance, 2001 Edition.* Available online at: www.oecd.org/oecd/pages/home/ display general/0,3380,EN-document-4-nodirectorate-no-27-22129-4,00.html (posted August 16, 2000).

Osberg, L., Smeeding, T., & Swabisch, J. (2002). *Income distribution and public social expenditure: Theories, effects, and evidence.* Syracuse, NY: Syracuse University.

Piachaud, D., & Sutherland, H. (2001). *How effective is the British government's attempt to reduce child poverty? CASE paper no. 38.* London, UK: London School of Economics.

Rosenbaum, J. E. (1995). Changing the geography of opportunity by expanding residential choice: lessons from the Gautreaux Program. *Housing Policy Debate, 6*, 231–269.

Ruhm, C. (2000). Parental leave and child health. *Journal of Health Economics, 19*, 952–955.

Smeeding, T. M. (2002). *Real standards of living and public support for children: A cross-national comparison.* Syracuse, NY: Syracuse University.

Smeeding, T. M., Rainwater, L., & Burtless, G. (2001). U.S. poverty in a cross-national context. In S. Danziger & R. Haveman (Eds.), *Understanding poverty* (pp. 162–189). Cambridge, MA: Harvard University Press.

Social Exclusion Unit (2001) *Preventing social exclusion: Report by the social exclusion unit.* London, UK: Cabinet Office.

Waldfogel, J. (2001a). Family-friendly policies for families with young children. *Employee Rights and Employment Policy Journal, 5*(1), 273–296.

Waldfogel, J. (2001b). What other nations do: International policies toward parental leave and child care. *The Future of Children, 11*(4), 99–111.

Waldfogel, J. (2001c). Research on poverty and anti-poverty policies. In S. Danziger & R. Haveman (Eds.), *Understanding poverty* (pp. 463–472). Cambridge, MA: Harvard University Press.

Waldfogel, J., Han, W., & Brooks-Gunn, J. (2002). The effects of early maternal employment on child cognitive development. *Demography, 39*(2), 369–392.

White, M., & Riley, R. (2002). *Findings from the macro evaluation of the new deal for young people.* DWP research report no. 168. Leeds, UK: Corporate Document Services.

About the Contributors

ROBERT H. BRADLEY is a professor in the Center for Applied Studies in Education at the University of Arkansas at Little Rock and adjunct professor of pediatrics, psychiatry, and public health at the University of Arkansas for Medical Sciences. Bradley received his PhD at the University of North Carolina in 1974. He was formerly director of the Center for Research on Teaching and Learning at UALR and director of the University of Arkansas University Affiliated Program in Developmental Disabilities. Bradley was a member of the board of editors of *Child Development* from 1996 to 2000 and is currently a member of the board of editors of *Parenting: Science and Practice*. He is also a member of the Steering Committee for the NICHD Study of Child Care and Youth Development and the Early Head Start National Evaluation Study. His primary research interests include the family environment and its relation to children's well-being, children living in high-risk conditions, child care, fathering, and early intervention. He is coauthor of the HOME Inventory.

JEANNE BROOKS-GUNN is the Virginia and Leonard Marx Professor of Child Development and Education at Teachers College, Columbia University. She is also Professor of Pediatrics and codirector of the Institute of Child and Family Policy at Columbia University. She specializes in policy-oriented research that focuses on family and community influences on the development of young children. Her research centers on designing and evaluating interventions and policies aimed at enhancing the well-being of children living in poverty. She has served on three National Academy of Sciences panels. The recipient of numerous awards, including the Jon B. Hill Award from the Society for Research in Child Development, the Cattell Award from the American Psychological Society, and the Distinguished Award for Policy from the American Psychological Association, Brooks-Gunn is also the author of 15 books and more than 300 articles.

ROBERT FLYNN CORWYN is a research associate at the Center for Applied Studies in Education at the University of Arkansas at Little Rock. Corwyn received his MA at the University of Arkansas at Little Rock and is currently in a PhD program at Memphis University. He has taught courses in gerontology, family sociology, research methods, and statistics. His research interests include adolescent delinquent behavior, poverty, and the relation between family environments and children's well-being.

THOMAS DELEIRE is on the faculty of the department of economics at Michigan State University. He previously taught at the Kennedy School of Government at Harvard University and at the Harris School of Public Policy Studies at the University of Chicago. From 2002 to 2003 he was Senior Economist for labor, health, and education for President Bush's Council of Economic Advisers. His research focuses on labor and health economics, and his recent work is on family structure, choice of occupation, household spending, and the effects of welfare reform on health insurance coverage. In other work, he has examined the impact of overtime regulations on hours of work, the effect of the Americans with Disabilities Act on the employment of disabled citizens, the extent of discrimination against disabled workers, and the role of tax-favored savings accounts in increasing national savings. He received his PhD in economics from Stanford University in 1997 and graduated magna cum laude from Princeton University in 1990.

GREG J. DUNCAN is the Edwina S. Tarry Professor of Education and Social Policy at Northwestern University. Prior to joining the Northwestern faculty in 1995, he was principal investigator of the Panel Study of Income Dynamics project at the University of Michigan and professor of economics. Duncan has published extensively on issues of income dynamics within and across generations, and on the impact of family and neighborhood poverty on children's development. He was a member of the Society for Research in Child Development Public Policy Committee between 1995 and 1999, the "Neurons to Neighborhoods" Committee on Integrating the Science of Early Childhood Development of the National Research Council/Institute on Medicine, and the Advisory Committee on Head Start Research and Evaluation in 1999 and 2000. He is currently a member of the NICHD Family and Child Well-Being Research Network and the MacArthur Networks on Successful Pathways through Middle Childhood and the Family and the Economy. He has directed the Northwestern University/University of Chicago Joint Center for Poverty Research since 2000.

RACHEL DUNIFON is Assistant Professor in the Department of Policy Analysis and Management at Cornell University. She received her BA in

Psychology from Davidson College and a PhD in Human Development and Social Policy from Northwestern University. Her research interests include studying the impact of social welfare policies on children, the associations between family structure, parenting, and child well-being, and the ways in which neighborhood characteristics influence parent–child relationships and child development.

ANDREW J. FULIGNI is Associate Professor in the Departments of Psychiatry and Psychology at the University of California, Los Angeles. He received his PhD in developmental psychology at the University of Michigan, and was previously an Associate Professor in the Department of Psychology at New York University. His research focuses on the family relationships and academic adjustment of adolescents from a variety of cultural groups, with a particular focus on the children of immigrant families. This work has been funded by a FIRST award from NICHD, a Faculty Scholars Award from the William T. Grant Foundation, and the Russell Sage Foundation. Fuligni was a recipient of the 2001 APA Division 7 Boyd McCandless Award for Early Career Contribution to Developmental Psychology, and has served on the editorial boards of the *Journal of Research on Adolescence* and *Child Development*.

MICHAEL J. GURALNICK is the Director of the Center on Human Development and Disability and Professor of Psychology and Pediatrics at the University of Washington. Over the years, Dr. Guralnick has conducted research and development projects in the fields of early childhood intervention, inclusion, social skills development, peer relations, and pediatric education. He has published more than 100 articles and book chapters (including seven edited volumes) and currently directs a major research project supported by the National Institute of Child Health and Human Development designed to determine the effectiveness of a comprehensive early intervention program in promoting the peer-related social competence of young children with developmental delays. Dr. Guralnick received the 1994 Research Award from the American Association on Mental Retardation, and the 1997 Distinguished Research Award from the Arc of the United States. He is a past president of the Association of University Centers on Disabilities, the Council for Exceptional Children's Division for Early Childhood, and the Academy on Mental Retardation, and is a former chair of the Mental Retardation and Developmental Disabilities Research Center Directors. He is currently the chair of the International Society on Early Intervention and the editor of the journal, *Infants and Young Children*.

ARIEL KALIL is Associate Professor at the Harris School of Public Policy at the University of Chicago. She received her PhD in developmental psychology from the University of Michigan. She has conducted research on the effects of welfare and the transition from welfare to work on mothers and children, barriers to the employment of welfare recipients, the influence of single parenthood, cohabitation, and nonresident father involvement on family processes and child development, and the transition to adulthood for teenage mothers. With funding from a William T. Grant Faculty Scholars Award, she is currently conducting a multimethod, interdisciplinary research project focused on the impact of parental job loss on family processes and child development. Kalil is the 2003 recipient of the Society for Research in Child Development (SRCD) Award for Early Research Contributions.

SHELLY LUNDBERG is Professor of Economics and Robert R. Richards Distinguished Scholar at the University of Washington and Director of the Center for Research on Families. She is also affiliated with the Center for Studies in Demography and Ecology, the Center for Labor Studies, and the Canadian Studies Center, and is an adjunct faculty member of the Women Studies Department. She received a BA from the University of British Columbia and a PhD from Northwestern University. Her research is focused in labor economics and the economics of the family, and includes both theoretical modeling (of discrimination and inequality and of family decision making) and empirical analysis (of fertility, labor supply, wage determination, and intrahousehold allocation of resources). Her current research includes projects on racial segregation and inequality, the relationship between family roles and labor market outcomes for American men and women, and the retirement and savings decisions of married couples. Her publications include studies of unemployment and restrictions on work hours, the effects of teenage childbearing, the enforcement of antidiscrimination policies in the labor market, and models of bargaining between married couples. Dr. Lundberg has served on many professional committees and review panels, including the Economics Advisory Panel of the National Science Foundation, review panels for the National Institutes of Health, and the American Economic Association's Committee on the Status of Women in the Economics Profession. She was a founding member of the MacArthur Foundation's Research Network on the Family, a multidisciplinary group of family researchers, and also the MacArthur Foundation's Inequality Modeling Group. Lundberg was a co-editor of the *Journal of Human Resources* from 1997 to 2002 and is currently an associate editor of *Labour Economics: An International Journal*, and a member of the editorial board of *Review of Economics of the Household*.

KATHERINE MAGNUSON is a Post-Doctoral Fellow at Columbia University School of Social Work. She completed her PhD in Human Development and Social Policy from Northwestern in June of 2002. Her research focuses on the effects of socioeconomic factors on children and families and research methodology.

ROBERT T. MICHAEL is Eliakim Hastings Moore Distinguished Service Professor in the Harris Graduate School of Public Policy Studies at the University of Chicago. He holds a PhD in economics from Columbia University and previously taught in the economics departments at UCLA and Stanford University. Michael served as CEO of National Opinion Research Center (1984–1998) and founding Dean of the Harris School (1989–1994; 1998–2002). He chaired the National Research Council's panel and coauthored its monograph *Measuring Poverty: A New Approach* (1995), is coauthor of *Sex in America* (1994), *The Social Organization of Sexuality* (1994), and *Sex, Love, and Health in America* (2001), and he is editor of *Social Awakening: Adolescent Behavior as Adulthood Approaches* (2001).

JENAE M. NEIDERHISER is an Associate Professor in the Center for Family Research within the Department of Psychiatry and Behavioral Sciences at George Washington University. She received her BS in psychology from the University of Pittsburgh and her MS and PhD from the Department of Human Development and Family Studies at Pennsylvania State University. Her research interests are in understanding how family relationships influence adjustment throughout the life span, and she is particularly interested in integrating this work with prevention and intervention. Neiderhiser is a member of the American Psychology Association and Division 7, the American Psychology Society, the Society for Research in Child Development, the Society for Research in Adolescence, the Society for Prevention Research, and the Behavior Genetics Association.

DAVID REISS is Vivian Gill Distinguished Research Professor in the Department of Psychiatry and Behavioral Sciences and Director of the Center for Family Research at George Washington University. Dr. Reiss received his medical training at Harvard Medical School, where he also completed specialty training in psychiatry. He is a graduate of the Washington Psychoanalytic Institute and is Teaching Analyst on its faculty. His clinical work focuses on family therapy and psychoanalysis. His research centers on the interplay between genetic and social influences on toddler, adolescent, and adult development. He directs his research toward the prevention of psychiatric disorders and is current co-chair of the Task Force on Prevention of the American Psychiatric Association. Dr. Reiss is also chair of the Selection Committee of the W. T. Grant Scholars Program and is a member of the Board of Neuroscience and Behavioral Health of the Institute of Medicine.

ELAINA ROSE is Associate Professor of Economics at the University of Washington, where she is also affiliated with the Department of Women Studies, the Department of South Asia Studies, the Center for Studies in Demography and Ecology, the Center for Statistics in Social Sciences, and the Center for Research on Families. Her work focuses on the economics of gender and the family in both developed and developing countries. She has written several papers on the problem of discrimination against girls in rural India, focusing on the role risk, consumption smoothing, and imperfect credit and financial markets in shaping patterns of intrahousehold allocation. Dr. Rose has received a grant from the National Institute of Health (NIH/NICHD) to study the change in marriage markets in the United States in the latter half of the 20th century. Her work with Shelly Lundberg on the changing relationship between household roles was sponsored by the National Science Foundation. This chapter is part of their ongoing research project involving the study of the role of gender in intrahousehold allocation in developed countries. Dr. Rose received her PhD in Economics from the University of Pennsylvania in 1993.

JANE WALDFOGEL is Professor of Social Work and Public Affairs at Columbia University School of Social Work. She is also a research associate at the Centre for Analysis of Social Exclusion at the London School of Economics. Waldfogel has written extensively on the impact of public policies on child and family well-being. Her current research includes studies of family leave, early childhood care and education, and child abuse and neglect. Waldfogel received her PhD in public policy from Harvard University. She is the author of *The Future of Child Protection: How to Break the Cycle of Abuse and Neglect* (Harvard University Press, 1998) and co-editor (with Sheldon Danziger) of *Securing the Future: Investing in Children from Birth to Adulthood* (Russell Sage Foundation, 2000). Her work has also been published in leading academic journals including the *American Economic Review, American Sociological Review, Child Development, Demography, Journal of Policy Analysis and Management, Journal of Human Resources, Journal of Labor Economics,* and *Journal of Population Economics.* From 2001–2003, Waldfogel was a member of the National Academy of Science's Committee on Family and Work Policies.

HIROKAZU YOSHIKAWA is Assistant Professor of Psychology at New York University, in community and developmental psychology. He received his PhD in clinical psychology at New York University. He has conducted research on effects of early childhood care and education programs, public policies, and prevention programs on the development of children and adolescents in poverty in the United States. He is currently conducting research on effects of experimental welfare reform and antipoverty policy demonstrations on children and families. He is also carrying out research on the prevention of HIV infection among Asian/Pacific Islander immigrant communities in the United States. In 1999, he served on the U.S. Department of Health and Human Services Advisory Committee on Head Start Research and Evaluation, a panel appointed to help design the national impact evaluation of Head Start. He currently serves on the Committee on Family Work Policies of the National Research Council, National Academy of Sciences. In 2001 he was awarded the Louise Kidder Early Career Award of the Society for the Psychological Study of Social Issues (Division 9 of the American Psychological Association), as well as the American Psychological Association Minority Fellowship Program Early Career Award.

KATHLEEN M. ZIOL-GUEST is a doctoral student at the Harris School of Public Policy at the University of Chicago. She received her BA and MPA at Indiana University–Bloomington. Ziol–Guest spent the 2001–2002 academic year as a Graduate Fellow in the Joint Center for Poverty Research at Northwestern University and the University of Chicago. She is an NICHD predoctoral Fellow in the Population Research Center at National Opinion Research Center (NORC) and the University of Chicago. Her research interests include absent biological father involvement, father investments in child well–being, and child support.

Author Index

Truman, S. D., 21, *30*
Trumbetta, S., 38, *47*
Trussell, J., 165, *179*
Tryon, A., 34, *46*
Tseng, V., 146, 149, 150, *160*, *162*
Tumlin, K. C., 140, *162*
Tuomilehto, J., 53, *82*
Turnbull, A., 127, *137*
Turner, G., 123, *135*

U

Upshur, C. C., 127, 129, 130, 131, *136*, *137*

V

Vaillant, G. E., 87, *118*
Vandell, D. L., 53, 58, *83*
Van Izendoorn, M., 22, *32*
Van Os, J., 43, *47*
Vargas, W., 221, *231*
Vaughn, S., 225, *231*
Vellet, S., 121, *136*
Ventura, S., 4, *29*
Vernez, G., 157, 158, *162*
Veroff, J., 95, *118*
Verropoulou, G., 51, *83*
Veum, J., 114, *118*
Vevea, J., 54, *82*
Vlietinck, R., 43, *47*
Vuchinich, S., 33, 39, *46*

W

Wachs, T. D., 24, *32*, 89, *117*, *118*, 121, *137*
Wadsworth, J., 253, *261*
Wadsworth, M., 53, *82*
Wagner, M., 131, 132, *134*, *136*, *137*, 215, *234*
Waldfogel, J., 247, 249, 250, 251, 254, *260*, *261*, *262*
Wales, T. J., 249, *262*
Warfield, M. E., 128, *137*
Warner, R. L., 163, 165, 166, *179*
Wasik, B. H., 133, *135*, 227, *230*
Wasserman, G. A., 10, *27*
Waters, E., 11, 12, *27*, *30*

Webster-Stratton, C., 41, *47*, 211, 212, 219, 220, 228, *234*
Weikart, D., 214, 225, *234*
Weisner, T. S., 125, 127, 129, 131, 132, *134*, *135*, *137*
Weisz, J. R., 218, *232*
Wells, N. M., 89, *118*
Wesley, P. W., 133, *137*
White, M., 259, *262*
Whitehurst, G. J., 14, *32*
Whiteside, L., 22, *32*
Whiteside-Mansell, L., 6, 10, *27*
Whitmore, J. K., 145, 146, 149, 151, 152, 157, *159*
Wichers, M. C., 43, *47*
Wiggins, J. S., 87, *118*
Wiggins, R. D., 51, *83*
Winkel, G. H., 3, *31*
Winter, P. D., 53, *82*
Witkow, M., 157, 158, *160*
Wohlwill, J. F., 6, 14, *32*
Wolak, J., 16, *28*
Wolf, A. W., 4, *30*
Wolfe, B., 163, *179*, 212, 221, 223, *232*, 241, 245, *261*
Wolke, D., 43, *45*
Wolpin, K. I., 223, *234*
Woon-Chia, L., 259, *260*
Wu, L. L., 181, 182, *208*

Y

Yates, W., 36, *45*
Yeates, K. O., 223, *235*
Yeung, W. J., 13, *32*, 165, *180*, 222, *231*
Yoshikawa, H., 215, 224, 225, *235*
Young, L. R., 204, *208*

Z

Zahn-Waxler, C., 21, *32*
Zaslow, M. J., 223, *233*
Zax, M., 125, 131, *137*
Zeisel, S. A., 131, *135*
Zhou, M., 145, 148, 150, *162*
Zill, N., 181, *207*
Zimmerman, W., 140, *162*

Subject Index